HOLOCAUST TRAUMA
Psychological Effects and Treatment

HOLOCAUST TRAUMA
Psychological Effects and Treatment

Natan P.F. Kellermann

iUniverse, Inc.
New York   Bloomington

Front Cover:
Exposure
An Oil on Canvas by Samuel Bak
Image Courtesy of Pucker Gallery
www.puckergallery.com

iUniverse books may be ordered through booksellers or by contacting:

iUniverse
1663 Liberty Drive
Bloomington, IN 47403
www.iuniverse.com
1-800-Authors (1-800-288-4677)

ISBN: 978-1-4401-4887-3 (sc)
ISBN: 978-1-4401-4885-9 (dj)
ISBN: 978-1-4401-4886-6 (ebook)

Library of Congress Control Number: 2009934592

Printed in the United States of America

iUniverse rev. date: 08/12/09

To my mother, Lilly Kellermann (1928–2009)
with gratitude and admiration

When the damage is done, the pain and the shame are there to stay, and the dead ... keep coming back like ghosts.

—Antoine Audouard

CONTENTS

ACKNOWLEDGMENTS

Much of what I know about Holocaust trauma comes from my work in Amcha—The National Israeli Center for Psychosocial Support of Survivors of the Holocaust and the Second Generation, where I served as the chief psychologist in the Jerusalem branch, as the executive director and as the project development director, since 1996. During the early years, I received regular supervision from D. Wardi and Y. Amit, and I was later stimulated by the continued professional interchange with Professor H. Dasberg, Dr. N. Durst, and the entire staff of Amcha. It has been a great privilege for me to be a part of this devoted team.

Some chapters are based on papers, which have been previously published in scientific journals. I would like to thank the publishers of these journals for permission to include them in this volume: (1) Gefen Publishing House for permission to republish papers originally published in the *Israel Journal of Psychiatry* (1999, 2001, 2008); (2) Taylor & Francis (Brunner-Routledge) for permission to reprint part of my paper originally published in the *Journal of Loss and Trauma* (2001); (3) The Guilford Press for permission to reprint part of my paper originally published in *Psychiatry, Interpersonal and Biological Processes* (2001); (4) George Halasz for permission to reprint part of his paper originally published in the *Melbourne Jewish Holocaust Centre News* (2008); and (5) *The Jewish Magazine* and *B'nai B'rith Anti-Defamation Commission Inc.* (2005) for the permission to reprint part of the contents of chapter 8. Some other material is based on presentations at public commemoration events, professional workshops, seminars, and congresses in various parts of the world.

FOREWORD

In introducing this book on Holocaust trauma, I would like to say a few words about the word *Holocaust*, or, in Hebrew, *Shoah*.

Shoah has only two syllables and four letters, but it is a very emotionally loaded concept. With the addition of the holy letter *H'* (Hebrew: 'ה), *the* Shoah has five letters. This clarification emphasizes that *the* Shoah was the only one; that there is none second to it. As such, the Shoah is still incomprehensible and has no rational explanation. It remains a gigantic riddle.

From a historical point of view, the Shoah began in 1935, when the racist and anti-Semitic Nuremberg laws (German: *Nürnberger Gesetze*) were passed. It continued until Victory Day on May 8, 1945, when Nazi Germany capitulated to the Soviet Union. This event is the subject of numerous historical, political, philosophical, theological, and even psychological and medical studies, and it is *also* an object of memory.

During the first decades after the foundation of Israel and until today, the Shoah was utilized as an object for the memory of the partisans, the ghetto fighters, and other victims as martyrs, as written on the entrance gate at *Yad Vashem* in Jerusalem. During the specific memorial ceremony on Holocaust Memorial Day called "Unto Every Person There is a Name," every victim is remembered. The memorial museum of *Yad Vashem* is exhibited for distinguished guests as a kind of tomb for the unknown soldiers within an army of six million. The Israeli parliament passed commemoration laws as well as laws bringing the Nazis and their cooperators to justice. In addition, a strong lobby was created for the return of victims' property, even though the survivors who live among us remained neglected for many years. The provision of individual reparations according to the Goldmann-Adenauer agreement was not properly respected until during the last decade, when there was a certain improvement, and pensions were equalized for those Russian immigrants who had also been war veterans in the Red Army.

Holocaust survivors who are living among us were part of the conspiracy of silence for many years. They attempted to be like other Israelis, living through the developmental phase of a Jewish national consciousness, which Zionist theory (Pinsker) called "auto-emancipation" (German: *Selbstemanzipation*). Until the 1980s, it was not a great honor to be a Holocaust survivor, except for the few ghetto fighters who founded the kibbutzim "Yad Mordechai" and "Lochamei Haghettaot" and who held seats in parliament.

Denial of being a Holocaust survivor was a psychological necessity for coping, and indeed Holocaust survivors thrived in society. After the phase of denial came the phase of ambivalence and doubt, occurring mainly around the years of military conflict in 1973 (The Yom Kippur War), 1982 (The First Lebanon War) and 1991 (The Gulf War), when national catastrophes threatened us. During these same years, a general empathy and identification with the survivors began, albeit with a lot of ambivalence and even dissociation. The general impression was that "we are all survivors—but not really."

Now, the survivors have become old. We have reached the next coping stage. After the denial and the dissociation, the memories return in an orderly fashion, bringing with them both delayed mourning and resilience. About a quarter of a million aging Holocaust survivors live among us. Most do not suffer from chronic illnesses or illnesses at all, even if a small group of lonely, grieving people at risk for psychosocial distress does exist.

Amcha is the only Israeli organization founded to provide preventive therapy and community mental health services for these survivors. Amcha was an initiative of a private businessman—Manfred Klafter—rather than the result of a public national effort. When the history of the psychosocial treatment of Holocaust survivors in Israel is written, Amcha's therapists will be remembered for their specific contributions. For example, a research study from Amcha in Beer Sheva found that membership in Amcha's psychosocial clubs improved the well-being of elderly participants so much that their visits to physicians decreased significantly. Amcha offers various group therapies in which survivors' past memories are integrated with the present. Survivors who were children in Europe are encouraged to express themselves in a nonverbal and artistic manner. Amcha has developed a wide range of therapeutic, rehabilitative, and integrative approaches to treating Holocaust survivors. Some of this pioneering work has been more fully described in a selected collection of my papers and lectures: *Trauma, Loss, and Renewal in Israel,* edited and published by Shefler et al. (2007).

But what is the meaning of the Holocaust that remains with us, *not* as a historical or therapeutic event, but as a continuing experience? Indeed, what was the Holocaust? I ask this on behalf of the survivors who have reached old age. What is the rational explanation and meaning of the Holocaust in our lives? And I ask in increasing amazement as we journey through the twenty-first century, after the denial, the dissociation, and the mourning.

Rabbi Yehuda Amital is a child survivor who was born in 1925 in Transylvania. Even though he is an Orthodox Jew, he doesn't accept the view that the Holocaust was a direct act of God. According to him, there is no theological explanation for the Holocaust. Instead, it was a part of historical events that resulted from spiritual acts and human states. Even the foundation of the State of Israel was not an answer to the Holocaust in the religious or messianic sense, according to him. Nevertheless, Rabbi Amital is a man of faith. Another Holocaust survivor—a Hungarian recipient of the Nobel Prize in literature, Imre Kertész—survived Auschwitz and Buchenwald as an orphan. He described his experiences there, in the shadow of death, as a source of strength. From a perspective of being seventy-three years old, he said that Auschwitz was the most significant event in his life.

These are all existential points of view, expressed in comforting words, but they do not offer any rational explanation. Nothing provides consolation for me. The answers to my questions will not come from us, from rabbis and authors, nor will they come from the generation after us, who are also involved. The oldest among the second generation are already around sixty, but most are middle aged. Will the third generation make sense of the Holocaust? Will they be able to suggest explanations when a decennium has passed? Will there ever be an answer?

Perhaps not.

But in the meantime, we in Amcha are helping the survivors. It is important that this work is being documented in various papers and books, such as this one. I hope Dr. Natan Kellermann's text will be widely read and utilized for the continued assistance of this vulnerable population or for others who are similarly traumatized. The lessons learned from our work in Amcha may prove as important as the work itself.

And if not for us, then for those who come after us.

The motto for this work is to "remember the past, and live in the present." But I want to add that the future is also important. Let me take this opportunity to strengthen the resolve of the therapists who take upon themselves the burden of this important work.

Haim Dasberg, MD
President, Amcha

Note: This foreword is based on a lecture presented at the Amcha conference on "Remembering the past and living in the present" in Tel Aviv on October 31, 2002.

PREFACE

The past is not dead. In fact, it's not even past.

—William Faulkner

At the age of fifteen, inmate A–8816 arrived in Auschwitz-Birkenau with her family in the last transport from the Satu Mare ghetto in May/June 1944. Upon their arrival, she was selected for work while her parents and younger brothers and sisters were sent to the gas chambers. After almost a year, and barely alive, she was liberated by the British army in Bergen-Belsen on April 15, 1945. Suffering from tuberculosis, she was then sent to Sweden for treatment and rehabilitation and stayed in hospitals and convalescence homes until 1950. Thereafter, she married and gave birth to two boys. I was the second of the two.

Even though I was born and grew up in a country far removed from the horrors of the Holocaust, I have lived with its images for my entire life. My mother, Lilly (Frischmann) Kellermann, was a fully functioning and loving mother, and told me very little about her traumatic experiences. But her Holocaust trauma has painfully permeated my inner life.

Imagining the Holocaust comes almost automatically to me. It's as if I have been there and have seen that before. Gruesome Holocaust associations fill my waking, and sleeping life and human suffering is a constant companion.

As have so many other children of survivors, I have apparently absorbed some of the psychological burdens of my parents and share their grief and terror as if I have experienced it myself. It is no coincidence that I became a psychologist and a psychodramatist and that much of my professional interest has focused on individual (Kellermann & Hudgins, 2000) and collective trauma (Kellermann, 2007).

Because, like a nuclear bomb that disperses its radioactive fallout in distant places even a long time after the actual explosion, any major psychological trauma continues to contaminate those who were exposed to it in one way or another in the first, second, and subsequent generations. Similar to radioactive waste, the emotional trauma cannot be seen or detected. It remains hidden in the dark abyss of the *unconscious* with its toxic and hazardous influence threatening the health of human beings for hundreds of years. Perhaps as a physical manifestation of such radioactive influence, I have lately lost all my hair to *alopecia universalis*, making me look almost like a *Muselmann* (a camp prisoner in the final stages of starvation to death). Publishing this book at this time might be a futile attempt to come to terms with this psychosomatic predicament and with my personal legacy.

From a more professional point of view, the purpose of this book is to present a comprehensive overview of the long-term psychological effects of Holocaust trauma. It will cover not only the direct effects on the actual survivors and the transmission effects upon the offspring, but also the collective effects upon other affected populations, including the Israeli Jewish and the societies in Germany and Austria. It will also suggest various possible intervention approaches to deal with such long-term effects of major trauma upon individuals, groups, and societies that can be generalized to other similar traumatic events. The material presented is based on the clinical and research experience gathered with hundreds of clients from Amcha—an Israeli treatment center for this population—on facilitating groups of Austrian/German participants in *Yad Vashem* and in Europe, as well as upon an extensive review of the vast literature.

CHAPTER 1

Holocaust Trauma

That attempt at the systematic destruction of an entire people falls like a shadow on the history of Europe and the whole world; it is a crime that will forever darken the history of humanity.

—Pope John Paul II

Imagine

Try to imagine how it was there and then.

Imagine the systematic destruction of an entire people.

Imagine the greatest evil.

Imagine the worst and darkest moments, from the mass slaughter to the indifferent masses: those who did not commit the crimes themselves but who knew and who saw but refused to stand up. Images of smoke and of mass graves; images of thousands of people being rounded up and sent away; images of fire.

Today, it seems unthinkable. Yet today we try to imagine it. We think of it, deliberately, to remember.

We do so to commemorate the millions who died in the Nazi onslaught.

We commemorate the victims of the Second World War who were brutally murdered. This includes not only the six million Jews, but also numerous other victims: the Roma and Sinti, the homosexuals, the Jehovah's Witnesses, the clergymen, the intellectuals, the communists, the disabled, and all those who resisted the Nazi regime.

All must be remembered and nobody should be forgotten.

We imagine the invisible faces of those left behind; the staring hopeless eyes of those who were barely kept alive. Imagine their loneliness and their sense of abandonment, and their silent despair as they walked in nocturnal procession toward the flames.

We utilize all our five senses for this mental process of imagination: sight, hearing, smell, taste, and touch. We see a child lying lifeless on the pavement in a ghetto. We hear the frightening sounds of the dogs barking. We smell the odors of the death camp. We feel the taste of dry bread in our mouths, and we sense the itching of lice on our cold bodies and the ache of hunger in our empty stomachs.

We see mass murder on an enormous scale: entire communities being forced into a wooden synagogue and burned to death or being shot in large pits in the forest, one on top of another. Infants and babies are thrown into burning fires. One after the other, Jews are systematically annihilated in the hundreds, thousands, and millions.

The nightmare continues to evolve as in the worst horror movie: Brownshirts are cheering as they burn down synagogues and books and smash the glass of Jewish shops and buildings in the night. SS soldiers are knocking on doors in the night, shouting *"Schnell! Raus! Verfluchte Juden!"* Entire families are sent to ghettos to starve and freeze and disappear. Those who remain alive are sent in crammed cattle trains to be slaughtered like animals.

Upon their arrival in the camps, they are separated from their families and either selected for slave labor or for death. Everything is taken from them: their suitcases, their clothes, their hair, their spectacles, and later, even their golden teeth. Those who get numbers tattooed on their arms have a chance to live a little longer while others are sent for immediate *processing*.

We imagine the last dreadful moments of suffocation when the Zyklon B (cyanide-based insecticide) gas is released through the satanic showers, and the last moments of farewells; the sounds of *"Shema Jisroel."* We watch as the *Sonderkommando* transport the bodies from the gas chambers to the crematoria and feel the heat from the flames of the ovens. Finally, we watch the smoke and white ashes from the chimneys, which rise to the clouds and cover the sky like smog.

Human beings have turned to powder and to dust and to nothing.

Then we switch our attention from the general to the specific: we imagine a father holding his child in his arms and watching it starve to death, without having any food to give it; we imagine the child lying next to his mother, searching for warmth, only to realize that she has frozen to death.

We imagine the death anxiety of all those who knew they were about to be shot, or hanged, or burned, or gassed, or whatever other method of murder was about to be enacted upon them. We imagine the heartbreaking separations between family members in which mothers gave away their babies in order to choose life. We imagine the impossible choices of life and death and the resignation of the *Muselmann* when his or her limits had been breached.

We try also to imagine what would have been if the Holocaust had not happened; if someone would have taken the threat seriously; if they had fled; if they had resisted; if someone had saved them; if the Allied Forces had bombed the railways or the camps; if Hitler had been assassinated; if, if, if! These hypothetical assumptions are festering in us like an unsolved riddle, multiplying like decomposing matter.

Imagining the horrors of the Holocaust cannot leave us indifferent. The images haunt us day and night and make our blood run cold and our hearts race with fear. If we really put ourselves in the place of the victims, it is a terrifying experience. Behind every single destiny, there is a chamber of cold horror. It does not leave us any rest. The images of death and torture will be a constant companion.

These are indeed terrible images; too terrible to really perceive.

How can we imagine such things? It is impossible! Putting ourselves in the place of the victims is not just emotionally painful. It is also a hard cognitive effort, because we try to turn the unspeakable and un-representable into something tangible and understandable.

We, who have not experienced it firsthand, simply cannot imagine such nonexistence.

Even if we try to imagine this reality through the eyes and voices of the survivors, we will stumble on our inner conceptual limitations. Even if we read such powerful narratives as Wiesel's *Night*, Levi's *Survival in Auschwitz*, *The Diary of Anne Frank*, Appelfeld's *Badenheim 1939*, Schwarz-Bart's *The Last of the Just*, or Spiegelman's (1991) Cartoon *Maus*, we cannot really comprehend how it was then and there. Drawing on a wide range of such texts, Rothberg (2000) demonstrated how the Holocaust as a traumatic event makes three fundamental demands on our representations: a demand for documentation, a demand for reflection on the limits of representation, and a demand for engagement with the public sphere and commodity culture, which are all so difficult to meet.

At the end of the day, and during the night, we are left with our own imagination, which is different from the reality experienced by the *victims* who perished and by the *survivors* who lived through it all.

Even if we try hard, we cannot really imagine the trauma of the Holocaust.

It is an impossible task.

As Freud (1930) wrote only a decade before the war: "No matter how much we may shrink with horror from certain situations—of a galley-slave in antiquity, of a peasant during the Thirty Years' War, of a victim of the Holy Inquisition, of a Jew awaiting a pogrom—it is nevertheless impossible for us to feel our way into such people" (p. 89).

Today, might this be true also for the survivors themselves? Perhaps they cannot really be in touch with that distant past either and recreate it in the present, even if they try hard. Describing the Holocaust will probably always be a re-presentation of the tragedy, a re-actualization of personal experiences, and a *secondary* narrative for everybody. But it will never be the *real thing*.

Remembering or Forgetting the Holocaust

In his poem "The Vow," Avraham Shlonsky (1972–1973), a survivor of the Holocaust, wrote:

> I have taken a vow: to remember it all, to remember—and to naught to forget. All along the millennia of our history—we recited on Passover night: "In every generation, a man must regard himself as though he had come out of Egypt."

Repeatedly, we are told that we must remember the Holocaust and that we must not forget.

"Why?" we ask.

And we are told: "So that it will not happen again."

This idea is based on the assumption of the American philosopher George Santayana (2005), who believed that those who cannot remember the past are condemned to repeat it.

During the Stockholm International Forum on the Holocaust—A Conference on Education, Remembrance, and Research in January 2000, the dictum was repeatedly mentioned. But while presenters mainly talked about what was important to remember—the victims, the sites, and the history—very little was said about *why* it was so important to remember. Clearly, however, we should not only remember the victims, and the Holocaust itself, but also its beginning, and the process that lead to the genocide, including the political and social environment at the time. Because in order for Holocaust education to become a *lesson*, it must concentrate also on the *road* to the Holocaust, in order for the students to make the apparently inevitable parallels with their lives today.

At this same conference, Bill Clinton, who was then the president of the United States, remarked: "We must deepen our study of the Holocaust and ensure that its lessons are taught in all our schools. The world must never forget how evil rose, took hold, and spread across Europe. The world must never forget the victims, their names, and their faces, how they lived their lives, how bravely they struggled for survival in the face of such unimaginable brutality. We must never forget what happened when governments turned a blind eye to the grave injustice outside their borders when they waited too long to act. To forget, as Elie Wiesel has said, would be an absolute injustice in the same way that Auschwitz was the absolute crime."

Well, I have lately started to feel that it would perhaps be good to forget some of it. Perhaps it would be good to stop thinking and talking so much about the terrible events of World War II? Perhaps it would be good to put an end to this sixty-year-old struggle at working through? Perhaps we should stop this endless mourning and get on with our lives?

But the truth is that we cannot forget.

The Holocaust has become a major collective trauma in Jewish history and, as such, it continues to leave its indelible mark on us. The long-term psychological effects of this event are obvious not only in the survivors who themselves experienced the persecution (chapters 2 and 3), and in their descendants who were vicariously affected (cf. chapters 4 and 5), but in the entire Jewish people, including those who live in and outside Israel (chapter 6). Holocaust memory is an insomniac faculty whose mental eyes have never slept (Langer, 1991; 1995). With the words of Yehuda Amichai (2000):

> I wasn't one of the six million who died in the Shoah; I wasn't even among the survivors. And I wasn't one of the six hundred thousand who went out of Egypt. I came to the Promised Land by sea. No, I was not in that number, though I still have the fire and the smoke within me, pillars of fire and pillars of smoke that guide me by night and by day. I still have inside me the mad search for emergency exit, for soft places, for the nakedness of the land, for the escape into weakness and hope ... Afterwards, silence. No questions, no answers. Jewish history and world history grind me between them like two grindstones, sometimes to a powder ... Sometimes I fall into the gap between to hide, or sink the way down.

The Holocaust is in our blood, in our bones, and in our minds. The terrible pictures return to us in our dreams and in our associations and we keep reexperiencing the tragedy over and over. We have thoroughly internalized its lessons and are constantly aware of the possibility of a new attempt of annihilation. It's not a question *if*, but *when* it will happen again.

It is therefore both impossible and unnecessary to tell ourselves that we must remember.

What we mean is perhaps that *they* should not forget. *They* are all the others; the other peoples of the world, some of whom were involved in the war and others who had nothing to do with it. What we mean is that they should learn from the Holocaust. So that *it* will not happen again. *It* means another genocide.

But *they* seem to have already forgotten most of it. Despite some public gestures of reconciliation, most people who are today living in the perpetrator nations of Germany and Austria (cf. chapter 7) have been successfully repressing most memories of World War II and left the working through of the past to subsequent generations (Duba, 1997). As a result, the ancient anti-Semitic sentiments, which were never eradicated despite everything, are again expressed in various circles. It is no longer politically incorrect to express anti-Jewish feelings, especially if they are concealed as anti-Zionist or anti-Israeli opinion. People living in other parts of the world are also showing increasing expressions of the "new" anti-Semitism, as was obvious from the conference on this issue in Melbourne in the beginning of 2005. While the Nazi Holocaust led to the attempt at total annihilation of the Jewish people, the recent "new" anti-Semitism may lead to "wiping Israel off the map" as stated by Iran's president Mahmoud Ahmadinejad (cf. chapter 8).

All of these new threats indicate that much of the world hasn't learned the lesson. And while there are various shades and grades of Holocaust denial, much of the world acts as if the Holocaust never happened.

So, what are the lessons of the Holocaust? What meaning should it have for future generations?

For the Jewish people, it provided the raison d'être for *the need* of a Jewish homeland and the justification for creating the Jewish state of Israel (cf. chapter 6). It became the legitimizing factor for the state's right to exist, and it underscored the urgency and vital necessity for pursuing its national interests. Contrary to popular opinion, however, this original significance has not lost its significance. Though the Holocaust in the future might be compared to a distant historic event, such as the exodus of Egypt, and be remembered and retold from generation to generation, it still has a profound effect on everything that happens in Israel today.

The Holocaust may be sometimes felt only as an undercurrent of vague energy without clear structure. But strong emotions easily evolve at every point of national crisis. At these times, the new trauma re-actualizes the old one. For example, during the withdrawal from Gaza in 2005, the settlers felt that they were exposed to a "pogrom" and in signs posted around Israel they accused the government of wanting to make this geographic area *Judenrein*.

For the non-Jewish world, however, the lessons of the Holocaust are much more difficult to spell out. Does the Holocaust have a lesson for the whole of people-kind, which is being ignored?

The obvious lessons of the dangers of malignant prejudice and racism, of cruel dictators and totalitarian regimes, and of the possibility of recurrent acts of genocide among human beings are easily taught. But what has the world learned to do in situations when dictators again rise to power and threaten another people with genocide, such as in Rwanda, Cambodia, Darfur, and today in Iran? Strangely enough, various countries who were all involved in the Second World War seemed to have learned a very different and almost opposite lesson from the Holocaust. As suggested by Frey (2005) in his book *The Hitler Syndrome*, the German population seemed to have learned to oppose universally all armed conflict and to choose peaceful means for resolving conflicts, while the United States (and perhaps the UK) learned that such major threats must be confronted with military means. The latter have learned from the Second World War that totalitarian regimes such as those in Iraq, North Korea, and Iran are real threats, which must be confronted head on and that terrorist organizations such as Al Qaida and other manifestations of the *Axis of Evil* may be as dangerous as Hitler.

In addition to these lessons, there are other more personal moral, theological, and existential lessons, which cannot be simply explained by the above political conclusions. In fact, in our efforts to digest the Holocaust, we become more perplexed and often raise more questions than answers. For example:

- *How could it have happened at all?*
- *Specifically, what happened then and there?*
- *What do we remember? And how could we forget?*
- *How can we talk about that which is impossible to*

perceive? Because our words are so inadequate, should we perhaps keep silent?

- *How could the perpetrators have been so cruel? Where they not human? Did they have no compassion?*

- *Why did the victims not resist? And why did they not escape when it was still possible?*

- *How did some people survive despite everything? Why did they survive?*

- *Could more people have been saved? Why were they not?*

- *Where was God? Where was the Rabbi?*

- *Where were the other (free) people and their governments? Why were there so few who did something to try to make it stop?*

- *What does the Holocaust say about people then-and-there and about people in general today? Are we (as human beings) basically good or bad? Could it have happened in another time and age? Could it happen again?*

These are all central questions that cry out for answers. It is difficult to remain indifferent to them as a Jew and as a human being. Living in this time and age, we cannot (and should not) stop asking these questions, even if they leave us disturbed and restless to the edge of insanity.

The questions and answers constitute a very disturbing lesson of the Holocaust that leaves us perplexed and uneasy.

Because it is an ugly one.

It tells the story of genocide and racial persecution, of unimaginable cruelty and nonexistent compassion. Anyone who learns about what happened will be unable to find some *sense* in it all. To the first question: "How could it have happened?" we respond with guilty silence and to the last one: "Could it happen again?" we nod in shame.

"Auschwitz and Hiroshima have shown us that death and violence belong to the most intimate and concealed parts of our identity. The monstrous and painful memories they have left behind overload or destroy the perceptual and representational systems of their victims, leaving behind a heritage that gives rise to cruel and violent forms of identification in themselves and their children" (Gampel, 2000, p. 61).

As we attempt to answer these questions, we are confronted with the forceful presence of the *ultimate evil* (cf. "Unconditional Hate" in chapter 8); the cruelty of human beings to each other, the mockery of basic human values, and the unlimited degradation of men and women. But at the same time, the history of the Holocaust also reveals great manifestations of compassion, courage, and heroism. In the study of the Holocaust, one confronts the categorical defiance of God, as well as the devotion to human values under the worst of conditions, including dire hunger, pain, suffering, and humiliation.

These two opposite learning experiences are perhaps the main lesson to be learned from the Holocaust. They have often been observed among survivors of the Holocaust and they have been variously depicted as posttraumatic stress disorder (PTSD) and posttraumatic growth (PTG). PTSD made people more vulnerable to stress, while PTG made them more resilient. While it is a paradoxical learning experience that has bewildered generations of trauma therapists, it seems to be a significant lesson of the Holocaust itself. According to Janoff-Bulman (1992), while survivors of trauma have learned that the world is evil and meaningless, that life is terminal and that people are unworthy, they have also experienced that there may be hope even in the worst of conditions. If we listen carefully to their stories, we will slowly come to appreciate this profound lesson.

As we become more accustomed to this stereophonic sound, we come to realize that this dual reality does not only include the assumptive world of the victims, but also of the perpetrators (who may not be only cruel), the rescuers (who may not be only saints), and the bystanders (who may not be only indifferent). While we have a tendency to look at these main actors of the Second World War in *black-and-white* terms, and try to understand them beyond the realm of normal human existence, we may come to understand and appreciate that they were all ordinary people of flesh and blood, like ourselves and everybody else.

Being confronted with the history of the Holocaust in depth, means that we are also facing ourselves today. This might be the main lesson for the world to digest when learning about the Holocaust. When they start to remember in this way, it will perhaps enable us to start to forget.

Remembering or forgetting Holocaust trauma was the subject of a workshop that I conducted on the International Holocaust Memorial Day, on January 27, 2008 at the Jewish Holocaust Centre Museum, Melbourne, Australia. The following is a description of this workshop.

A Workshop Example

(written by George Halasz, 2008)

"This afternoon's trauma workshop fulfilled many hopes to find comfort through a deeper understanding of how to cope with our inner demons. Attended by over thirty participants, aged from their mid-twenties to eighties, survivors, their families as well as nonsurvivors, came to listen, learn, and share reflections. As we formed a large circle, Natan invited us to share how we cope with tragic memories of the Holocaust: should we only remember, or is it finally time to forget, to move on?

To explore some of these sensitive issues, Natan placed three chairs in the middle of the circle, to represent the first, second, and third generation, and called on people to trade places as part of a series of mini role plays. Taking on any one of these assigned roles, we started to open up, to explore experiences from any one of the roles of a Holocaust survivor family; what it felt like, from the inside, to be a survivor's son or daughter, a parent or child, or grandchild. Which subtle messages were communicated from one to the other within this highly emotional system?

A tearful and distressed granddaughter's words focused our minds and hearts to acknowledge the insufficiently worked-through 'trauma' of a grandmother. This prompted Natan to transform the moment when he borrowed a black case from one of the participants and invited us to imagine that it contained the survivor's trauma. Thus, we could look at different ways that we deal with it, holding onto it, putting it 'out of sight, out of mind' under the chair, embrace it, or hand it over to others. Trauma was thus 'enacted' and became externalized, concretized, and visible. This allowed us to make new links to sources of our otherwise unknown distress. The trauma was actualized.

The 'trauma' of our hidden 'demons' previously known to reside in the deeper layers of our unconscious as fears, terrors, feelings of chaos, abandonment, helplessness, anger, or rage thus became more tangible and less overwhelming. Because such intense feelings are often 'acted out' in different phases of our life cycle, either as risk-taking or aggressive and damaging behaviors, now they might be easier to handle.

As additional participants delved deeper and encountered and conquered more 'demons,' a stirring sense of curiosity motivated one Holocaust survivor who hitherto had been silent to read from his recently written manuscript, a story told for the first time after sixty years. Containing and attempting to control that tangible 'trauma-filled black case' contrasted with our usual paralyzed response to trauma, and helped us to overcome our sense of chaos, our loss of control.

The afternoon's encounter offered hope that such overwhelming feelings might be gradually transformed, and as the stories opened up to reveal ever deeper layers of otherwise hidden hurt, we felt that we were able to share together a theme that had previously been so full of pain. As feelings and thoughts were voiced, they could be 'seen,' and at the same time their owners experienced a sense of relief.

A child of survivors recalled how she went home from Natan's last workshop two years ago, and for the first time in her life had cried deep tears of relief that she had stored inside her during a lifetime of silent pain, unknown to her till she took part in that workshop. The experience had changed her life, she said.

In this workshop also, many layers of silent distress were exposed for the first time. And at the same time, for some, increased resistance blocked off further understanding. Natan took great care to explain that it was all right to stop exploring, to take a rest, or even to leave the memories alone. We all need to respect our safety zones, to decide when to confront, and when to support, and to nurture those emerging feelings that threatened to overwhelm us.

As the transmission of Holocaust trauma was mentioned, one grandmother attempted to soothe the tearful granddaughter, and herself, by defensively exclaiming: 'No, no, no, we did not pass on any of our trauma to you, and you do not need to be upset.'

Natan gently but firmly guided such repeated and all too familiar misunderstandings between the generations. For some of us, such moments galvanize our steely resolve not to open up again. We do not want to be exposed and vulnerable, and we are afraid to open up to someone who might deny the reality of our feelings. In such situations, we decide it is better to cut off from all feelings, not to risk being rejected.

Yet, to not share can, and does, compound the burden of trauma as it fuels further family conflicts. Sadly, misplaced efforts of reassurance and clichés like 'that was in the past, we must look to the future' merely inflame feelings of fury or silent rage.

So, it became apparent how families transmit trauma, even if unintended, and sadly persist to deny this reality. Instead they fall into lifelong patters of family communications that misread each other's moods of sorrow and pain. Such patterns can start early in life, in the nursery, as mothers and fathers silently witness their baby's cries. These moments can persist or may be triggered decades later, at the other end of the life-cycle, when it's the turn of the grown-up children to care for their aging parents and grandparents.

A particularly poignant moment for me in the workshop occurred when Natan (as the second generation) recalled from his own family experience a deep sense of pleasure as his daughter and mother shared, and talked about his mother's past. He relived with us that intimate moment with heartfelt words, gestures, and such a warm smile that elicited knowing reactions in kind from all the participants.

This was more than just professional care. Natan shared his pleasures and sorrows from the depth of his humanity. He blended with consummate clinical skills a sense of understanding that was an antidote to the complex sense of ache, emptiness, futility that Holocaust survivor families endure for decades.

Again and again, we asked 'Should we speak?' 'Is it better not to speak?' 'What should I say?' 'How should I say it?' There were no simple answers. We need to be reminded that to keep our minds open to listen, to hear, to ask, and to answer, to tell each other our stories calls for great and intense effort. This was the secret and the message of the workshop: That we can attend to the gaps inside only by opening up to those gaps.

While reassurance is necessary at times, it is not sufficient to repair, to fill those unmeasurable gaps that trauma has excavated in our minds and hearts; the memory of murdered loved ones, abandonment, torture of body, mind, and soul.

In the final moments of the workshop, the black case was opened and we could learn what was inside it. What a surprise! Only the owner had the right to open it, when she felt the time was right. The black case could be opened, in the right place, at the right time, when the owner felt that it was safe enough. As she did, we felt much relief. We even laughed. There were no demons inside. Of course, for survivors and their next of kin, the box contains their black memories, they have black cases by the trainload, half-buried and half-exposed, often battered, blood-stained, soiled, and beyond recognition.

Survivors do not have the luxury of the symbolic black case. There will always be a difference between 'real trauma' and its symbolic representation. However closely that approaches to realism, the real and its representation will always be in a relationship, approximating to an infinite gap.

As this trauma workshop reminded us, we should not confuse the survivor's real experience and the imagined. Yet in the minds of their children, there is the blurred zone of transitional trauma, the 'transmitted trauma' that many, including me, feel transmitted as real" (Halasz, 2008, pp. 17–18).

What is Holocaust Trauma?

Simply, Holocaust trauma is a trauma caused by the Holocaust.

The word *Holocaust* describes the systematic killing of approximately six million Jews by the Nazis in death camps and elsewhere during the Second World War. The corresponding Hebrew word is *Shoah*, which means total destruction and refers to the almost complete annihilation of Jews in Europe by Nazi Germany and its collaborators. Historically, it started from the Nurnberg laws in 1936 and lasted until May 8, 1945. *The Holocaust has become an emotionally loaded and mysterious concept, conceived as something incomprehensible like a riddle* (Funkenstein, 1993), even though it has been the object of historical, philosophical, theological, political, and also psychological investigations.

The word *trauma* conveys not only the terrible events that occurred during the Holocaust, but also (and particularly) the stressful reactions of the people who survived the ordeal, including the sense of horror and helplessness experienced by the persecuted individuals. Because the events were so severe, intense, and long lasting, the likelihood of developing some kind of posttraumatic stress response after the war was very high.

Although this definition of Holocaust trauma may be seen as straightforward and simple, it raises some further, more complicated questions. For example, can the event—the *Holocaust*—be compared to other genocides in the history of humankind and/or to other stressful and overwhelming traumatic events, and are these posttraumatic responses similar to or different from other stress responses that have been reported in the literature?

The first two questions deal with a more quantitative comparison of the Holocaust with other genocides and with other stressful events; the third one attempts a more qualitative comparison of the various traumatic stress responses and the different kinds of suffering of the multitude of trauma survivors (further discussed in chapter 2).

Can the Holocaust Be Compared to Other Genocides, or Was It a Unique Event?

Comparing the Holocaust with other genocides, mass killings, and massacres evokes heated discussions and stirred-up emotions. On the one hand, there are those who insist that the Holocaust was a unique event and that it cannot be compared to any others. Elie Wiesel (1997), for example, views the Holocaust as an extraordinary event that "transcends history." On the other hand, there are those who hold that genocides have been perpetrated all through history, and that they are still happening today, and that the Holocaust merely is one such event that is similar to the others. In his book on the Holocaust and other genocides, Smith (2002) ties the teaching of the Holocaust to an analysis of the genocides in Armenia, Bosnia and Kosovo, Rwanda, Tibet, and Somalia. In addition to these two views, there are those who emphasize that while the murder of six million Jews indeed was an extraordinary historic event, these victims should be regarded as only a part of the total fifty million civilian and military casualties of the Second World War.

In a collection of essays edited by Rosenbaum (1996), both of these sides were represented, including advocates and detractors of the *uniqueness thesis* in the field of comparative genocide. Similarly, Charny (1991) presented a critical bibliographic review of different kinds of genocide, utilizing the events from the Holocaust as a guideline. A middle position was suggested by Huttenbach (1996), in his "Apologia Rationalis" of the *Journal of Genocide Research,* which clarified that there were many points from which the Holocaust could learn from genocide studies, but that the *Final Solution* still remained the event in which genocidal thought and deed had received its highest articulation to date.

Comparing the suffering of different groups of trauma survivors with one another is of course a futile exercise. Sooner or later, such a comparison will lead to a situation in which one or the other group feels offended because their suffering is minimized as compared to the other group. All survivors want to feel that their tragic events were *special* and *unique* and that their emotional pain is justified. A survivor of several concentration camps might for example feel offended by comparing his or her experiences with that of the Armenians. Armenians would feel an equal sense of indignation if their suffering was not acknowledged as a genocide of enormous proportions. The Roma and Sinti (Gypsies) express similar outrage over the fact that their Holocaust trauma has not been sufficiently acknowledged.

We may also observe a similar competition for sympathy among different kinds of Jewish Holocaust survivors; between those who fled, those who were in the ghetto, those who were confined to work camps, in (one or several) concentration camps, or on the death march, etc. Even within the camps, inmates compared their own destiny to others, such as those who were "only" working in the *Canada*-barracks or in the kitchen, while they themselves were sent to work in some terrible quarry or in the gas chambers. On the other (positive) side of the weighing scale, there were, of course, also those who compared themselves with the many victims who didn't have a chance to survive, and who perished. Beyond the fact that such sentiments evoke resentment in most trauma survivors, they also raise profound social, psychological, and moral questions. Behind it all, there seems to be a kind of a *hierarchy* of suffering between various kinds of trauma survivors. The group that suffered more would get the "first prize" and would be entitled to the most sympathy, compassion, and understanding, as well as monetary compensation, while the other group would be neglected and dismissed.

In his speech at the opening forum of the Swedish forum for human rights, professor Yehuda Bauer (2000) tried to settle this question by emphasizing the fact that the (Jewish) Holocaust was an *unprecedented* event, explaining that there has *not yet* been a similar genocide of this magnitude in the history of humankind: "There have been other genocides, after all; and the number of the other victims of Nazism in World War II is much larger than that of the Jews. No one suffered more than the other; we must not compare suffering with suffering—it would be immoral to do so. But there is something unprecedented, frightening about the Holocaust of the Jewish people that should be taught: for the first time in the bloodstained history of the human race, a decision developed, in a modern state in the midst of a civilized continent, to track down, register, mark, isolate from their surroundings, dispossess, humiliate, concentrate, transport, and murder every single person of an ethnic group as defined not by them, but by the perpetrators; not just in the country where the monster arose, not just on the continent the monster first wished to control, but ultimately everywhere on earth, and for purely ideological reasons. There is no precedent for that. And it happened to a people whose legacy is an important component of human civilization, whose traditions have influenced major religious and social movements, whose culture is thousands of years old" (p. 898).

Thus, according to Yehuda Bauer, there is still no other genocide that compares to the Holocaust, neither in its intensity of evil; nor in the pain of individuals made to suffer precisely because they were a specific group of people; not in the ghastly scope of its cruel ambitions; not in the combination of twisted ideas and wicked actions that, for a time, threatened to engulf our entire world. The Holocaust was unique in its scope, magnitude, and methodology. It was the most systematic, merciless, and effective mass murder in human history, a disaster of enormous proportions that we are only now beginning to grasp. This fact is what makes this event so much more malignant than many of the other genocides.

Can the Holocaust Be Compared to Other (Non-genocidal) Stressful Events?

Any other traumatic event, such as being hit by lightning, seeing someone get killed, battlefield experiences, being abused or raped or tortured, being incarcerated in a prison, being kidnapped or taken hostage by terrorists, being involved in a severe automobile accident, being diagnosed with a life-threatening illness, or experiencing violent personal assault, may be equally painful and lead to similar posttraumatic stress reactions.

None of these events, however, can be compared to the Holocaust on any of the above criteria. In addition, even if we observe the immense losses and insurmountable grief of the survivors of the recent natural disasters in which entire families where wiped out, we must conclude that "it's not the same."

The reason for this difference between Holocaust trauma and other traumatic events may be found in the work of Keilson (1979/1992) on *Sequential Traumatization in Children.* According to him, the Holocaust was basically different from any other trauma because of the extreme nature of the continual events occurring during three traumatic sequences: (1) the impact of military invasion followed by the occupation of the country and the mobilization of hate toward the Jews; (2) the registration, persecution, deportation, destruction of families, and mass orchestrated extermination; and (3) the psychosocial consequences after the war. The sequence of these events together transcends what we usually conceive as one *trauma*. Rather, it became a prolonged *chronic horror existence* of extreme dimensions that made it essentially different from other, more limited, stressful events. Recent studies (Turner & Lloyd, 1995; Turner, Finkelhor, & Ormrod, 2006) support the conclusion that the impact of trauma is not only *cumulative* (the more times a traumatic event is experienced the greater the impact), but also *additive* (exposure to additional different types of trauma is correlated with greater impact), and *summative* (the combination of events plus impact is what individuals carry forward through time inscribed in memory, sense of self, and behavior).

Contrary to other survivors of war trauma, Dasberg (2003) pointed out that survivors of the Holocaust were victims of massive genocide perpetrated on a passive civilian population. The length of exposure to a series of many different and cumulative traumata was unusually long. The entire multigenerational family was endangered and often annihilated, including children. Properties, homes, and ties to their country of origin were irretrievably damaged. After liberation, additional traumatic events occurred in most instances. Finally, children were caught by the genocide during their early development with adult aftereffects.

The unique quality of the Holocaust also lay in its *merciless cruelty*. For the Nazi killing squads, persecution and mass murder was not enough. There was also dispossession, terror, concentration, humiliation, degradation, starvation, torture, and systematic annihilation. The victims were tortured in the most vicious ways before they were finally killed; they were experimented on, they were forced to cooperate in the killing factories, they were torn between hope and despair without reason, and they were dehumanized and treated like parasites to be exterminated. This psychological dehumanization was perfected all through the war, and reached its climax in 1944. For example, in the infamous camp of Sobibor, the SS guards continued to invent new ways to murder the Jews, pushing them with umbrellas off roofs to resemble parachuting, stabbing them in their backs with a small knife when the workers bent over to pick up branches, sewing up their trousers after putting rats inside, and throwing babies directly into garbage pits. Such extraordinary cruelty was not implemented in a haphazard manner, but with a systematic and calculated strategy in which almost everything was carefully recorded as revealed in the recently opened gigantic *Bad Arolsen* archive with its sixteen miles of file drawers and shelf space.

All of this contributed to the feeling that the events of the Holocaust was an extraordinary genocide and that every one of the few survivors who returned from that Hell to bear witness, had a unique story to tell. This was the story of their Holocaust trauma. The present book is an attempt to describe it.

Holocaust Trauma Today

"Fifty years ago no one would have imagined the topic of the Holocaust being as vibrant and as relevant as it is today" (Laub, et al., 2007, p. 49). Even though so many years have passed since the war, the *actuality* of the Holocaust has increased in recent years. In fact, there seems to be a widespread and growing interest in anything related to the Holocaust during the last decade.

In his pioneering edited book *Survivors, Victims, and Perpetrators: Essays on the Nazi Holocaust*, Dimsdale (1980) observed that the concentration camp has acquired a general allegorical meaning: "There is something about the camps that stirs us profoundly and resonates familiarity.... For many, the image of man in the camps is quite simply the image of man and his fate, thrown into a world that is hostile, with no chance for escape and no real chance for change. The way that man deals with his feelings about such a condition, the way he goes on to create a world within these confines, may not be dissimilar to the way that millions coped with their immersion in concentration camps" (p. 174).

As represented in a massive archive of documentary and fictional writings, films, artworks, television programs, and in new museums and exhibitions, the Holocaust reverberates in our present. Holocaust education has become a field of its own and is increasingly promoted in schools and universities all over the world. An increasing number of people visit the memorials and participate in the yearly commemoration ceremonies. Apparently, the Holocaust has "come out from hiding" and it is now confronting the world with its profound secrets.

As a result of this newly recognized actuality, Holocaust trauma has become a paradigm for genocide and traumatology research in academic settings. For example, in an international conference on the "Holocaust as the Paradigm of Psychic Trauma in the Twentieth Century," held at Tel Aviv University in 2007, this new paradigm of psychic trauma was addressed from a variety of interdisciplinary perspectives. It is my hope that the present book will further facilitate such cross-fertilization through the clarification of basic concepts and processes involved in the long-term traumatization and transmission of war trauma. Possibly, the experience gained in the diagnosis and treatment of Holocaust survivors and their families may be of help to mental health professionals who work with other survivors of trauma, even though these might be different in many ways from the trauma inflicted upon Holocaust survivors during World War II.

Despite the fact that the Holocaust continues to retain its unique character and symbolism, perhaps the time has come to universalize some of its lessons, given that it was apparently not the last genocide perpetrated against humankind. According to Salpeter (2001): "If the conversion of the Holocaust into a symbol of ultimate evil can help in future struggles against genocide, that would be one more contribution that the Jewish people have made to the universal values of humanity" (p. 11).

CHAPTER 2

Holocaust Trauma in Holocaust Survivors

There is more to survival than staying alive.

—Hill (1991)

More than half a century after the Second World War, the long-term aftereffects of Holocaust traumatization on the last survivors are far reaching. When retiring from work or experiencing deteriorating health, terrifying nightmares and flashbacks reappear in aging survivors who, over the years, had kept themselves excessively busy in order to repress their painful memories. There is frequently a contradictory effort both to remember and to forget, both to approach and to avoid the traumatic event in a compulsively repeated fashion. Like a broken record that is spinning around and around, intrusive experienced images and painful memories keep coming back, while at the same time there is a conscious effort to avoid them and not to think about them. Thus it seems that Elie Wiesel (1978) was correct in stating that "time does *not* heal all wounds; there are those that remain painfully open" (p. 222).

While Holocaust survivors and their families make every effort to continue their lives without being constantly reminded of the terrible events of the past, traumatic memories kept returning with all their accompanying emotions. As Judith Herman (1992) pointed out in her book *Trauma and Recovery*, "Atrocities refuse to be buried" (p. 1). They keep penetrating the conscious and unconscious minds of the survivors and their offspring until they are properly remembered, mourned, and worked through within a safe, healing relationship.

The awareness of such late Holocaust traumatization has evolved during the last thirty years. Until then, survivors had lived normal lives and appeared healthy on the outside; they were careful to keep much of their suffering concealed within themselves. During the 1980s, however, some people started to open up, and there was suddenly a sense of urgency to provide emotional support *now or never*. The woes of aging, retirement, illness, and the deaths of their spouses created new emotional crises that activated the old trauma. As a result, many began to seek professional help for the first time in their lives, and the psychological needs of this population became more widely acknowledged and investigated. However, services that were heretofore provided were found to be insufficient and largely inadequate. Mental health professionals seemed to avoid this chronic patient population and showed signs of *Holocaust victimophobia* as well as various counter-transference responses that reinforced the conspiracy of silence that had prevailed for so many years.

Amcha—the Israeli Center for Psychosocial Support of Survivors of the Holocaust and the Second Generation—was founded in 1987 to meet the needs of this population in Israel. Similar support centers were also founded by local communities around the world.

In 1995, the medical and psychological literature on Holocaust survivors and their children had already grown to almost 2,500 publications (Krell & Sherman, 1997). Since then, the field has continued to grow even more. A recent HistCite (2008) search produced over 2,700 references to papers and books on the Holocaust published between the years 1962–2008.

Definition and Demographics

A *Holocaust survivor* was defined broadly as any persecuted Jew who lived under Nazi occupation during the Second World War and who was thus threatened by the policy of the Final Solution but managed to stay alive. This included persons with widely different Holocaust experiences; for example, those who were confined to a ghetto, those who experienced forced labor in a work camp and/or incarceration in a concentration camp, those who were in hiding or lived under false identities, refugees who were forced to leave their families behind, or those who fought with the partisans. All of these people were affected in one way or another, either under constant threat of being killed, suffering significant losses, or living under the shadow of imminent persecution.

Naturally, many non-Jewish people were similarly affected, but for various reasons they received much less attention. The mentally and physically handicapped were exposed to forced sterilization, the homosexuals were persecuted for being "socially aberrant," the Roma and Sinti were murdered *en masse* as were the Jehovah's Witnesses (if they did not renounce their belief), and scores of political, religious, and intellectual leaders in Poland and many other occupied countries were killed, while the "working population" was viewed as "subhumans" and sent to forced labor camps. Millions of other non-Jewish civilians were also persecuted and suffered tremendously under the Nazi regime. While not a focus of the present chapter, their emotional suffering should also be acknowledged, and there is still much work to be done to provide some psychosocial support also to these populations, according to their specific needs (e.g., Radebold, 2005).

The exact number of Jewish Holocaust survivors in Israel and around the world is unknown, but there have been many different estimates. According to DellaPergola (2003) the total number of survivors in the world (according to a broad definition) at the time was 1,092,000, with the majority (511,000) living in Israel, 174,000 in the United States, 146,000 in the former Soviet Union, 197,000 in Western Europe, 32,000 in Eastern Europe, and 32,000 elsewhere. Based on a much more narrow definition of a survivor, a much lower number was presented by Brodsky (2005) in her study of the characteristics and needs of Holocaust survivors in Israel. She estimated that there were about 283,000 survivors in Israel (of whom 40,000 had been in concentration camps, 70,000 in hiding or in work camps, 95,000 who had been persecuted, and 78,000 who had fled). This estimate was based on 76 percent of the total number of European-born citizens over the age of sixty-five, according to the Israel Bureau of Statistics (373,000). This quantity decreased to 300,000 in 2007, of which only 228,000 are assumed to be Holocaust survivors.

All these estimates should be considered as the high end of the spectrum. The minimum number of Jewish survivors in Israel in 2005 would be 62,000, which is the amount of former enslaved and forced laborers who received compensation from the German Foundation "Remembrance, Responsibility, and the Future" through the Claims Conference. The number of survivors worldwide receiving monthly pensions from Germany and, via German reparations, through Israel, has been as follows: (1) BEG Damage to Health (as of 1998): 86,138; (2) Israeli program (as of 1999): 22,000 (approximate); (3) Article 2 (as of 1999): 48,948; and (4) CEEF (as of 2000): 13,479. Total: approximately 170,565 (Swiss Banks, 2000). In 2008, the approximate amount of such survivors eligible for some kind of disability pension in Israel was about 90,000. This would be the present final *minimum* figure of Israeli Holocaust survivors, according to a more strict definition (not including the *second circle* of survivors, many of whom are new immigrants from the former USSR).

Because of the inevitable effects of aging, the total amount of these survivors will decrease significantly in coming years. The average Holocaust survivor who was born in 1928, and was sixteen years old in 1944, turned eighty years old in 2008. A child survivor who was born in 1938, and was only six years old in 1944, turned seventy years old in 2008. With an average life expectancy in Israel of 78.3 for men, and 82.3 for women, there will be few survivors still alive after 2014. While there is no definite scientific evidence of a lower life expectancy in this population than in the general population, there is a definite possibility of premature aging as a late effect of their hard life conditions, especially if such conditions occurred during puberty (Ohry & Shasha, 2006).

Major Periods of Postwar Adjustment

Five more or less distinct periods of postwar adjustment may be delineated, during which Holocaust survivors began to gradually cope with their war experiences:

1. The first posttraumatic period directly after the war involved an *emotional crisis*. While searching for surviving relatives, they embarked on the journey of *surviving survival*, which involved recuperating from physical illnesses as well as trying to come to terms with their emotional scars and losses. From hospitals and displaced persons camps, they searched for a new home in Palestine/Israel, the United States/Canada, Australia, Europe, or elsewhere;

2. The second period of *immigration and absorption* (1950s) confronted the survivors with the harsh reality of their new home country. Those who chose to immigrate to Israel were hit especially hard. Contrary to their expectation of *coming home*, many experienced great disappointment with the lack of empathy from the local Israeli population. As a collective group, they were marginalized and ridiculed for not having defended themselves sufficiently and for having gone "like sheep to the slaughter";

3. The third period of social adjustment and *reintegration* into society (in the 1960s to 1970s) involved building a new life, a new family, new language and culture, and a new financial platform. The majority of survivors took on the challenges and opportunities afforded them by their new Israeli environment and used effective coping strategies in their adjustment to postwar living conditions (Harel, 1995). Everybody made an effort to *move on* and leave the tragic past behind;

4. The fourth period of *aging and regression* (1980s, 1990s, and later) became a period in which the repressed memories returned and demanded resolution, either because of old age, new trauma, or because the survivors were less busy in their daily lives. As a result, some new treatment programs for Holocaust survivors were created in the 1980s;

5. The fifth period (2000s to present) involved *recognition* by society of the survivors' extraordinary accomplishments. Survivors, who were previously considered less than heroic, were now invited to document their life stories in Holocaust museums, in schools, and in society at large. This shift resulted in a general feeling among survivors of a final social acceptance, and a sense of pride for what they had succeeded to achieve *despite everything.*

During the first three periods of postwar adaptation, few people wanted to talk or hear about the Holocaust. In fact, most survivors tried to put the past behind them and focused instead on the future. This involved a conscious effort not to think too much about the past, and to repress their traumatic experiences as much as possible. This effort came either because of the inner feelings of the survivors, or from the feeling that they were misunderstood by others when they opened up. A *conspiracy of silence* (Danieli, 1985) developed, in which the survivors themselves kept quiet about their experiences, and others did not ask too many questions.

The Eichmann Trial in 1961 changed all that. This tribunal is generally considered the major historical event that ended the profound silence of the survivors. According to Yablonka (1999; 2004), the trial changed the way Israelis perceived the Holocaust, because it forced people to confront its harsh realities for the first time. Testimonies at the trial led to a wave of sympathy and respect from other Israelis, who until then had neither understood the suffering nor recognized the courage of the survivors. While many survivors still chose to keep their memories to themselves, the Holocaust became less loaded with social taboo, and it has become a more acceptable theme for private and public discourse ever since. Parallel to this change of attitude toward the Holocaust in the public sphere, there was also a gradual change in the attitude of many individual survivors, who started to share their experiences with their families and others, a process that is still continuing to this day.

Talking about the Holocaust or keeping silent remains a major issue for survivors all over the world, as emphasized in the German book *Breaking the Silence: Berlin Lessons of the Late Effects of the Shoah*, edited by Rossberg and Lansen (2003).

The Mental Health of Holocaust Survivors

Holocaust survivors clearly differ from one another in a great many ways, in their prewar personality make-up, in their various traumatic war experiences, and in their postwar readjustment. Of all these differences, their varying vulnerability and resilience to stress are perhaps the most striking in rendering them more or less susceptible to mental disease. While a majority of survivors showed an unusual degree of psychic strength in overcoming the effects of their traumatic experiences and multiple losses (many fought in Israel's wars and helped shape the state in every area since its establishment), a clinical minority continued to suffer from emotional scars for many years after the war.

In the following sections, I will give an overview of some of these emotional effects on the survivors, as they have been described in the vast research literature assembled of their pathology and health ever since the war. However, before presenting the findings of these studies, it is important to delineate some of the major historical milestones in this research, in order to later clarify the underlying assumptions of health and sickness, which guided the professionals engaged in each phase of this research.

History

The psychological assessment of Holocaust survivors has a rich and varied past and has continued in intervals almost since the release of the first emaciated camp inmates. The first professional attempt to interview survivors was probably done by the American psychologist David P. Boder, who traveled through several European displaced persons camps in 1946, electrically recording interviews with over one hundred camp survivors concerning their recent experiences. Boder (1949; 1952) published some of these interviews in his book, *I Did Not Interview the Dead,* and many were recently republished by Niewyk (1998) in an oral history book, *Fresh Wounds.* These accounts illustrate the fragmented cognitive mental state of the survivors immediately after the war; their sense of shock and bewilderment, their attempt to comprehend what had just happened to them; and their worries about relatives and concerns for their future.

Early research by mental health professionals, such as Bruno Bettelheim (1943; 1979) and Viktor Frankl (1947), was mostly based on autobiography and observations of their own behavior and that of their fellow inmates. These historical accounts of life and death in the camps still represent some of the most striking psychological observations of how inmates thought and felt and struggled with their day-to-day survival during the war, even though they may be written in a more distant fashion than the eloquent publications of poets and writers, because no mental health professional can be more successful in capturing the human predicament in the shadow world of the Holocaust than authors, such as Primo Levi, Paul Celan, Nelly Sachs, Elie Wiesel, Aharon Appelfeld, Imre Kertész, and several others (Lang, 1988; Langer, 1991; 1995; Schiff, 1995; Sicher, 1998).

The first actual studies on Holocaust survivors, however, were apparently done in Scandinavia, only a few years after the war. In Sweden, Getreu (1952) reported on *Smedsbo,* a boarding school for concentration camp survivor adolescent girls and boys from 1945 until 1948 (more of this study will be reported in chapter 3). In Denmark, the psychiatrists Herman and Thygesen (1954) described the concentration camp syndrome (*Konzentration-lagersyndrom*) on the basis of detailed research carried out already in 1947 (Thygesen et al., 1970). In Norway, Leo Eitinger (1964; 1980), who was himself a camp survivor, started to work with the local survivors almost immediately after returning from captivity, and found that almost all of them suffered from some serious mental disorder. Eitinger's greatest achievement was in his meticulous studies of *Mortality and Morbidity after Excessive Stress* (1973), in which he concluded that the severity of the mental disorder was correlated with the severity and duration of the concentration camp experiences, and not related to the patient's organic or premorbid personality. This was a revolutionary idea at the time when chronic psychiatric disorders had to be the result of some form of tainted personality and disposition, rather than the result of excessive stress (such as Nazi persecution). In fact, these studies contributed greatly to define the way we today understand posttraumatic stress disorders and enduring personality changes after catastrophic experience. Most importantly, this new diagnosis helped survivors receive some acknowledgment of their emotional suffering and war disability pensions (*Wiedergutmachung*) (Pross, 2001) for mental disabilities, rather than only for the physical impairments.

As a result of this pioneering work, psychiatrists from all over the world were called upon to examine the emotional state of Holocaust survivors, and write recommendations for indemnification claims. One of these psychiatrists was Niederland in the United States, who was appointed by the German authorities in 1953. On the basis of the earlier diagnosis suggested by the Danish psychiatrists, Niederland (1964) coined the term *The Survivor Syndrome*, which became the predominant diagnosis of Holocaust survivors with emotional problems at the time. His clinical observations of over eight hundred survivors in a series of publications in the 1970s and 1980s (Niederland, 1971; 1972; 1981; 1988), helped greatly to improve the understanding of this population.

During the following years, an international research network was established with Robert Lifton, Ulrich Venzlaff, and Henry Krystal, who published handbooks, such as *Massive Psychic Trauma* (Krystal, 1968) and *Psychic Traumatization: Aftereffects in Individuals and Communities* (Krystal & Niederland, 1968; 1971). This early groundbreaking literature described the diverse and devastating psychopathological effects of Holocaust trauma upon the survivors (Chodoff, 1963), and opened doors for this client population to receive improved diagnosis and treatment.

Israeli psychiatrists, such as Winnik (1967), Klein (1968), Robinson (1979), Dasberg (1987), Hertz (1990), Davidson (1992), and others were also examining survivors for the German authorities on a regular basis and published their findings, sometimes from a psychoanalytic perspective. One of the first publications originating from Israel on the persistent effects of internment of survivors of the Nazi concentration camps was written by Shuval (1957), as a by-product of her study of adjustment problems of immigrants in Israel. She did not find survivors to be more distrustful of the outside world than other immigrants. In 1962, Levinger, an Israeli neuropsychiatrist, himself a refugee from Nazi Germany before the Holocaust, published a statistical descriptive study on the psychiatric evaluation of eight hundred such cases.

Such research continued uninterrupted all over the world with increasing intensity. In his review on the research on long-term effects of the Holocaust upon the survivors, Lomranz (1995) concluded that over the course of twenty years, 182 studies had been published (an average of 9–10 studies per year). Most of these, however, lacked a control group, or even when used (in only 35 studies), these were inappropriate. The majority of publications were clinical reports of Holocaust survivors who were being evaluated for psychiatric treatment and/or compensation and they presented a gloomy picture of severe symptomatology with considerable affective, cognitive, and behavioral impairments. The usual complaints of such survivors included: (1) massive repression, numbing of responsiveness, amnesia, alexithymia (a lack of words for what they felt); (2) intrusive memories, Holocaust-related associations, shattered assumptions; (3) anhedonia, suicidal ideation, depression, chronic state of mourning; (4) survivor guilt; (5) sleep disturbances with terrifying nightmares; (6) problems with anger regulation and in dealing with interpersonal conflicts; (7) excessive worries, anxieties, catastrophic expectancy, fear of renewed persecution; (8) suspiciousness, paranoia, isolation from the community, lack of trust, loneliness; (9) utilization of survival strategies *from there*; and (10) low threshold for stress (Kellermann, 2001c).

This detrimental view of survivors was frequently criticized for being based on nonrepresentative clinical case reports, with an overemphasis on psychopathology. When considering this critique, it is important to remember that the early work was done within a specific historic context, where survivors were struggling for both recognition and compensation and that these early studies helped them gain both. In addition, it counteracted the widespread *Holocaust-victim phobia,* which was predominant among mental health professionals and which often led them to keep a safe distance from this "radioactive" client population (Danieli, 1981b; Solomon, Neria & Ram, 1998).

The psychopathology of Holocaust survivors nevertheless remained a controversial issue during all these postwar years. Any statement describing this population in general as disturbed would evoke intense protest, because it would stigmatize already-disempowered people (Herman, 1992). Contrary statements that this population was *not* disturbed would evoke equal protest on the grounds that "nobody who went through the Holocaust could remain insulated from emotional scars." The arguments for and against were more emotional than informative. During the last decade, this situation has largely changed. Apparently, it has now become easier to reconcile both views on the grounds that they can be equally true and, in fact, complement one another. Holocaust survivors *were* of course emotionally affected by the Holocaust, but they were not necessarily *disturbed,* in view of the fact that their various emotional responses should be regarded as *normal responses to an extremely abnormal situation.* This position will be further discussed below within its proper historical context.

The following six assumptions of mental health and disease in Holocaust survivors have evolved during the last six decades:

1. Severe mental disease

Immediately after the war, survivors who showed signs of mental distress were assumed to be suffering from some kind of prewar organic and constitutional illness or personality disorder that continued after the war. Simply put, *a disturbed person before the war was disturbed also after the war.* The severe mental disease had nothing to do with the war (and the German authorities were not responsible).

Some of these survivors were patients with schizophrenia before the war and many of them were hospitalized in psychiatric institutions after the war. In an early study, Natan, Eitinger, and Winnik (1964) compared two such groups of hospitalized patients, one of whom were camp survivors and the other who were immigrants from the former Soviet Union. They found that camp survivors showed a more chronic course and a more mixed picture of anxiety and depression than the control group.

Many years later, Terno et al. (1998) assessed elderly Holocaust survivors in a long-stay psychiatric setting, most of who were diagnosed with chronic schizophrenia and had been hospitalized since the Holocaust. Though they assumed that the chronic nature of the illness and the massive lifelong psychological disintegration was caused by the Holocaust, this is not yet substantiated with sufficient evidence (even though Reulbach et al., 2007 found that *late schizophrenia* was associated with the highest category of persecution). It is more probable that such illnesses indeed have an organic source. One reason for this is that the prevalence of Holocaust survivors with these illnesses is approximately the same as in the general population. We may assume, however, that even with such a severe disease, the prognosis and symptomatology of the disease will be affected by the patient's war experiences.

Recently, Davidovitch and Zalashik (2007) analyzed the attitude and treatment of mentally ill Holocaust survivors in Israel. Thousands of these survivors who suffered from mental problems were hospitalized for decades in various psychiatric and geriatric hospitals. A few years ago, about three hundred of these chronic survivors were moved to hostels, old-age homes, and other nonhospital facilities to receive more humane care.

2. Holocaust traumatization

After a prolonged battle in the courts and as a result of extensive psychiatric evaluations, survivors who did not fit within previous psychiatric classification labels started to be diagnosed with a new specific syndrome, which was assumed to be caused by the extreme trauma that they had experienced. Simply put, they had been healthy before the war, but had become mentally ill from their war experiences.

Given that many survivors were in a very bad emotional state, a new name had to be found to describe their mental status. The *KZ Syndrome* (Bastiaans, 1974a; 1974b) or *Survivor Syndrome* was created for this purpose. This new syndrome clearly indicated that this mental disorder was a result of the maltreatment and the stress, rather than because of some earlier precondition.

According to this view, anyone could become mentally ill if they experienced extreme stress. As a result of such a new psychiatric perspective or *pragmatic shift*, when the World Health Organization published their new classification of mental disorders in 1992 (ICD-10), they included a category called "Enduring personality change after catastrophic experience." According to Krystal and Danieli (1994), the "emerging descriptions of survivors' problems helped to shape awareness of the posttraumatic pattern and to form a prototype of what came to be recognized as PTSD in DSM-III" (pp. 1–2). Further research on the prevalence of PTSD in Holocaust survivors will be presented below.

3. Chronic traumatization

Some years later, a third view developed, based on the assumption that traumatic disorders, rather than gradually easing up, were instead aggravated in numerous cases. This phenomenon came as a surprise to many clinicians because "in the early postwar years it was optimistically believed that the mental disturbances in most of the survivors would gradually subside after a period of adaptation, but unfortunately these hopes have not been realized. In daily clinical practice, psychiatrists are faced with large numbers of these patients in whom the psychological sequelae have actually deepened with the passage of time" (Winnik, 1967, p. 8).

Many controlled studies conducted during the last decades have substantiated this observation with empirical evidence (Eaton, Sigal, & Weinfeld, 1982; Levav & Abrahamson, 1984; Carmil & Carel, 1986; Keilson, 1979/1992; Kuch & Cox, 1992; Bower, 1994; Yehuda et al., 1995; Sadavoy, 1997; Favaro et al., 1999; Landau & Litwin, 2000; Brom, Durst, & Aghassy, 2002; Joffe et al., 2003; Shmotkin, Blumstein, & Modan, 2003; Ben-Zur & Zimmerman, 2005; Freyberg & Freyberg, 2007; Stessman et al., 2008; Levav, 2009). These studies showed that the mental health and psychosocial adjustment of Holocaust survivors were worse than other comparable populations.

Several studies also indicated that survivor symptoms persist into old age (Sadavoy, 1997; Letzter-Pouw & Werner, 2005). In a recent comprehensive demographic survey of the general elderly population in Israel, Brodsky (2005) reported that Holocaust survivors increasingly suffer from problems related to mental health such as depression and sleep disorders, frequent feelings of loneliness, negative appraisal of their own health status, and from problems related to mobility outside the home, to a much higher extent than comparable elderly groupings.

4. Late-onset traumatization

The fourth view was based on the assumption that survivors might have been healthy before the war, and also functioned adequately after the war, but that they could develop *late effects* from the war, as a result of anxiety-provoking associations, a new trauma, or simply in old age, *thirty, forty, fifty* or *sixty* years after the war. According to this view, survivors would be *at risk* of developing a mental disorder all through life, but especially at times of renewed stress and retraumatization. This view also represented a new perspective, because people had hitherto assumed that emotional effects occurred during and immediately after a stressful event, and not many years later. An extensive overview of the scientific evidence for such late-onset posttraumatic reactions was presented by Dasberg (2003) in an expert opinion to the German court.

5. *Resilience*

During the last decade, a fifth view evolved in contrast to the earlier ones, which put too much emphasis on the psychopathology of the survivor. This new perspective regarded survivors as being healthy before the war, and observed that a majority seemed to have recuperated very well after the war, suggesting that they were basically *strong* and *resilient* which made them survive in the first place (Anthony & Cohler, 1987; Sigal, 1998). Proponents of this view based this on the argument that, apparently, most survivors never received a psychiatric diagnosis, nor did they require any mental health treatment.

This assumption takes the health-promoting or *salutogenic* factors, such as growth, adaptability, and resourcefulness of the survivors into account (Shmotkin & Lomranz, 1998), rather than only the *pathogenic* or disease-causing ones. This view was largely based on the work of the Israeli medical sociologist Antonovsky (1979; 1987), who stumbled upon this idea while studying problems of menopause in female camp survivors. What surprised him was not that they had health problems, but that they were in good health and that their ability to heal remained intact despite their ordeals.

Several researchers have made similar observations (e.g., Suedfeld, 1997; 2001; 2002), emphasizing the resilience (Bonanno, 2004; Ayalon, 2005) of Holocaust survivors. In his paper on the "Skewed image of the Holocaust survivor," Lomranz (2000) concluded that even though there might be some disturbances on the part of the survivors, they did not suffer from more psychopathology than others. Studies such as Antonovsky et al. (1971); Harel, Kahana, & Kahana (1993); Krell (1993); Leon et al. (1981); Shanan & Shahar (1983); Segal (1986); Shanan (1989); Lifton (1993); Cohen et al. (2001); Sigal & Weinfeld (2001); Kahana, Harel, & Kahana (2005); and Lurie-Beck, Liossis, & Gow (2008) also provided additional data indicating the positive coping skills of survivors. Such studies showed that there were no more serious problems in survivors than in comparative groups.

Other studies also demonstrated that Holocaust survivors were able to establish a productive and successful existence, as well as a happy family life. Over the years, there has also been an emergence of studies that document the substantial contributions that survivors have made to their communities (Helmreich, 1992). Finally, *Yad Vashem* in Israel recently devoted a Holocaust Memorial Day to the celebration of the survivors for such achievements.

In a recent meta-analysis of fifty-nine prior studies of more than twelve thousand Holocaust survivors, Barel (2009) concluded that Holocaust survivors in Israel seemed to cope better with the traumatic late effects than those living in the United States and Australia. She explained that, "On the one hand, the difficulties connected to life in Israel through wars and problematic financial situations would intuitively mean a less supportive environment for coping with trauma ... These studies, however, seem to support an opposing view, which argued that the 'national sense of purpose' in Israel and 'togetherness' offer a more supportive environment than elsewhere. The fact that the troubles of war and pressures that come with it are shared by everyone could help reduce trauma and isolation rather than augment it."

6. *Complex traumatization*

A sixth view evolved from these earlier perspectives. This included a more complex picture of adult and child survivors who seemed to function well and who had never applied for psychiatric treatment, but who admitted that they had suffered tremendously from deep emotional scars ever since the war. The nonclinical population of Holocaust survivors, described by Robinson et al. (1990), is a good example of such a complex combination of disorders. They were described as suffering after the war and as still suffering from the results of persecution, but they nevertheless succeeded in coping and adjusting, being successful at work and in society, and they managed to raise warm families. Such a *mixed picture* was also found by Cohen, Brom, & Dasberg (2001), who observed that while child survivors were indeed suffering from PTSD and were vulnerable to stress, they did not show any marked psychosocial symptoms.

This mental state demanded a more in-depth clinical analysis than those that had been hitherto attempted, including an additional factor which had been absent from earlier research. This factor was the *hardening* effect that sometimes demanded a high price in terms of emotional restriction, but which also was helpful in the psychological adaptation to extreme stress. It had been earlier described by Dasberg (1987) in his review of the comparative studies conducted on nonclinical populations of Holocaust survivors. Recently, in their longitudinal study of survivors, Yehuda et al. (2009) also found *either* a worsening *or* an improvement of trauma-related symptoms over time in persons with and without PTSD earlier in time.

What we can conclude from this additional perspective of a *complex traumatization* is that any diagnostic label—including PTSD—might be insufficient when describing such a *mixed* patient population. According to Brom, Durst, & Aghassy (2002), "PTSD is not and has never been suitable to describe the complex constellation of symptoms that have been observed in Holocaust survivors. The deep-seated injury and lack of basic trust, the extreme restriction of emotions and characterological difficulties (Krystal, 1981) are not adequately accounted for by the criteria of PTSD. Even now, more than 55 years after the end of World War II, no diagnostic conceptualization has been proposed that can cover the complexity of the clinical phenomena of help-seeking Holocaust survivors" (p. 199).

7. Paradoxical integration

This brings us to the present phase in which we are trying to integrate the above diverse observations of Holocaust survivor postwar adjustment, which often appear to be paradoxical in nature. When trying to reach a comprehensive appraisal of the survivor of extreme trauma, we attempt to include *both* vulnerability and resilience; both severe traumatization and *also* extraordinary growth; both softness and hardiness, both periods of severe suffering and symptomatology *and* periods of emotional balance and creativity. In addition, we try to acknowledge both victimization *and* legacy, which hitherto have been so difficult to appreciate in combination, both among individual survivors and within the society at large (Updegraff & Taylor, 2000).

Any informed discussion about the health and disease of Holocaust survivors must take all of these assumptions into account, rather than only a few *either-or* conceptions of mental health. Within such a broad and integrative view, we might be better able to analyze and summarize the abundant cumulative research available on the various aspects of the mental disease and health of this population and suggest more effective treatment alternatives.

From the point of view of psychopathology, it is clear that the clinical population of survivors who ask for help are suffering from a combination of posttraumatic symptoms with some kind of depression. From the point of view of health and adaptation, it is equally clear that there were an abundance of health promoting factors at work during the early and late working-through of Holocaust survivors. No *either-or* perspective can adequately describe the survivor and no simple psychiatric label, including PTSD, will be all-encompassing for all individuals. In the sections below, we will therefore reexamine the early and late studies on the prevalence of PTSD, complicated mourning, and health promoting factors in Holocaust survivors.

Posttraumatic Stress Disorder
(PTSD) in Holocaust Survivors

When professionals today study the consequences of stressful events on older people, they usually describe them as a manifestation of a posttraumatic stress disorder.

This was not always the case. Twenty years ago, references to PTSD were conspicuously absent from the Holocaust survivor literature (Yehuda & Giller, 1994). But clinicians and researchers seem lately to have become less opposed to diagnosing Holocaust survivors with PTSD. A good example is Henry Krystal, one of the early authorities in the field, who initially (1968) found the existing category of *traumatic neurosis* inappropriate for describing concentration camp survivors. Many years later, however, he started to advocate the diagnostic criteria of PTSD for this population, in a *spirit of compromise* (Krystal, 1993, p. 841) and in order for the treatments of Holocaust survivors to be covered by public health care (Kellermann, 1999).

Researchers have undergone a similar change. For example, while Wilson, Smith, & Johnson (1985) did not include Holocaust survivors in their comparative analysis of PTSD among various survivor groups, Weisaeth & Eitinger (1993), almost a decade later, did. Hence, during the last few years, an increasing number of studies (Yehuda, et al., 1994; Kaminer & Lavie 1991; Kuch & Cox, 1992; Valent, 1995a; Conn, 2000) have applied the formal diagnostic criteria for PTSD to Holocaust survivors. Advocating this research philosophy, Yehuda & Giller (1994) concluded that "if Holocaust survivors had been considered from the vantage point of either having or not having posttraumatic stress syndrome, this might have helped clarify prior observations of other aspects of posttraumatic adaptation, such as affect dysregulation, character changes, psychiatric co-morbidity and resilience, and might have provided a more cohesive literature" (p. 13). Kolb (1985) was in agreement with this latter view, suggesting that Holocaust survivors should be investigated in the light of what is known about traumatized people in general.

We are therefore in a position today to suggest that the DSM-IV disorder most suitable to this clinical population would be *Chronic Posttraumatic Stress Disorder*, with depression (Conn, 2000) as a frequent associated feature (Yehuda et al., 1994). According to the DSM-IV (American Psychiatric Association, 1994), this type of anxiety disorder includes the following common features, frequently observed in a clinical population of Holocaust survivors: (1) exposure to a traumatic event that invoked intense fear, helplessness, or horror; (2) the trauma is reexperienced, for example, through recurrent distressing recollections; (3) avoidance of stimuli associated with trauma, and a numbing of general responsiveness; and (4) symptoms of increased arousal (e.g., sleep disturbances, irritability, concentration difficulties, and startle responses).

However, because PTSD may be felt as a grave underestimation of the trauma of the Holocaust, comparing the prolonged suffering of the Holocaust survivor erroneously with the stress responses of comparably limited traumatic events such as car accidents, earthquakes, or rape, the term *complex* trauma or the distinct subcategory called *victimization sequel disorder* may be added as a more precise denomination because, according to Herman (1992), "survivors of prolonged abuse develop characteristic personality changes, including alterations in affect regulation, consciousness, self-perception, perception of the perpetrator, relations with others, and alterations in systems of meaning" (p. 121).

How common is PTSD among Holocaust survivors? The *prevalence* of PTSD in a general population of adults who have experienced a stressful event is about 9 percent (Kessler et al., 1995; Breslau et al., 1998). But among tortured war veterans, or among civilians who have been exposed to purposeful bodily harm, the chance of developing PTSD has been repeatedly observed to be much higher. Such increased susceptibility to PTSD also holds true for the prevalence rates among Holocaust survivors even though these rates may vary greatly from study to study. According to Dasberg (2003), the prevalence of a full-blown PTSD in elderly Holocaust survivors, half a century after the war, was reported by different studies as being between 39 percent and 65 percent. But he also emphasized that the prevalence of *single* posttraumatic complaints and symptoms would be even higher.

It is my estimation from Amcha in Israel that *at least* 50 percent of all Holocaust survivors have suffered from immediate or delayed PTSD at some period in their postwar life. While a majority of these survivors seem to have recovered well, a clinical population of 15–25 percent remains chronically traumatized and in need of specialized psychosocial support at any specific point in time.

In an extensive review of the literature on the epidemiology of elderly Holocaust survivors and war combat veterans, Sadavoy (1997) observed that while survivor syndromes persist into old age, patterns of expression vary. Holocaust survivors appear to have adapted well to instrumental aspects of life, whereas combat warriors may show less functional life-adaptation. Persisting symptoms in all groups include marked disruptions of sleep and dreaming, intrusive memories, impairment of trust, avoidance of stressors, and heightened vulnerability to various types of age-associated retraumatization. Some of these symptoms will be further described below.

Sleep disturbances are perhaps one of the most common symptoms of Holocaust traumatization. Here is a common example:

An elderly man complained of severe sleeping problems. He awoke almost every night in a sweat, unable to fall back to sleep. Since being less active, painful memories from the Holocaust had returned with all accompanying affects and he was overwhelmed with terror. He recounted a recurrent nightmare in which Gestapo soldiers hunted him on motorcycles. It was forbidden for Jews in the ghetto to be out at night and he ran for his life until arriving at the door of his house, which was closed and locked. Standing in front of the large door, he shouted and called for his father to open the door. He shouted "Papa! Papa!" but nobody opened the door. While shouting aloud, he became aware of his wife trying to wake him up and he realized that it was only a dream. But he was unable to fall asleep again, remembering how his family had been slaughtered and how he had been forced to do things that could never be forgiven. The fact that he was still alive was an absurd accident because life had lost its meaning for him. "Before there was *life*," he said, "now it is just an *existence*."

Empirical research has confirmed this clinical impression. Rosen et al. (1991) found that (forty-five years after liberation) survivors had significantly greater sleep impairment than healthy comparison subjects, but less impairment than depressed patients (except for more frequent awakenings due to bad dreams). These sleep disturbances and frequency of nightmares were significantly and positively correlated with the duration of the survivors' internment in concentration camps. Similarly, Pillar, Malhotra, & Lavie (2000) found that patients with PTSD often suffered from bad sleep disorders and nightmares. He found that such patients complained of difficulties falling asleep because of hyperarousal, but once they fell asleep their sleep was actually deeper. They concluded that if the *sleep deepening* mechanism was dominant they experienced an increased percentage of slow-wave sleep, but if the *hyperarousal* mechanism dominated, the final result would be insomnia.

In addition to sleep disturbances, Holocaust survivors respond with habitual panic when exposed to *triggers* that in some way symbolize the Holocaust. Such Holocaust-associated triggers may include any or all of the following:

- *Crowded trains, cattle wagons, train stations;*
- *Barking dogs, (especially German shepherds);*

- *Standing in line, selections, roll-call;*
- *Wooden shoes, uniforms, SS signs, striped clothes;*
- *Crematoriums, pizza ovens, burned flesh;*
- *Gas, gasmasks, biological warfare;*
- *Extermination (of insects), cleansing;*
- *Music by Wagner, German language, everything Made in Germany;*
- *Separations, death, leave-taking, loss;*
- *Exhaust fumes, barbed wire, fences;*
- *Swastikas, Neo-Nazism, cruelty, Holocaust denial;*
- *Other catastrophes, disasters, and genocides;*
- *Familiar smells, sounds, tastes from the war.*

Any of these triggers may create a violent emotional response in the survivor who at that moment is thrown back to a life-threatening situation during the Holocaust. In addition, happy occasions such as weddings, Jewish holidays, and family celebrations may also evoke sudden grief reactions, as they remind survivors of their immense loss and all the people who are absent because they were so brutally killed.

In addition to the above examples, elderly Holocaust survivors frequently associate hospitals and old age homes with concentration camps and they tend to respond with anxiety and frustration when being admitted to such *total* institutions. To help alleviate such stress, Paula David (2003) from Baycrest in Canada compiled a manual for caretakers, in which she listed some of the most common triggers in hospitalized survivors, along with possible aversive reactions, their source in the Holocaust past, and suggested response tips for caretaking personnel. An attempt to shave a resident, for example, may evoke a violent protest because of the memories it brings back to the shaved heads in the camp. Other such triggers described in the book included "taking a shower or a bath, fear of public or strange toilets, lack of privacy, small spaces, crowded conditions, medical history-taking, requests for medical procedures, receiving injections, wristband identification (depersonalization to a number), lining up for treatment, unpleasant smells, illnesses and feeling unwell, secure areas, locks on doors, physical restraint, limited access, flashlight examination (searchlights), family members or visitors saying goodbye (memory of final separations), foreign language or heavy accents, loud voices and sounds, crying or screaming, left/right selections, routines and schedules, determined meal time and food presentation, insufficient provision of food, hunger pangs, hoarding of food, Jewish holidays, specific hospital clothing, relocation, and dentist treatment (gold fillings)" (pp. 51–59).

However, nothing is more emotionally disturbing for survivors who have experienced starvation than the discarding of food. Sindler, Wellman, and Stier (2004) confirmed that food attitudes were influenced by Holocaust experiences. Five themes emerged: (1) difficulty throwing food away, even when spoiled; (2) storing excess food; (3) craving certain food(s); (4) difficulty standing in line for food; and (5) experiencing anxiety when food is not readily available. Empathy for those currently suffering from hunger was also reported. In their study of binge eating, Favaro et al. (2000) similarly found that people who have survived a period of extreme food deprivation are more likely to develop binge-eating behavior than others.

As recently shown in a study by Marcus & Menczel (2007), malnutrition during childhood and adolescence often led to *osteoporosis* later in life and the prevalence of *osteoporosis* was significantly higher among female Holocaust survivors than a comparative population.

In addition to their past Holocaust trauma, survivors also have to cope with changes occurring as a result of aging: loss of spouses and long-term friends, lack of financial resources, social isolation, loneliness, and functional impairment. Such normative stressors tend to *reactivate* the past traumatic experiences and increase the number of elderly survivors who suffer from emotional problems.

The impact on survivors of such cultural historical-normative events as wars, economic crises, or the absorbing country's reception of the immigrant, has received increasing attention (Charny, 1991). Contrary to the view of an inoculating effect of the Holocaust upon survivors that leads to greater resilience in dealing with stress, some Holocaust survivors seem to have become more vulnerable to such new stressful events rather than less. In these survivors, defenses to ward off anxiety and depression that had been successful earlier in life have become harder to utilize at a more advanced age.

Yehuda et al. (1995) investigated how the present and the past *add up* when looking at the suffering of an individual survivor. They found that Holocaust survivors with PTSD reported significantly greater cumulative trauma and recent stress than survivors without PTSD and with comparison subjects. The severity of PTSD symptoms, including both cumulative trauma and recent stress were significantly associated. Similarly, in their study on the psychological effects of the Persian Gulf War on nonclinical survivors, Solomon & Prager (1992) found that survivors tended to perceive higher levels of danger and report more symptoms of acute distress than comparison subjects. As expected, survivors who had homes being hit by SCUD missiles were most retraumatized (Robinson et al., 1994). Lamet & Dyer (2004) also found that increased symptoms of posttraumatic stress remained with the Holocaust survivors after the September 11 event. Characteristic themes included paralleling the present with the past and reliving the past, empathy with current victims, reawakening and awakening and hope for the future generations. Zloof et al. (2005) found both resilience and vulnerability in survivors who were exposed to the threat of terror in Israel. However, Schreiber et al. (2003) found no differences in the coping behavior between survivors and nonsurvivors who had heart surgery.

Baider & Sarell (1984) found that Holocaust survivor cancer patients showed lower coping potentials overall and that they reported significantly higher psychological distress than controls (Baider, Peretz, & Kaplan De-Nour, 1993), but there were no differences in other coping indicators. In a recent similar study, Hantman & Solomon (2007) tried to determine whether elderly Holocaust survivors were affected differently from nonsurvivors by the adversity of aging and cancer. They again found a significant difference between survivors and nonsurvivors in posttraumatic symptoms and their intensity, with survivors having significantly more PTSD symptoms. However, additional analysis of the various survivor subgroups (victims, fighters, and those who made it), *victims* were shown as suffering from PTSD and psychiatric symptomatology to a higher degree and had more difficulties in coping with the problems of old age than the other groups.

Holocaust survivors exposed to new stressful events are not only retraumatized by these events, they also face a significant *cumulative traumatization,* which is added to the earlier traumatic experiences. For example, some Israeli survivors who recently experienced terror attacks during the Palestinian uprising responded with extraordinary fear and bewilderment to the military tension, as it brought back terrible memories of people being blown to pieces during the bombardment of the Second World War. Such Holocaust recollections are of course especially common when entire families are being destroyed, leaving only a single child alive, and when pregnant women, senior citizens, and new immigrants are brutally killed in such a "pogrom."

The worst responses are seen when elderly Holocaust survivors who lost everything during the Second World War, are again burying their own children, their grandchildren and/or their spouses. "It all comes back again to me," they say. "It is like it was *then and there.*"

Trauma can evoke a wide variety of psychological symptoms, and responses to trauma should perhaps be better understood within a spectrum of conditions rather than as a single, well-defined disorder (Herman, 1992; Cook, 2002). Complicated bereavement and grief with depressive features, is a related, but separate, clinical manifestation of Holocaust trauma frequently observed in survivors.

Traumatic Loss, Depression, and Complicated Grief

Holocaust survivors do not only suffer from anxiety and posttraumatic stress, but also from various forms of late grief reactions and general melancholia. Yehuda et al. (1994) found that *depressive symptoms* in individuals who have been traumatized are more severe when associated with a concurrent PTSD. Similarly, Trappler, Cohen, & Tulloo (2007) found that the prevalence of depression and PTSD symptoms was very high among survivors. Most importantly, depressed Holocaust survivors seem to have significantly worse psychological and social functioning than depressed controls.

Many Holocaust survivors show a uniform melancholic clinical picture, with sad affect and restrained expression. Their narrative is often accompanied by excessive crying and they sometimes communicate self-reproach, helplessness, and overt pessimism. Among elderly survivors, there are also aggravating cognitive problems, concentration difficulties, forgetfulness, and irritability. Physical signs include loss of appetite, sleep disturbances, lack of energy, aches and pains, and a general sense of fatigue.

All such signs of depression invariably lead to the question of suicide in survivors. Eitinger (1993) observed that, "overwhelmed by unfounded feelings of guilt combined with feelings of hopelessness, Primo Levi became melancholic to such a degree that he committed suicide, many years after his liberation. Or was he—were we—ever completely liberated? He committed suicide just like Jean Améry, the Austrian philosopher who escaped to Belgium, was caught and tortured by the Gestapo as a Belgian resistance fighter, sent to Auschwitz as a Jew, and "liberated" in 1945. Like Paul Célan, the Romanian-born poet and survivor, who lived in France after the war and wrote the most moving poems. Or like Jerzy Kosinsky, the Polish-born Holocaust survivor who became such a successful writer here in the U.S." (p. 9). From detailed biographies of famous survivors who committed suicide during and after the war, Lester (2005) also analyzed such suicidal behavior in Holocaust survivors to try to understand why there seemed to be more incidents of suicide after the war than during the war. Similarly, Titelman (2006) discussed such suicide-nearness from a psychoanalytic perspective, and exemplified it with the life and death of Primo Levi.

Severely depressed Holocaust survivors are apparently a high-risk group for attempted suicide and this population has been the object of increased attention and research lately. For example, Clarke et al. (2004) examined the impact of past exposure to the Nazi Holocaust on the development of suicidal ideation in a sample of depressed older adults. They found that severity of depression and exposure to the Holocaust was independently associated with suicidal ideation. The chronic stress produced by these traumatic events may have predisposed survivors to cope ineffectively as they age, thus resulting in suicidal ideation. In addition, Barak et al. (2005) found that the incidence of attempted suicide was three times higher for Holocaust survivors (24 percent) as compared to other elderly mental health patients (8 percent) before admittance to a psychiatric hospital in Israel. Finally, in a review of published reports on suicide among Holocaust survivors, Barak (2007) confirmed an increased rate of suicidal ideation and suicide attempts among elderly Holocaust survivors. All these findings emphasize the need for preventive measures in depressed survivors so that suicidal risk may be contained as much as possible.

Additional signs of the inner pessimistic world-view of survivors were described by Janoff-Bulman (1992) as "shattered fundamental assumptions" about the world that is no longer the same as before the trauma. This world is no longer benevolent and meaningful and human beings are no longer worthy. The trauma taught survivors that *bad things* can really happen, that people may really become victims, and that they have no real worth as human beings in this world. In addition, according to Lifton (1979), death imprint and death anxiety are cardinal features of survivors of massive trauma. Death imprint means a "radical intrusion of an image-feeling of threat or end of life" (p. 169), an all-encompassing sense of hopelessness and the end of existence.

When observing such symptoms, we need to differentiate between: (1) *common unhappiness,* which is so common in old age; (2) grief because of a recent loss; and (3) mild or major depression, which is sometimes *masked* by physical symptoms. In most Holocaust survivors, such a clinical picture is frequently complicated by the fact that they have been stuck in the process of unresolved grief for more than half a century, and that this prolonged mourning process has been a part of their existence for most of their lives. The concept of *traumatic bereavement* was suggested to describe this state of mind in a recent paper by Witztum & Malkinson (2009).

For our present purposes, we will here focus on this latter state of *complicated mourning*, and describe some of its main characteristics. Complicated mourning among Holocaust survivors is characterized by a dysfunctional adaptation to loss: blocked feelings, rigidified relationships, and stopped time. Upon further analysis it becomes apparent that images of the deceased preoccupy the mind of the bereaved; also, there is a persistent yearning for the lost object, overidentification with the deceased, and misdirected anger and ambivalence both toward self and toward the other (*why did you leave me?*).

The state of complicated mourning was caused by the fact that, during and immediately after the war, it was apparently impossible to grieve for the following reasons: first, mourning was postponed and suppressed because people had just disappeared; there was often no dead body, no grave, no date of death, and no concrete evidence that the loved person had really died. As it is very difficult to realize loss without concrete evidence, they continued to ask: "Were they really dead?" Survivors who were in doubt and yearned for some closure, continued to endlessly search for traces of their lost family members. With some tangible evidence of their death, survivors could embark on some kind of delayed mourning process. But for the very young survivors who didn't know anything about their parents, regaining closure was especially difficult. Because they didn't have even a small trace left from their family (no pictures, no relatives who could tell their stories, no family history), they started to doubt their own memories and question if there had been life before the Holocaust.

Second, there were too many separations without leave-taking. Parents might have promised their children that "they would return" and children got suddenly separated from their parents never to see them again. All this led to difficulties in acknowledging death because *hope* that the significant other would return one day had helped them to continue to struggle to survive all through the war. "If I knew they were dead, I would not have continued to struggle," they say. To give up such fantasies of future reunion would also endanger their meaning to life, and threaten to throw them into a deep depression with suicidal ideation.

Third, mourning was often impossible during the war even if survivors realized that their family members had died. Even if they were witnessing the executions with their own eyes, survivors had to keep their emotions in control to have a chance to survive. During the subhuman conditions of starvation, threat, and fear, *those who cried, died*, and any overt expression of weakness diminished the chances of survival.

Fourth, the magnitude of loss seems to have been too large to contain within a human mourning process. The enormous multitude of people who died a traumatic death, under the most terrible circumstances, seems to have been too hard to digest, even though the moments of sudden and final separation are forever imprinted in their souls. The atrocities were too overwhelming and they left a sense of emptiness, which cannot be expressed in words. Such *unrepresentability* of trauma has been described variously as alexithymia, numbness, amnesia, etc. (Van der Hart & Brom, 2000), and seems to be an overt sign of massive and primitive repression.

Fifth, when the loss was realized after the war, there were so many other things to do, so many other tasks to fulfill other than mourning. The recuperation from starvation and illnesses, the realization that there would be a future after all, and the struggle for a new existence prevented the survivor from being too preoccupied with the past. Some reported that they simply had insufficient energy to grieve, because all their efforts were focused on rebuilding a new existence, on creating new families, and/or on fighting for a new country. Most survivors decided to *leave the past behind* and make themselves busy instead of giving in to sadness and grief. Refusing to grieve was also a way to deny victory to the Nazis, and not to show weakness and defeat. Finally, mourning was impossible because there was insufficient social support available to the majority of survivors, to enable them to grieve within a social context and among peers. The absence of close family and friends led to a profound sense of alienation and isolation, which sometimes continued for the rest of their lives.

Health-Promoting Factors and Late Working Through

The Holocaust apparently left invisible scars upon the minds and souls of many survivors, leading to chronic emotional problems such as posttraumatic stress disorder and complicated mourning. Other survivors, however, seem to have escaped comparatively unharmed.

What is the difference between these two groups of survivors? Why do only some people who experience trauma develop PTSD? Yehuda (1999) tried to answer these questions and searched for the biological factors that are associated with susceptibility to PTSD as well as other factors that might serve to protect individuals from developing this condition. A growing body of research on resilience was also trying to find the factors that determine why some people rebounded from adversity, strengthened and more resourceful, while others remained paralyzed, depressed, and panic-stricken (Suedfeld, 1997). Some of the answers to these questions lie in the various more or less adaptive coping strategies (Suedfeld et al., 1997) that were utilized by Holocaust survivors during and after the war.

Valent (1995b; 1998) described eight such more or less adaptive survival strategies to cope with traumatic stress: rescuing, attaching, asserting, adapting, fighting, fleeing, competing, and cooperating, which all act as specific bio-psycho-social functional units.

Other successful coping strategies of the Holocaust survivors "who made it" were described by Helmreich, in his book *Against All Odds* (1992, p. 267). He suggested that there are ten general traits or qualities that were present in those survivors who were able to lead positive and useful lives after the war. These are: (1) flexibility—adaptation to a new environment; (2) assertiveness and taking initiative; (3) tenacity—refusal to take *no* for an answer; (4) optimism—a future-oriented approach to life; (5) intelligence, or professional skill; (6) distancing ability—removing the trauma from consciousness; (7) group consciousness and belonging to a certain support group; (8) assimilating the knowledge that they survived; (9) finding meaning and a sense of coherence in one's life; and (10) courage. These traits more or less summarize the various protective factors reported in the trauma literature.

There is no doubt that survivors utilized such survival strategies *more or less* systematically and successfully, not only during the war, but all through life. It is important to emphasize, however, that all such individual coping occurred within a social context, and that there has been an enormous social change in the entire realm of Holocaust survivor awareness during the last two decades. As a result, many of the more affected survivors, who might have been suffering tremendously during the first periods after the war, later found a more balanced emotional state, in which they started to implement some of the more successful coping strategies described above.

During the last decades, many Holocaust survivors clearly have found more inner balance, have gained more recognition and have been blessed with the fruits of their struggles on various private and public levels. This inner balance has enabled some survivors to start to write and publish, paint and exhibit, and become active in Holocaust education on a wide scale. All of these activities helped to counteract the tendency to repress their traumatic memories and make these more available for conscious working through.

Most importantly, however, many survivors have now received professional counseling and support, which helped them to gradually come to terms with themselves and their tragic past. In the following section, I will delineate some of the main principles in such counseling and support.

Treatment of Holocaust Survivors

Eitinger (1993) wrote:

Survivors are of course in need of help, for all their somatic ailments, but still more for their psychological isolation, their feeling of having lost their anchorage in the world and in humanity, their feeling that nobody cares if they are alive or not. If we manage to reverse this tragic evolution by establishing at least traces of inter-human relationships and reduce the deep existential isolation, then we have made an important step.

When do Holocaust survivors apply for help? Holocaust survivors in general do not readily apply for professional assistance with their psychological ailments. Because they are used to being self-sufficient and managing by themselves, they apply for help only after a long period of hesitation. If they do turn to help, it may be because of any of the following reasons: (1) after a new catastrophe, a terrorist attack, a national crisis such as the threat of war; (2) aging, illness, weakness, and fear of death; (3) a powerful Holocaust trigger that has evoked overwhelming depression and/or death anxiety; (4) death of spouse, siblings, friends from the war, or their children; (5) new possibilities to get financial compensation, but their application was declined; (6) children leave home and the survivor becomes lonely with unacceptable dependency needs; (7) new revelations of Nazi atrocities, the trial of Nazi perpetrators, e.g., during the Demanjuk trial 1986–93; (8) when there is too much time and too much emptiness and a wish to fill the free time with something creative and fulfilling; and (9) when everything is in order and the survivors feel that *now* the time has come to tell their stories and to work through their Holocaust experiences.

Upon entering treatment, survivors do not want to be treated as psychiatric patients and they initially show little interest in psychotherapy. Most apply for help with significant doubts. When they do, however, their need for symptom alleviation is often pressing and urgent. It is therefore important to establish a trusting relationship quickly and to give some hope that the efforts in overcoming their resistance to seeking help have been worthwhile. Obviously, a major way of doing this is to make them feel understood and accepted as they are within a framework of fellow-survivors. Entering into the private world of the client and becoming thoroughly at home in it seems to be a prerequisite for such a relationship.

Talking or keeping silent about the Holocaust? After establishing as much safety and trust as possible, the central importance of Holocaust experiences on the lives of the survivor will be emphasized. For this purpose, survivors are invited to recount what they remember from the war already at the beginning of their contact. Survivors who have repressed their painful memories commonly respond ambivalently to such an invitation to retell their war experiences: "Why open old wounds and re-actualize the pain? Why bring out the frightening ghosts from the past? Why not let them sleep? What good does it do to meddle in those terrible memories that happened so many years ago? Let's try instead to forget and go on with life as it is today!"

Such ambivalence is based in part on the difficulties in verbalizing traumatic memories, as expressed by Elie Wiesel (1978):

> How is one to speak of such things and not lose one's mind, and not beat one's fists against the wall? It is as impossible to speak of them as not to speak of them. Too many corpses loom on our horizon; they weigh on every one of our words; their empty eyes hold us in check. One would have to invent a new vocabulary, a new language to say what no human being has ever said (p. 236).

Frankl (1959) similarly explained how former prisoners often disliked talking about their experiences: "No explanations are needed for those who have been inside and the others will understand neither how we felt nor how we feel now" (p. 6). Despite such resistances, however, most survivors today want to retell their stories if they feel that there is somebody who is really willing to listen to them.

The struggle to forget and remain silent on the one hand, and the urge to memorialize and to talk on the other, are both central to the survivor's attempt to organize experience. According to Nutkiewicz (2003), the therapeutic nature of oral testimony makes it a unique platform for both of these conflicting forces to work themselves out, by transforming the (private) narrative of suffering into a (public) narrative of witnessing. In his book on *Listening to Holocaust Survivors*, Greenspan (1998) also emphasized the importance for the survivor to build a narrative of his or her experiences. Such an autobiographic story will be rooted in *two* sets of memories: in meanings and identifications salvaged from wider life histories and in the reduction and, finally, dissolution of those meanings within the destruction itself.

While it is impossible to give any general recommendation about talking or keeping quiet, from the perspective of healing trauma, it is generally agreed that letting out what was hitherto kept in is better than attempting to repress and forget painful memories (Herman, 1992). In other words, memorialization takes precedence over amnesia. In addition, the commemoration of the Holocaust and the acknowledgment of its legacy are surely an essential part of collective working through.

On an individual basis, however, the balance between forgetting and remembering is usually not a conscious and intentional activity. Survivors continue to reexperience the trauma (in vivid recollections and nightmares) while they desperately try to put the past behind them in order to regain some kind of inner balance and emotional equilibrium. Talking about their Holocaust experiences in therapy may in a paradoxical fashion provide some emotional relief. A woman had insomnia and nightmares for many years. She would dream that she was back in the camps and that she was going to die. Once she gave testimony and began writing her memoirs, the nightmares subsided and she slept better. Retelling her story again and again seemed to have helped her. The mere verbalization of memories and the very act of translating feelings into words may thus help to reorganize experiences and make them easier to digest (Freud, 1958). Thus we may conclude that people whose lives have been darkened by the shadow of the Holocaust need to find a way to communicate their experiences, either verbally or nonverbally.

However, while we may agree on the benefits of talking about the Holocaust with survivors, many questions remain regarding the more or less suitable treatment approaches for this population. For example, which therapy approach should be recommended? What works best for whom in which context? Do we recommend long-term, medium, short, or time-limited treatment? In which cases do we suggest individual, group, family, milieu, or psychopharmacological treatment? Should psychotherapy be supportive and reeducative or explorative and reconstructive? Obviously, with such a wide variety of presenting problems, it is impossible to give any specific recommendations. Furthermore, while there is a rich literature on the manifestation of Holocaust traumatization, comparatively little is written about actual treatments with this population (Chodoff, 1980).

Research on the treatment of Holocaust survivors is very scarce. The few studies reported are mostly anecdotal single-case studies, and, as far as I know, there are no published accounts of controlled treatment studies for this population (Sadavoy, 1997). Among the more recent case studies, Seritan, Gabbard, and Benjamin (2006) described a patient with major depression and PTSD who received brief psychodynamic psychotherapy. In this therapy, exploration of early trauma during the Holocaust linked to current stressors took center stage as well as identifying a focus of loss. In another paper, Shamai & Levin-Megged (2006) explored how Holocaust survivors experienced therapy. Overall, their findings contradict the traditional perception, in which the goal of therapy was defined as one of integrating the traumatic narrative with the entire life story. Successful therapy was rather experienced when the traumatic narrative was put into a capsule separated from other parts of the life story.

The treatment of elderly Holocaust survivors differs somewhat from that of their younger brothers and sisters (the *child survivors*) as well as from other, more recently traumatized people. Loss of past and recent family members and the companionship of children, diminished strength and decreasing physical ability, combined with the recurrence of Holocaust memory to accelerate mental distress. In order to suit their personal requests and their individual therapeutic needs, a wide range of treatment alternatives may be suggested. A combination of psychological, social, and occupational approaches, including individual and/or group psychotherapy, psychosocial milieu therapy, and social casework, would be the ideal multimodal option. In addition, as the survivors grow older, there should be a continuous effort to develop more innovative treatment approaches and psychosocial services in their homes to meet the new needs that arise because of aging.

Modest treatment goals and limited therapeutic objectives are proposed with this elderly, fragile population. Except for the obvious focus on mitigating the wounds of the Holocaust, therapy also aims to alleviate the anxieties of aging: to help them deal with depression and grief, with problems of retirement and inactivity, with difficulties in living alone and in becoming dependent on others, and to prepare for an approaching death. A social club, home visits by volunteers, and various group activities may be provided to fill the void of the interpersonal isolation, to increase morale, and to counteract withdrawal and mental deterioration.

Specific rehabilitation activities may also be suggested, such as suitable voluntary work for an active older retired person and the development of appropriate recreational facilities, such as hobbies, lectures, and discussions. Physical exercise classes are offered both as a release of muscle tension and as a means to get their minds off whatever is bothering them. Social casework aims to help resolve problems of housing, health, occupation, socialization, and recreation on a more practical basis. Proper information and guidance is sometimes all that an older person requires to continue to maintain self-respect and independence. Psychopharmacological drugs, including selective serotonin reuptake inhibitors (SSRIs) are sometimes added as an adjunct to psychotherapy in cases of major depression, severe anxiety, and chronic sleeping disturbances.

The following *phases* can often be delineated in the psychotherapeutic treatment of Holocaust survivors. The first stage of therapy is to establish a safe and trusting relationship in which survivors feel accepted and understood. This demands specialized understanding and experience on the part of the psychotherapist as well as considerable attention to the therapists' own counter-responses. Survivors are thereafter encouraged to tell their personal life story, including memories of experiences happening before, during, and after the Holocaust and relate these to the present. Traumatic incidents are addressed directly and, if possible, the accompanying emotions, thoughts, and physical sensations are explored in depth. The emotional working through of the personal meaning of these events (as remembered) thus follows the reconstruction of the actual events. This invariably involves a phase of emotional ventilation and mourning the multiple losses of the past and the present within the confines of a safe, holding environment. Such reconstruction of the trauma requires a sustained immersion in the past experience and a descent into the abyss of mourning and depression. Sometimes, this period might feel like surrendering to tears that seem to be endless. But after many such reconstructions, the moment comes when telling the story no longer arouses such intense feelings for the client. When this happens, the trauma has become a memory like other memories and it begins to fade.

Finally, an attempt is made to reach some degree of resolution or transformation of the traumatic past. This may involve some reconnection with the hitherto neglected traumatic past (e.g., in terms of commemoration), a transformation of the personal meaning of the Holocaust (e.g., in terms of finding a profound personal meaning of survival that replaces guilt) or some integration of the trauma within one's own and one's family's history (e.g., to pass on the legacy of the Holocaust to the next generations). Frankl's (1959) logotherapy, in which survivors are encouraged to work through existential issues around the meaning of life, may be suitable in this stage.

Naturally, resolution of Holocaust traumatization is never complete. According to Friedländer (1992), some amount of "deep memory" of that which essentially remains inarticulate and unrepresentable, will always remain as unresolved trauma just beyond the reach of meaning. In addition, there will always remain a considerable amount of anger, sorrow, fear, and yearning for another reality. But there may also be a sense of completion and of pride for having done so much of what was possible under the specific circumstances.

Most Holocaust survivors seem to need a broad range of psychosocial support, rather than only a specific psychiatric treatment. There are different methods of psychotherapy, including humanistic, existential, psychodynamic, and interpersonal approaches, which all may be suitable for this population. But in the long run, a variety of both individual and group rehabilitation methods will be most effective for the chronically traumatized survivors. For survivors with interpersonal problems, some kind of group therapy with or without elements of reparenting might be the treatment of choice. In addition, creative and expressive techniques such as art, movement, drama, and music therapy may be helpful in various phases of the healing process.

Cognitive therapy is often especially helpful, as it *tunes in* to many of the intuitive survival strategies utilized during the war. This approach is based on the assumption that it is not necessarily the terrible things that happen to people that causes them to be emotionally affected, but rather what they make of these events. From their own life experience, many survivors have learned to reformulate their experiences into various new cognitive structures that helped them to cope better with stress. For example, many have learned to persuade themselves that "things could be much worse" or to say "let's see what this situation is bringing me in terms of challenges and opportunities" instead of complaining about their "bad luck" or "the evil world." Still others are searching for a (more profound) meaning in what is happening, and those who find such a meaning will be able to cope much better than those who do not.

Naturally, specific trauma therapies, such as cognitive behavioral therapy (CBT), eye movement desensitization retraining (EMDR), somatic experiencing (SE), autogenic training, breathing and relaxation exercises, as well as stress management techniques, will also be helpful in the more classic cases of traumatization disorders. The goal in these approaches is to regulate affect, to come to terms with helplessness and to work through specific traumatic experiences on a mental and physical level.

When complex mourning is predominant, grief-resolution therapy with leave-taking rituals may be recommended. Such rituals may include a personal visit to the camp, the "old country," or the hometown of the survivors. Lighting a candle for the deceased relatives in these places may become a transforming experience. Such rituals would also include writing autobiographical material, making a documentary video film, or finding some kind of transitional object that will help one to move on in life from the frozen earlier position. The clinical benefit of video testimony in the alleviation of posttraumatic symptoms was found even among a group of long-term hospitalized psychiatric inpatients (Strous et al., 2005). Whatever can help the survivor to find closure on a spiritual dimension may also be suggested, including specific mourning ceremonies, such as sitting *Shiva* during a specific time, even if the loved person died more than half a century ago.

Even if many of these approaches are powerful and effective in themselves, their ultimate success will depend on the ability of the survivors to find a very personal meaning with their Holocaust trauma. If they found such an inner meaning, they may emerge from their Holocaust traumatization with renewed strength and a stronger existential presence. While some survivors have found such a deep meaning in altruistic ideals, others have found the creation of the Jewish homeland of Israel to be the *raison d'être* for their continuing survival and existence.

But there is nothing as powerfully healing for survivors as seeing their own grandchildren grow up and thrive.

CHAPTER 3

Holocaust Trauma in Child Survivors

These kids were literally "too scared to cry."

—Terr (1990)

Sam's childhood came to a brutal end when he was eight years old. He had been going to school for only two years like the other children in the small town in Romania where he grew up. Then the war started, and he was sent off to work. The basic right to be a child was taken from him and from his friends: "My brother and I worked in the municipal bathing house and we earned only pennies. But there was no choice because father was sent into forced labor and mother was very ill."

Like all the Jews in Europe, he was forced to wear a yellow star and he was later dispatched to clean a Romanian army base. "The freezing cold is accompanying me until this day. Nobody cared about the fact that we were only two small children. We were hungry and afraid. We were not sent to concentration camps like the Jews from Hungary, Poland, and other places, but we were also persecuted and suffering," he would later say.

To this day, Sam is not recognized as a Holocaust survivor and he doesn't get any compensation. He came alone to Israel and settled in the town of Rehovot, married, and had two children. Two years ago, his wife passed away, leaving him all alone (again). In Amcha he found a new family of friends.

How does an eight-year-old child cope with suddenly losing his mom and dad? How does it feel for a small boy to hide under a bed, waiting for the Gestapo to come at any moment? How does it feel for a child to be on the run for years? These are the common traumatic experiences that children endured during World War II.

"One thing is clear. These are children who were deprived of their childhood and who were forced to grow up, literally overnight. One day they were at play. The next, they were foraging for food for their entire families or were responsible for the welfare of their younger brothers and sisters in horrendous circumstances. One day a child was a member of a large family; the next day found this same child abandoned and hiding in caves, forests, and convents, usually with strangers. They were indeed children grown old before their time, elderly children" (Krell, 2006, p. 2).

Indeed, child survivors were prevented from having a normal childhood. Because of the circumstances in which they grew up, they became *little adults* with premature responsibilities. As a result, they are constantly struggling with an alter ego child within them that search for (infantile) need satisfaction.

A female child survivor exclaimed: "I had no real childhood. As a child, I had to be an adult. It was dangerous to be a child. I had to hide the child within me and pretend to be someone else. Therefore, the child inside me is still yearning to be acknowledged and taken care of. But people find it strange to meet an old woman who is really only a child, and I am careful not to disclose this secret of mine. But when I'm around children, they feel it immediately."

The manifestation of Holocaust trauma is different in child survivors than in older Holocaust survivors because children are at the same time more vulnerable and more malleable than adults. Mental health professionals therefore must approach them differently when they apply for help. Most obviously, they often need something less verbal because they cannot easily describe their childhood experiences in words. This chapter will give an overview of the specific manifestations of Holocaust trauma in child survivors and suggest possible treatment approaches for this vulnerable population (cf. Anthony, 1974).

Child Survivor Characteristics

Very few Jewish children survived the Second World War in Europe. Those who did survive settled in places such as the United States, Canada, Australia, the United Kingdom, and Scandinavia or in Israel. But these countries failed to acknowledge child survivors as a specific group of Holocaust survivors until many years after the war. At the first child

Holocaust survivor conference in 1991, they met to form a distinct group. According to Loew (2001): "The child survivors had been neglected for 40, 50 years, really. And the only people that were significant were the adult survivors. But child survivors were thought to be people without much memory—they were only children, they didn't have much memory. They don't count because they're too young. But we do count!" (p. 22).

An additional reason for the *late bloom* of this survivor group might have been that many of them kept silent about their past for such a long time, almost as if they *remained in hiding*, even after the war. Krell (1999), who himself was such a *hidden child* during the war, commented on this reserved stance: "Silence is the language of the child survivor. We might have talked after the war ... but adults persuaded us to get on with life, forget the past. Adults, who themselves had survived and suffered so much, inadvertently diminished the experiences of the children. In the aftermath, in that silence which enveloped our existence, what needed saying was not said."

Because children perceive and remember things differently than adults, they also cope differently with trauma. Apparently, the long years of confinement, deprivation, and family separation forced them to adopt a variety of different and extraordinary survival strategies that continue all through life. Such early trauma reverberates across the entire life span of the child survivor and it is therefore not surprising to find a specific clinical picture in survivors of the Holocaust who were less than sixteen years old when the war ended. This population has been extensively studied by, for example, Keilson (1979/1992), Kestenberg (1982; 1985; 1998), Kestenberg & Brenner (1986; 1996), Robinson & Hemmendinger (1982), Kestenberg & Kahn (1998), Gampel (1988), Laub & Auerhahn (1993), Moskovitz (1983 1985), Dasberg (1992), Durst (1995; 2008), and many others.

For example, in their study on the impact of Holocaust trauma on child development, Kestenberg & Brenner (1996) found that the Holocaust forced these children to mature more rapidly and incompletely (p. 59). Dasberg (2001) summarized the main impact of such premature maturation on the development of the child survivors: "1) a lack of functioning parents or caretakers, who are initially filled with fear and worry, then either disappear, die, or may even return, although as changed persons, after liberation, and 2) being at the mercy of strangers in the Holocaust world *and* afterwards. The child survivors are both gravely deprived and at the same time (severely) traumatized children" (p. 22).

As of this writing, child survivors have reached pension age and are between sixty-five and eighty years old, depending on their age at the end of the war. Obviously, age made a big difference in terms of the developmental phase in which the war trauma occurred. As a result of this variability, it would perhaps be more correct to divide this population into additional subgroups, according to their age and developmental needs at the time of their Holocaust trauma (Keilson, 1979/1992). Experiencing the horrors of war at various stages of their cognitive, emotional, and personal growth made them suffer impairment and developmental arrest in the same phases of growth. The trauma would be differently perceived depending on their ability to comprehend what was going on. Thus, there would be different kinds of fixations in specific stages of trust-mistrust, autonomy-doubt, guilt, and identity, according to the developmental phases described by Erikson (1959; 1962).

According to this theory, Durst (2008) suggested that it is possible to divide child survivors into five age groups, each with its own normative phase of development and specific posttraumatic response: (1) the toddlers and small infants (0–3); (2) the early childhood (3–5); (3) the middle childhood (5–8); (4) the latency kids (8–12); and (5) the adolescents (12–15). Thus, a child who, for example, experienced the war at age five would be expected to suffer from separation anxiety later in life. As a result of such developmental arrest, child survivors struggle with the following emotional issues all through life: (1) learned helplessness; (2) abandonment and isolation; (3) interrupted mourning of loss; (4) identity problems; (5) memory loss; and (6) primitive defenses, which will all be discussed in more detail below.

First, as child survivors learned early in life that external forces over which they had no control shaped their destiny, there is a strong sense of learned helplessness and a *victim mindset* in which they feel at the mercy of others. In addition, the lack of safety, predictability, and trust, together with overwhelming fear, powerlessness, and loss of control, became a permanent learning experience that continued to limit their sense of independence and autonomy all through life.

Second, there is an inherent feeling of abandonment, existential loneliness (Durst, 2008), or a vague sense of being unwanted, which lead some child survivors to constantly trying to prove their worth. Others feel a sense of detachment from the world. Such child survivors still feel that they must remain in hiding and that they are somehow isolated from others and also from themselves. This alienation reinforces their self-imposed silence and repression of their inner lives, until they feel that the outer world accepts them as they really are. Conflicting feelings of guilt for having left their parents and siblings are sometimes mixed with anger for not having been properly protected.

Third, the multiple and early loss of parents and family continues to haunt them throughout life. Children were separated from their parents and siblings in a variety of terrible ways. They were handed over to foster parents or to convents and given false names. They were pushed out of trains or left behind and hidden in attics, cellars, or forests. They were put on trains and sent away to distant countries or they were brutally torn from their parents in concentration camps. Seldom was it possible to say goodbye and for any proper leave-taking and mourning to take place. Interrupted grief with a frequent and long-standing tendency to deny the overwhelming loss therefore continues to be a lifelong struggle for many child survivors. As a result, normative separations later in life may also be very stressful and interpersonal relations are sometimes kept shallow to prevent a future painful separation.

Fourth, identity problems frequently arise in child survivors who were forced as children to take on a false identity in order to survive during the war. For a significant period of their youth, such children were exposed to a radically different socialization experience, which created at least an identity-confusion and at most a total repression of their earlier sense of self. In some of the latter cases, adolescents found it very difficult to return to their former families and resume using their original names after the war. Their return to normal life after the war was almost as difficult as the ordeals of war itself. Having to leave their adopted parents and return to their biological parents, who were often nonfunctional and severely ill, demanded extraordinary adjustment capacities. In addition, many had to get used to new surroundings in their new countries of immigration, with different cultures and languages. To make this process a little easier, some made active efforts to repress the past as much as they could and put the life of the old country behind them.

Fifth, loss of memory leaves a void forever in the inner world of the adult child survivor. The absence of any childhood memories creates a breach in the natural flow of the life narrative. Infant child survivors therefore continue to search with fervor for something within or outside of themselves that can bring traces of the past (and their parents) back. They may look for preverbal signs, such as a familiar smell, a sound, or an image that can evoke some fragment of their mothers and fathers and original homes, and thus to reexperience and feel again something from their lost childhood.

A child survivor who was separated from his parents of whom he has no memories before the age of five remembers only one thing from his childhood; how he was walking in mud with soldiers all around. Someone was holding his hand, but he doesn't know who it was. He only remembers that he would fall and that someone picked him up. After more than fifty years, he still feels that he is walking deep in mud and needs someone to hold his hand and lead the way.

Finally, as a result of overwhelming pain, powerlessness, and isolation, primitive defenses were frequently developed in order to survive emotionally. Such defenses served to help them not to feel anything as children, and certainly not to express their feelings, because "Children, who cried, died." But when perception of reality became too threatening and overwhelming, *speechless terror* left experiences beyond words. Thus affects were often dissociated and totally forgotten. As adults, this is sometimes manifested in a kind of emotional encapsulation, psychic numbing of responsiveness, and total amnesia of the past. Less dramatic survival strategies include not being seen, not standing out, and being quiet, obedient, and well behaved.

A thirteen-year-old girl is sitting on a windowsill, apparently detached from the outside world after a pogrom, in which her father had been taken away and beaten at the police station. He was later shot and thrown into a mass grave and she never saw him again. As if encapsulated from all affect, she was reading a book, keeping her overwhelming emotions all locked in. But the emotional development of her life had stopped at that moment. She never created a family of her own and, now in her late sixties, it is as if she is still sitting on the windowsill waiting for her father to return.

Similar to their older brothers and sisters, however, many child survivors also manifested a remarkable capacity for resilience (cf. Lev-Wiesel & Amir, 2003). For example, in their book on the children of Buchenwald, Hemmendinger & Krell (2000) tell the stories of countless child survivors who not only struggled for normalcy and emotional well-being, but who mostly succeeded to overcome the horrors and losses that they had experienced during the Holocaust and who made successful careers in their adult lives.

While often (too?) well adjusted and well functioning in their daily lives, child survivors remain a vulnerable group, carrying high risk for emotional instability and distress (Dasberg, 1987a). Some are obsessively preoccupied with the untouchable memories of the past, while others have avoided them totally. When they are called upon to cope with recurrent situations of stress, they tend to reexperience the painful moments of separation and loss from the past and then suffer from periods of behavioral dysfunction and increased anxiety and depression.

Review of Descriptive and Empirical Research

One of the first attempts to rehabilitate traumatized child survivors was probably described by Getreu (1952). In his early paper on "Practical Pedagogy" at a boarding school in northern Sweden (Smedsbo 1945–1948), the work with mostly orphaned girls was documented. The girls, who were between the ages of fifteen and eighteen had been liberated from concentration camps only a few months or years earlier. My mother also spent some time in this school and remembered it as a very important step in her own recuperation and as a kind of reentrance into society after the war. Getreu (1952) wrote:

> Imprisonment in the camps, which had lasted on average one year, had left deep scars. First of all, it had destroyed the physical shape of the students, manifested in the fact that many of them weighed only 30–35 kg when they arrived in Sweden. Many had become ill because of the inhuman conditions in the camp, mostly with TB. As a result, almost everybody received medical supervision and pneumothorax treatment. Two girls died from these illnesses…. Psychological stress upon the children was severe. Torture had been a daily occurrence in the camps and the students were burdened by memories, which kept appearing in all expected and unexpected contexts. In the beginning they told each other and us a lot about their experiences in the camps. Every conversation during the first weeks ended usually with some reference to the camp. Referring to the known saying "All ways lead to Rome," a girl commented that during "that time, all ways led to Auschwitz." The sight of a chimney during a walk led their thoughts to the high chimneys of the gas chambers in the camp. Some hens on the road reminded them of their old homes and how they themselves once had fed the hens, which could evoke severe weeping attacks. One girl, who handed out oranges in the evening, could with a mixture of irony and humor say: "Now I am almost like a *Blockälteste*" (a prisoner with a special position in the compound). They dreamt about the camp and often woke up during the night (pp. 44–45).

Another early investigator of the lives of children during the Holocaust was Dwork (1991), who wrote about children in hiding, ghettos, transit camps, slave labor camps, and even in concentration camps. Similarly, the British historian Gilbert (1996) documented the stories of 732 young concentration camp survivors, including about 80 girls.

The first actual psychological study on child survivors, however, was initiated by Sarah Moskovitz (1983) and later published in the book

Love Despite Hate: Child Holocaust Survivors in their Adult Lives. She interviewed twenty-five children between the ages of two and fifteen who were raised together outside London following their postwar arrival, and who had been earlier studied by Freud and Burlingame (1943; Freud & Dann, 1951). For many, her book was a revelation that children also could be survivors, that they had also endured severe psychological trauma, and that they needed special care.

According to Metzger-Brown (2007), "In the early 1980s, a decade after the author began her first treatment, Milton and Judith Kestenberg cofounded the International Study of the Organized Persecution of Child Survivors of the Holocaust and began semistructured, audiotaped interviewing of these child survivors. Moskovitz on the west coast and Gampel (1992) in Israel joined this effort, followed by Krell (1983, 1985a, 1985b), a child survivor, in Vancouver, Canada, who had begun videotaping the interviews with child survivors. Thus began a concerted focus on listening to child survivor stories in a new way, validating for them the importance of their traumatic memories from the war" (pp. 53–54).

Together, they collected a formidable record on over 1,500 child survivors, filling thirty-five linear feet of transcripts of interviews that focused on the children's trauma and their resilience. Florida Atlantic University Libraries received these original audiotapes, transcripts, and ephemera with Kestenberg's annotations, medical and sociological information, depositions, and autobiographical and creative writings. Her work with the children became a forerunner for interviewing protocols now used all over the world. Some of the results of these interviews were reported in the book on children surviving persecution, in which Kestenberg & Kahn (1998) collected a series of essays with historical information about children during World War II and firsthand reports of interviews of these youngsters many decades later.

Valent (2002), who is both a child survivor and a psychiatrist, interviewed ten child survivors and reported their stories in more or less their own words. Each of them described how their worlds were shattered piece by piece, and in some cases, how being surrounded by death and torture became an almost normal part of their day-to-day lives. A brief commentary after each personal story suggested how that specific person's experiences had shaped his or her worldview.

Most of these descriptive studies indicate that child survivors of the Holocaust suffer from what Judith Herman (1992) called *Complex PTSD*, highlighting that the person endured a series of traumatic experiences over a long period of time resulting in psychological fragmentation and loss of a sense of safety, trust, and self-worth.

Empirical research tried to validate such clinical impressions. Keilson (1979/1992) was perhaps the first to do a systematic follow-up of 204 Dutch Jewish war orphans in their late twenties to early forties, who had survived the war. Except for coining the term *sequential traumatization*, Keilson emphasized the importance of documenting not only the war experiences themselves, but also the periods before and after the Holocaust. In particular, Keilson studied the relation between the age of the child during the war and the influence this had on the development of psychopathology later in life. He concluded that the younger child survivors tended to suffer more from a neurotic character development while the older children tended to suffer more from anxiety and those aged over fourteen tended to suffer more from chronic depression. Generally speaking, he concluded that the younger the survivor, the more traumatic the circumstances and the more damaging the impact of their war experiences.

Controlled empirical research on the child survivors, however, has been very scarce. One of the exceptions was the study by Cohen, Brom, & Dasberg (2001), who used a controlled double-blind randomized design to look at symptoms and coping of child survivors fifty years after the Holocaust. The results indicated a slightly higher level of psychosocial symptoms in the child survivors than in the control group, a high level of PTSD symptoms (intrusion/avoidance tendencies), and achievement motivation based mainly on the fear of failure. Surprisingly, the child survivors viewed the world more positively than the control group, which may be understood as a greater need to compensate for the lack of security suffered in childhood by creating a meaningful world in a chaotic reality.

In their study on attachment and traumatic stress, Sagi-Schwartz et al. (2003) similarly found that child survivors who were now grandmothers showed more signs of traumatic stress and more often lack of resolution of trauma than comparison subjects, but that they were not impaired in general adaptation.

Recent studies have shown that certain groups within the child Holocaust survivors have more psychological distress than others. For instance, child survivors who were in foster families were found to have a lower quality of life and more psychiatric symptoms than child survivors who had hid in the woods and/or were in concentration camps (Lev-Wiesel & Amir, 2000). Moreover, a group of child survivors who had lost their original identity (name and knowledge of biological parents) had a lower quality of life than a comparison group of child survivors who knew their original identity (Amir & Lev-Wiesel, 2001). Similarly, Robinson et al. (1997) found that orphan child survivors did worse than those who had a surviving parent.

In addition, Amir & Lev-Wiesel (2003) investigated PTSD symptoms, psychological distress, and subjective quality of life in a group of forty-three child Holocaust survivors and a community sample of forty-four persons who had not personally experienced the Holocaust. Results showed that the child survivors had higher PTSD symptom scores, higher depression, anxiety, somatization, and anger-hostility scores; and lower physical, psychological, and social quality of life than did the comparison group. The findings suggest that the psychological consequences of being a child during the Holocaust can be long lasting.

Lev-Wiesel and Amir (2004) conducted a number of comparative studies on the various long-term effects of different kinds of child survivors, depending on if they had endured the war in Catholic institutions, Christian foster families, concentration camps, or in hiding with partisans. They found that survivors who had been with foster families scored significantly higher on several of the measures of distress, whereas survivors who had been in the woods and/or with partisans scored significantly higher on several of the positive measures. Similarly, Robinson et al. (1994) found that different forms of persecution influenced the state of the survivor in different ways. Survivors of extermination and labor camps, as well as survivors in hiding, suffered from depression, while those who had been with partisans did not suffer from depression after the war.

The present findings support earlier findings showing that being a child survivor is indeed a vulnerable position in late adulthood. Robinson, Rapaport-Bar-Sever, & Rapaport (1994) studied 103 child survivors about fifty years after the war and found that most survivors still suffer from psychological distress symptoms and that their suffering from these symptoms is even more severe than immediately after the war.

Van der Hal-Van Raalte (2007) investigated the link between deprivation and trauma during earliest childhood and psychosocial functioning and health in later life in 203 *baby* survivors born between 1935 and 1944. Quality of postwar care arrangements and current physical health independently predicted lack of well-being in old age. Loss of parents during the persecution, year of birth of the survivors (being born before or during the war), and memories of the Holocaust did not significantly affect present well-being. Lack of adequate care after the end of World War II is associated with lower well-being of the youngest Holocaust child survivors, even after an intervening period of sixty years. Results showed mild to severe present-day repercussions of the Nazi persecutions, and a potentially moderating effect of the sense of coherence on later life impact of Holocaust survival experience.

Reulbach et al. (2007) investigated if child survivors may be a high-risk group for developing psychosis later in life. To answer this question, ninety-three medical files of Holocaust child survivors from sociomedical expert reports of the restitution offices in Germany were analyzed. These reports indicated that late onset schizophrenia was significantly associated with the highest category of persecution, which suggests that the exposure to the stress during the war might lead to severe mental illness. Considering the secondary gain effects of this population, however, the results of this study is highly biased.

A final study compared Jewish and non-Jewish child survivors in Poland. In this study, Lis-Turleiska et al. (2008) found that current PTSD was almost twice as high in Jewish (55.6 percent) as opposed to non-Jewish survivors (30.9 percent), whereas no differences were found between these groups for depression and social isolation.

In concluding this section, we are now in a position to define a *typical child survivor syndrome* (Kellermann, 1999) in more detail. Survivors of the Holocaust who were less than sixteen years old when the war ended usually present a somewhat different clinical picture from their older brothers and sisters.

These were severely traumatized children who survived in hiding or in very difficult circumstances, sometimes with changed identities and in total isolation from their families of origin. Extraordinary psychological adjustment strategies were developed by these children in order to survive mentally, including dissociation, psychic numbing, and denial. As expected, such early traumatization reverberates across the entire life span of the child survivor and many of the early strategies are maintained all through life. Some are obsessively preoccupied with the vague remnants of the past while others have avoided them totally.

While often well adjusted and well functioning in their daily lives (mental state seems to be correlated to the intensity of childhood trauma they suffered), they are a highly vulnerable group, carrying high risk for emotional instability and distress. When they are called upon to cope with recurrent situations of stress, they tend to reexperience the painful moments of separation and loss from the past and then suffer from periods of behavioral dysfunction and increased anxiety and depression. Suspicion and distrust in interpersonal relations are often added emotional components.

This clinical picture of the child survivor of the Holocaust seems in many ways similar to the above-mentioned diagnostic label *Complex PTSD* of the DSM-IV. However, the specific characteristic of this group of child survivors is the various kinds of developmental impairments, depending on their age of traumatization.

Typically, developmental arrest in early ages manifests itself as various forms of personality disorders, with the adult personality structure being dominated by more or less unfulfilled needs of the traumatized child from the past. Clearly, however, because of the great variation in traumatic experiences and ages of traumatization, the Child Survivor Syndrome includes different elements, as described by Valent (1995a) in his comparison of child survivors of the Holocaust with other traumatized children.

Treatment of Child Survivors

As part of the initial assessment, a qualified therapist will determine the need for psychotherapy. This decision will be based on such things as the child survivor's current problems, history, level of development, ability to cooperate with treatment, and what interventions are most likely to help with the presenting concerns. If suitable, psychotherapy would be recommended in combination with other treatments, such as medication, behavior management, or family therapy.

Naturally, the relationship that develops between the therapist and the patient is very important. The child survivor must feel comfortable, safe, and understood, in order for him/her to be able to express his/her thoughts and feelings and to use the therapy in a helpful way. According to Krell (2001), child survivors need to be aided in overcoming their fear that their experiences and feelings of intense sorrow and rage will not be understood by others. How best to appreciate and validate the child survivors' feelings remains a significant challenge for the therapist.

As I have already pointed out above, treatment of these juvenile traumatized people at later ages must take into consideration the specific trauma period and the specific demands of the actual life period. Kestenberg & Brenner (1996) and Brenner (2004) suggested that clinicians working with survivors of historical trauma are well served by knowing about the actual circumstances that their patients endured. The reconstruction of the traumatic period and the opportunity to develop a coherent narrative— often for the first time—may be one of the important achievements in therapy. In addition, the therapist is confronted with an adult in which there is an abandoned child, and in whom memories of the past are broken or do not exist at all. Often, these clients are not in tune with their hidden feelings of yearning and their hidden pain, or they do not usually reveal them (Durst, 2008).

Psychotherapy may help in a variety of ways. Obviously, child survivors will receive general emotional support, resolve conflicts with people, understand feelings and problems, and try out new solutions to old problems. Goals for therapy with child survivors may also be more specific (change in specific behavior, improved relations with friends or family), or more general (less anxiety, better self-esteem). The length of psychotherapy depends on the complexity and severity of problems.

Psychotherapists and survivors themselves have written extensively about treatment for the long-term effects of posttrauma (e.g. Williams & Sommer, 2002). However, there is little scientific data validating their methods (Ratiner, 2000; Solomon & Johnson, 2002; van der Kolk, McFarlane, & van der Hart, 1996). What has become increasingly apparent, however, is that severely traumatized children tend to view people in power, such as therapists, who challenge their boundaries, as dangerous aggressors, even when those people intend simply to express disagreement. If survivors do not feel strong enough to counter effectively, they might feel violated.

Such emotional characteristics makes the treatment of adults who were traumatized as children a very delicate matter. Beyond the obvious focus on supportive therapy, there are great variations in directiveness, time-span, and overall therapeutic strategy. Initially, brief sessions may be suggested to hesitant clients in order to provide a setting in which memory processing, problem solving, and symptom alleviation may occur. The aim of such sessions is to bring the client to an emotional equilibrium and adequate functioning as rapidly as possible. For this purpose, existing defenses and coping mechanisms are strengthened within a framework of positive thinking and cognitive reframing. In addition, the client is encouraged to identify sources of stress in the present, to observe his or her physical reactions to such stress and to find ways to control overwhelming affects. Relaxation training, meditation, guided daydreaming, desensitization procedures, and similar techniques may be used for this purpose. Because much emotionally painful material is out of the reach of words, it may be more easily uncovered and contained within expressive therapies such as art, creative writing, music and/or movement therapy. Group interaction and communal sharing may provide further resources for coping with the stressors of life.

Over thirty child survivors participated in such a group session that I facilitated during a recent child survivor conference in Jerusalem. Many of them knew one another from earlier conferences and there was an apparent sense of cohesion in the group, a sense of *we* who had endured the same hardships during our childhood. This allowed each one at a time to share deeply about their past and present tragedies, and I was surprised to hear that some of them said that this was the first time that they had opened up and ventilated their hidden agenda from the war. Apparently, some utilized these experiential group sessions during conferences as the only *once-a-year ventilation opportunity* in their lives.

In such a group therapeutic setting, Dasberg, Bartura, and Amit (2001) observed that aging child survivors faced the double task of coming to grips with the stresses of aging and of their psychobiological development, as well as the recurrence of the traumatic memories, and losses of their almost forgotten, disregarded, denied, repressed, or dissociated childhood memories. In addition, and probably as a result of their own lack of adequate parenting, these group members also shared concerns about their own children and about child-rearing problems in general.

While the purpose of such initial sessions is symptom alleviation and/ or resolution of concurrent family issues, treatment of child survivors will ultimately have to deal also with the experience of Holocaust trauma itself. A more explorative psychotherapeutic approach may therefore be suggested to work through some of the repressed or dissociated material of their traumatic childhood.

Classical psychoanalytic psychotherapy with this population, however, seems to be of little help. The suitability of psychoanalysis for this population was discussed in a roundtable discussion with mental health professionals, who were themselves also child survivors. Dori Laub (in Laub et al., 2007), who was one of the panelists, shared his own experience with classical psychoanalysis: "I switched to a Jewish analyst in New Haven, and for five years, five times a week, nothing happened [*group laughter*]. Not even the fact that I was hurting, you know, that I was mourning. After five years he said to me, I think you don't like me. I said, you bet [*group laughter*]. So I switched to a third analyst at the Institute who was tolerant enough to allow that and who said, 'I know that you want to get out.' Yeah, [*laughs*] to finish. He said, 'Okay, I'm happy to help you get out,' and it took another three years. So the man really picked up what it was about" (p. 29).

If long-term explorative psychotherapy is at all recommended, it should be based on some kind of psychology of the self (Kohut, 1978-1991) rather than on insight-focused interpretation of unconscious conflicts. Step-by-step, such an approach aims to strengthen the self in terms of making it more caring and able to regulate overwhelming affect. This may help the child survivor to finally face the terrible experience of having been abandoned and often violently torn from their close families. Moving back and forth between grief/sadness and anger/fear, this process invariably stands at the center of trauma (Shoshan, 1989, p. 193). Until such memories are brought to the surface, progress toward assimilation of the images indelibly etched in the minds of child survivors is stalled.

In a personal account of her own journey of healing with the dramatic title *A Child Survivor of the Holocaust Comes Out of Hiding*, Metzger-Brown (2007) describes the important ingredients of psychotherapy with child survivors. The following account explains why the first psychotherapy did not succeed:

> It was as if somewhere the relationship between my analyst (BL) and me stopped growing. I liked him and felt connected to him, too, but somehow I hesitated in opening up the concrete wall surrounding the core of my innermost feelings. I would learn much later, in my second therapy, that what I was safeguarding was the world of strong feelings, unresolved sorrow, grief, and rage; it was the world of torrents of unwept tears and the myriad of childhood losses. It was the guarded space where a child survivor of a terrible war still harbored the hope that someone, somewhere, would help her feel *safe enough* and *secure enough* to reach out beyond a wall that she, as yet, could not see clearly. BL was not going to be that someone for me; I had a halo around him and protective barriers around myself; I did not recognize either (p. 61).

This was very different from the second therapist, who came across more as a *real person* and who was thus able to create a sense of safety in treatment:

> I consider myself fortunate for the psychotherapeutic relationship that did develop with my second therapist (GR), who was also a psychiatrist. Thinking back, I would emphasize that central to my developing a sense of trust and safety with GR was my focus on trying to get to "know" him as a "real" person through cues I could pick up not only from his words, but from his actions, his nonverbal behavior. All the information that I gathered contributed, eventually, to my feeling secure enough to begin to ask GR questions about himself. This is the heart of what I want to emphasize in this paper: my second therapist was "less hidden" and more interactive with me, which added to my feeling of greater safety in the situation. GR "moved around." I could "see" how he listened to me, not only patiently and quietly, but with a compassion and kindness that was communicated through his responses. If I said something that touched him, his facial expression would show it and I could tell that he was listening and that he cared. Significantly, our nonverbal exchanges

became much more pronounced than a simple nod of the head
or a leaning forward to show that he was attending (p. 66).

Traumatic experiences may thus be slowly worked through within such
a "real" holding relationship in which the therapist functions like a good
mother figure that protects, reassures, and encourages the client. Through
vicarious identification with the parental figure of the therapist, the child
survivor is thus provided with a kind of *corrective emotional experience*
in which he or she can draw new strength to cope with the past loss. In
addition, such an experience may give him or her new perspectives of life
and new sources of identification.

CHAPTER 4

Holocaust Trauma in Children of Survivors

For a long time, I recounted to my children that the six-digit number tattooed on my forearm was the telephone number of an old friend.

—Siegi Hirsch, a survivor from Auschwitz

During the course of psychotherapy, a man reports fragments of dreams: "I am hiding in the cellar from soldiers who are searching for me. Overwhelmed by anxiety, I know that if they find me they will kill me on the spot … Then, I am standing in line for selection; the smell of burning flesh is in the air and I can hear shots fired. Faceless and undernourished people with striped uniforms march away to the crematoriums. Then, I am in a pit full of dead, skeletal bodies. I struggle desperately to bury the cadavers in the mud, but limbs keep sticking up from the wet soil and keep floating up to the surface. I feel guilty for what has happened, though I do not know why. I wake up in a sweat and immediately remember that these were the kinds of nightmares I had ever since I was a child. During a lifelong journey of mourning, I have been travelling back to the dead; to the corpses and graveyards of the Second World War with a prevailing sense of numb grief for all those anonymously gone."

From the content of this dream, the man could have been a Holocaust survivor. But he was not. He was the *child* of a survivor. His mother had survived the Auschwitz-Birkenau concentration camp. But he, himself, was born long after the war had ended in a country far removed from the horrors of the Holocaust. Why was he dreaming such dreams half a century after the war? Why are children of Holocaust survivors still experiencing the effects of the Holocaust as if they themselves had actually been there? How do we explain that the so-called second generation seems to share the grief and terror of their traumatized parents? Was the trauma of the parents somehow transmitted to them?

The observation that the psychological burdens of Holocaust survivors have been thus passed on to their children is not a new one. Over a period of three decades, more than five hundred papers have been published on the transmission of trauma from Holocaust survivor parents to their offspring (Kellermann, 1997). Despite this vast literature, however, several questions remain to be answered about this complex process of transmission of Holocaust trauma. What was in fact passed on from parent to child? How does the transmission occur? What is the relationship between parental psychopathology and mental distress in the children? Do parents invariably and inevitably transmit and are children equally susceptible? The purpose of the present chapter is to further discuss these issues and present a model in which they can be viewed more consistently.

Transmission Terminology

A review of the literature suggests that there are a multitude of different terms that describe trauma transmission. Regarding the term *transmission*, Albeck (1993) suggested that we talk about *intergenerational* aspects of trauma, instead of trauma transmission, and the concept was changed accordingly within the International Society of Traumatic Stress Studies in the early 1990s. Despite this, I feel *transmission* is a useful and adequate concept and I have therefore retained it here. In addition, concepts such as *secondary* and *vicarious* traumatization have been suggested in order to differentiate this phenomenon from the *primary* and *direct* traumatization of the first generation. But such transmission includes also the effect on spouses and caretakers. Emphasizing the generational interchange specifically from parent to child, the transmission process is delineated as either *trans-generational* (e.g., Felsen, 1998); *inter-generational* (e.g., Sigal & Weinfeld, 1987); *multi-generational* (e.g., Danieli, 1998); or *cross-generational* (e.g., Lowin, 1983). However, because the trauma was invariably passed on from one or both of the parents, *parental* transmission would perhaps be the most adequate term (Dasberg, 2000).

Earlier literature on the transmission of Holocaust trauma (e.g., Schwartz, Dohrenwend, & Levav, 1994; Felsen, 1998) have further differentiated between on the one hand *direct and specific* transmission (a mental syndrome in the survivor parent leads *directly* to the same *specific* syndrome in the child), and on the other hand *indirect and general* transmission (a disorder in the parent makes the parent unable to function as a parent which *indirectly* leads to a *general* sense of deprivation in the child). While such a differentiation seems to be valid, it confuses aspects of the process of transmission, which are more or less *overt and covert, manifest and tacit* and *conscious and unconscious*. It further fails to clearly separate the etiology (or assumed *cause*) of the transmission from the manifestation (or assumed *effect*) of the transmission. There is as yet no consensus as to how to define the field, some focusing on its descriptive meaning whereas others include possible explanations of its etiology.

In order to limit such ambiguity, I will differentiate between the *process* of transmission (*how* the trauma was carried over from one generation to the next), and the *content* of transmission (*what* was in fact transmitted) (Levine, 1982). The first would contain the assumed cause of transmission, in terms of what parents did to their children, and the second would contain the effect, in terms of the psychological responses of the child. While both perspectives apparently involve direct and indirect (as well as specific and general) aspects, the basic differentiation of parental influence and infant/child response is essential for making sense of the various theories and research findings within this field. The underlying model for the parental transmission of Holocaust trauma may thus be characterized as a functional relationship, in which the behavior of children of survivors (B) is a function (f) of Holocaust survivor parents' childrearing behavior (P), leading to the formula: $B = f(P)$.

However, there is seldom a clear and simple linear connection between P and B. As Prince (1985), pointed out:

> The mechanism of second generation effects is seen as an extremely complex one in which cumulative trauma of parental communication, the aspect of the parent-child relationship determined by the Holocaust context, and the historical imagery provided by the parent and by other cultural processes are mediated by interaction with normative developmental conflicts, family dynamics independent of the Holocaust, variables of social class, culture, Jewish heritage, and immigrant status (p. 27).

The above simple paradigm therefore needs to be expanded to include various psychological responses of children of survivors (B1, B2, B3, etc.) to a variety of parental factors influencing the process of transmission (P1,

P2, P3, etc.) under different circumstances (C1, C2, C3, etc.). In such an expanded model, the simple question: "Are children of Holocaust survivor parents affected by their parents?" is replaced by the more elaborate and appropriate question: "*Which kinds of Holocaust survivor parents influence which kinds of children in which ways under which circumstances?*" This functional relation may be described by the following formula: 2nd Gen. B1, B2, B3, etc. = f (Parental P1, P2, P3, etc.) + (C1, C2, C3, etc.).

In order to more fully describe this complex process, I will here describe some of the contents of that which was transmitted, present an overview of the prevalent theories of trauma transmission, and discuss some of the *mitigating* and *aggravating* factors that are assumed to increase or decrease the development of specific second-generation psychopathology.

Content of Transmission

What was passed on to the child? What are the manifestations of trauma, if any, that can be observed in children of survivors? While the content of transmission has been also described in positive terms as a *legacy* and/or as a capacity for resiliency, it has most often been negatively associated with some kind of psychopathology. Most frequently, the transmission has been assumed to contain some kind of secondary posttraumatic stress disorder, suggesting that because many Holocaust survivors suffer from PTSD, their offspring will also suffer from such a syndrome (Baranowsky et al., 1998).

The existence or nonexistence of any manifestations of psychopathology in the offspring of Holocaust survivors has been the subject of the greatest disagreement. While psychotherapists usually observed and described various kinds of emotional distress in this population, researchers failed to confirm these observations with more objective and reliable instruments. An overview (Kellermann, 2001b) of the empirical research concluded that most controlled studies with nonclinical populations failed to confirm the assumption of increased rates of psychopathology in the offspring of Holocaust survivors compared to control groups. Similarly, Levav et al. (2007) did not find differences in psychopathology and other health dimensions among 430 offspring of Holocaust survivors who were compared to offspring of European-born parents who did not reside in Nazi-occupied territories in an Israeli national health survey. Finally, in a meta-analytic investigation of secondary traumatization involving more than 4,400 nonclinical participants, Van Ijzendoorn et al. (2003) found no evidence for the influence of the parents' traumatic Holocaust experiences on their children. Their series of meta-analyses showed that children of Holocaust survivors were, in general, well adapted. But under conditions of extreme stress, latent vulnerability to maladaptive and prolonged posttraumatic responses may come to the surface, even in the children of Holocaust survivors (Yehuda et al., 1998a). As an example of this vulnerability, Baider et al. (2006) found that children of Holocaust survivors, when diagnosed with breast cancer, reported more psychological distress than patients with nontraumatized parents.

Thus we are no longer asking if children of Holocaust survivors in general are more disturbed than others. Rather than continuing to investigate this question, we should try to delineate the specific characteristics of this clinical subgroup of children of Holocaust survivors. According to clinical experience and empirical research, this clinical population, compared to other people with emotional problems, seems to have specific disturbances more or less focused on difficulties in coping with stress and a higher vulnerability to PTSD.

Apparently, problems are usually centered on the following areas (Kellermann, 1999):

1. **Self.** Impaired self-esteem with persistent identity problems; overidentification with parents' *victim/survivor* status; a need to be superachievers to compensate for parents' losses; and carrying the burden of being *replacements* for lost relatives. In his book *The Children of Job,* Berger (1997) observed that many of these second-generation *replacement* children tried to get over the feeling of living in the *presence of absence* through writing books and making films. Dave Greber (2000), a son of Holocaust survivors, reflected upon what the children of survivors represented to their parents:

> Sometimes it was everyone and everything they lost. So I was not David Greber, but my father's brothers Romek and Moishe and Adamek, and his father David; my brother wasn't Harvey, but Herschel, my mother's beloved brother, or Aharon, her father; my sisters were named for our grandmothers and aunts Sarah and Leah and Bella and Molly, loved ones our parents last saw when they were eighteen and were being separated for transportation to camps from which they never emerged. Representing six million dead is a grave responsibility, and a terrible burden for a child to carry.

2. **Cognition.** Catastrophic expectancy; fear of another Holocaust; preoccupation with death; stress upon exposure to stimuli that symbolizes the Holocaust; vicarious sharing of traumatic Holocaust experiences,

which dominate the inner world. Chani Kurtz (1995) gave the following example:

> In fact, I still have a problem with buying my children clothes with vertical stripes. Silly? Perhaps. But in my parents' photo album is a picture of my father in his concentration camp garb. I carry that photo in my mental album, too. Nor can I forget my father's reaction when I bought myself a pair of those cute little Dr. Scholl clogs that were so in style when I was a teenager. "Wooden shoes?" He stared at me, not angry, just bewildered. "Wooden shoes? I've already worn wooden shoes enough to atone for my children, and for my children's children, and for their children after them."

Another child of survivors shared the following experience: "During an ordinary dental examination, the dentist suggested that it would be best to remove my wisdom teeth. In a morbid manner, I immediately started to think of the gassed corpses who were stripped of their golden teeth. It was just a quick thought without much affect; a registration followed by repression. But it made me feel all sweaty and scared" (Gottschalk, 2000).

3. Affectivity. Annihilation anxiety; nightmares of persecution; frequent dysphoric moods connected to a feeling of loss and mourning; unresolved conflicts around anger complicated by guilt; increased vulnerability to stressful events.

A daughter of two survivors of Auschwitz, who was born in a DP-camp in 1948, suffered from debilitating clinical depression for her entire life. Her parents had lost five children in the camp, including a pair of twins, and were mentally scarred for the rest of their lives, apparently unable to care adequately for their only surviving child. As a result, she endured severe deprivation during most of her childhood and her life remained a constant struggle of survival against suicidal ideation and dreams of the horrors her brothers and sisters had endured before being killed. Antidepressant medication and a supportive family of her own were of little substantial help.

Holocaust associations that evoke panic anxiety attacks are very common among children of Holocaust survivors. Such intrusive images were reported by Gottschalk (2000) in a daughter of survivors who was reliving the Holocaust trauma of her mother on a daily basis.

These images … invade me in a suffocating way. Like in the

morning when there are so many cars and exhaust fumes, I think: "Don't breathe," and I think that this is how they would gas people, redirecting the exhaust pipes into the trucks full of prisoners. My mother was almost gassed, you know. They dragged her to the showers, but found out they did not have enough Zyklon B. So they failed ... another twist of fate! But I think about it ... I think about it twenty times a day, a hundred times a day!

Gottschalk (2000) analyzed a series of deep interviews with children of Holocaust survivors and found that these children were inclined to: (1) produce and suppress (in)congruent emotions; (2) trace boundaries; (3) hierarchize suffering; and (4) compensate for parental difficulties with emotion management to adjust to various kinds of emotional dynamics that characterize survivor families. As a result, these children tended to suppress negative emotions, suppress rebellious impulses, internalize the parents' suffering, and minimize the severity of their own suffering.

4. Interpersonal functioning. Exaggerated family attachments and dependency or exaggerated independence and difficulties in entering into intimate relationships and in handling interpersonal conflicts. In a controlled, double-blind study, Brom, Kfir, & Dasberg (2001) found that daughters of Holocaust survivors tend toward slightly more problematic relationships, i.e., either very close or very distant relationships, indicating some problems in the realm of separation-individuation. Helen Motro (1996) shared some of the contents of a group for children of Holocaust survivors that used to meet on Holocaust Memorial Day:

We gather to talk about our ability and our inability to love, to be lovable, to deserve love. We hardly mention the war at all. We don't have to; it's always there in the background, axiomatic. After all, the war is our template. One of us might say, "When I was six and wouldn't eat enough, my mother shouted at me: 'Mengele I survived—but having you will kill me!'" And we others listening will nod and know what our friend means. Not all of our fathers beat their sons when the boys came into the house wearing black boots. Not all of our mothers froze us out as teenagers because they themselves survived by abandoning their own mothers at fifteen in the camps. No, most of us had parents who loved too much, who smothered us with their care, their solicitude, their ever-present, all-enveloping anxiety.

Some of these relational themes were recently described by Wiseman & Barber (2008) in their book *Echoes of the Trauma* in which they combined the *core conflictual relationship theme* method with narrative-qualitative analysis.

Models of Trauma Transmission

How does transmission of trauma occur? How can a trauma be transmitted from one generation to another? At first glance, the concept of transmission is difficult to grasp. It is as if saying that someone's headache is caused by the fact that his father was hit on his head by a stone some fifty years ago. Or, that a woman is afraid of becoming pregnant because her mother had lost a child during the war. Explanations like these, which connect past experiences of a parent with a present state of mind in a child, may be regarded as at least farfetched and at most ridiculous.

Most people, however, would agree with popular folk wisdom that "an apple does not fall far from the tree," and with the notion of "like father, like son." In addition, bacteria may be transferred from one person to another in the spreading of disease and various physical forms of passing something over from one body to another, or from one place to another, are parts of our daily experiences. The transmission of sound waves in telecommunications is a commonly accepted phenomenon and may serve as a suitable analogy that also illustrates the process of trauma transmission. Thus, in the same way as heat, light, sound, and electricity can be invisibly carried from a transmitter to a receiver, it is possible that unconscious experiences can also be transmitted from parents to their children through some complex process of extra-sensory communication. In fact, such quasi-naturalistic terminology is frequently applied when describing how the *vibrations* within a Holocaust family *atmosphere* may affect the offspring in a variety of indirect and subtle ways.

Four major theoretical approaches to understanding trauma transmission have been suggested: (1) psychodynamic; (2) sociocultural; (3) family systems; and (4) biological models of transmission. These are summarized in table 1.

Table 1
Models of Trauma Transmission

	Theory	Medium	Transmission Factor
1	Psychodynamic	Interpersonal Relations	Unconscious displaced emotion
2	Sociocultural	Socialization	Parenting and Role Models
3	Family Systems	Communication	Enmeshment
4	Biological	Genes	Hereditary vulnerability to PTSD

Like an infectious disease, Holocaust trauma is highly contagious and may be transmitted by direct or indirect contact. Utilizing such descriptive analogies, we may theorize that any Holocaust trauma may cause one of more of at least three different kinds of strains or types of *virus*: loss, guilt, and/or catastrophic anxiety. Each of these virus strains will be infective for anyone who is living in the proximity of the people carrying the virus, such as close family, friends, and others who are susceptible to the disease. But the virus may be also considered to be highly resistant in many people and it may be expected to develop only under certain conditions and within certain contaminated premises. As Holocaust trauma usually spreads slowly over a long period of time, the overt signs of being affected may be seen only after several years. When it has taken root, however, it will linger on and remain potent forever. If this occurs, it may affect the entire human physiology of a person, including the nervous, musculoskeletal, circulatory, respiratory, gastrointestinal, urinary, reproductive, immune, and endocrine system, and its psychosomatic expressions may be profound. The way these processes work, however, will be the object of future research.

Thus, in the same manner that the transmission of a virus needs a mediating agent, such as a mosquito, which carries the virus from one person to another, a trauma also needs a mediating agent to be carried from parent to child. But various theories assume different mediating agents. For example: (1) according to psychoanalytic theory, the *unconscious* is in itself infectious, being highly malignant if it is not acknowledged. However, if the parent becomes aware of his or her immense loss and starts to work through the emotions, they tend to disappear and will not be transmitted to the children; (2) *parenting* is the mediating agent in socialization theories.

Overprotection, punishment, and enmeshment would contribute to a higher risk for absorbing the trauma of the parent, while a healthy dose of separation-individuation would counteract such a detrimental influence; (3) in family systems theory, *communication* is the mediating agent. If the trauma is talked about in a *balanced* manner, it will be easier for the child to digest it. On the other hand, if it is talked about too much or too little, it will become malignant; and (4) biological approaches view blood, hormones, genes, and DNA to be the transmitting factors determining hereditary predispositions.

1. Psychodynamic and Relational Models of Transmission

Almost one hundred years ago, Freud (1913) was probably one of the first to describe the intergenerational transmission of "certain dispositions" in his book *Totem and Taboo*: "I have supposed that an emotional process, such as might have developed in generations of sons who were ill-treated by their father, has extended to new generations which were exempt from such treatment ... We may safely assume that no generation is able to conceal any of its more important mental processes from its successor.... The unconscious understanding of all the customs, ceremonies, and dogmas left behind by the father made it possible for later generations to take over their heritage of emotion ..." (pp. 158–159).

The field of Holocaust transmission has long been dominated by psychoanalytically oriented theories (Kohout & Brainin, 2004). According to these theories, emotions that could not be consciously experienced by the first generation are given over to the second generation. "The child thus unconsciously absorbs the repressed and insufficiently worked-through Holocaust experiences of survivor parents. Transgenerational transmission is when an older person unconsciously externalizes his traumatized self onto a developing child's personality. A child then becomes a reservoir for the unwanted, troublesome parts of an older generation. Because the elders have influence on a child, the child absorbs their wishes and expectations and is driven to act on them. It becomes the child's task to mourn, to reverse the humiliation and feelings of helplessness pertaining to the trauma of his forebears" (Volkan, 1997, p. 43).

Psychoanalytic authors further emphasized the transmission of Holocaust traumatization through an unconscious process of identification and a failure in achieving self-object differentiation. Specifically, Rowland-Klein & Dunlop (1998) propose a form of projective identification as an explanatory mechanism to the transmission of trauma that "brings together diverse aspects of the observed phenomena: projection by the parent of

Holocaust-related feelings and anxieties into the child; introjection by the child as if she herself had experienced the concentration camps; and return of this input by the child in the form of ... problems" (p. 358). From a similar psychoanalytic frame of reference, Kahn (2006) illuminated this process by referring to early developmental influences of traumatized parents, identification with these parents, and role induction (of deceased victims).

As a result, the children would feel the need to live in their parents' Holocaust past (Kogan, 1995, p. 26). Auerhahn & Laub (1998) described how "the massive psychic trauma shape the internal representations of reality, becoming an unconscious organizing principle passed on by parents and internalized by their children" (p. 22). Throughout this process, parents tended to displace their own repressed grief upon their children who would then be seen as "memorial candles in Holocaust cape" (Wardi, 1992, p.40).

For example, a daughter of a Holocaust survivor remembers how she was buying a dress with her father as a child. Looking at herself in the mirror with her new dress, she caught a glimpse of the reflection of the face of her father behind her. He suddenly looked pale with grief and bewilderment. Asking him what was going on, he told her for the first time that he had had a daughter before the war and that he recognized the remarkable resemblance between her and his first daughter who had died at about the same age as she was now. From that point on, the woman understood why her father had always looked at her with some amount of sadness and why she herself had felt a kind of unexplainable grief throughout her life.

Adding to the above formulations, relational psychoanalytic models of trauma transmission described children of survivors as also being shaped by a matrix of unhealthy relationships with their parents with whom they struggle to maintain their ties and from whom they try to differentiate themselves at the same time. Repetitive patterns of interpersonal behavior, based largely on internalized self and object representations, continue to control their lives. Such undifferentiated relations have been described in various case studies (Barocas & Barocas, 1980) and in empirical research reports (Kellermann, 2001b).

2. Sociocultural and Socialization Models of Transmission

Transmission in culture (Heller, 1982) has always been a central postulate of anthropology, and the passing down of social norms and beliefs from generation to generation is well described in social psychology. Social learning and socialization models of transmission focus on how children of survivors form their own images through their parents' childrearing behavior; for example, their various prohibitions, taboos, and fears. Numerous studies indicate that abused children often grow up to be child abusers themselves (Blumberg, 1977), that teenage motherhood and early marriage seems to be passed on from mothers to their daughters and that an inclination for gambling and alcoholism seems to be passed on from parent to child.

In comparison with psychoanalytic theories that focus on unconscious and indirect influences, social learning theories emphasize conscious and direct effects of parents on their children. In much of this literature, Holocaust survivors have been described as inadequate parents. Their multiple losses were assumed to create childrearing problems around both attachment and detachment. For example, overt messages conveyed by Holocaust survivor parents, such as "Be careful" and "Don't trust anybody!" were assumed to have left their indelible marks. The exaggerated worries of such anxious parents may have conveyed a sense of an impending danger that the child may have absorbed.

Countless studies have confirmed the relationship between childrearing practices and behavioral traits in the child (Sears, Maccoby & Levin, 1957). Patterns of parental rejection, overprotection, overpermissiveness, and harsh, inconsistent discipline upon the developing child have been regarded as most influential. Empirical research on children of Holocaust survivors, however, has yielded contradictory evidence regarding the parenting behavior of Holocaust survivors when investigated with classical parenting instruments. Kellermann (2001a) investigated parental behavior with a new self-report instrument that also included salient Holocaust dimensions and found four major kinds of parental rearing behaviors: transmission, affection, punishing, and overprotection. While the second-generation group rated their parents higher on transmission, other differences in childrearing practices were small, if taken as a whole. These findings largely support the descriptive literature on trauma transmission, while at the same time refuting the view that Holocaust survivors function more inadequately than other parents do.

We may assume, however, that Holocaust survivor parents influenced their children not only through what they *did* to them in terms of actual childrearing behavior, but also through whom they *were* in terms of inadequate role models. As pointed out by Bandura (1977), children learn things vicariously by observing and imitating their parents. Children of Holocaust survivors may be assumed to have taken upon themselves some of the behaviors and emotional states of their parents. A middle-aged child of two Holocaust survivors with a very low tolerance for stress described her parents in the following manner: "My father used to scream during the night and my mother screamed during the day. Both were highly disturbed and could not tolerate anything that might upset them. I had to be careful always as a child not to come home late, not to be ill, not to show any signs of distress, and to be as quiet as I possibly could be." Growing up with such tormented parents must in itself have been a kind of cumulative trauma for the woman, but some of her own anxious behavior was clearly learned through modeling.

3. Family Systems and Communication Models of Transmission

Unconscious and conscious transmission of parental traumatization always takes place in a certain family environment, which is assumed to have a major impact on the children.

Though Holocaust survivor families certainly differ from one another in many ways (Danieli, 1981a), the more pathological families are described as tight little islands in which children came into contact only with their own parents, with their siblings, and with other survivors. In such highly closed systems, parents are fully committed to their children and children are overly concerned with their parents' welfare, both trying to shield the other from painful experiences (Klein-Parker, 1988). Through mutual identifications, parents live vicariously through their children and children live vicariously in the horrific past of their parents. Considering such powerful family dynamics, it is not surprising that problems around individuation and separation (Klein, 1971; Barocas & Barocas, 1980; Freyberg, 1980) and attachment (Bar-On, Eland, Kleber et al., 1998) were often observed.

A forty-three-year-old man, a lawyer by profession, brought his disturbed mother for consultation. His appearance was candid and strong, but when he spoke, one could immediately notice a sense of insecurity and low self-esteem. He was single and had never built a life of his own. His eighty-year-old mother, on the other hand, was a strong-willed, dominant lady whose hysterical personality and anxieties were all too obvious. She was fully self-centered without any real concern for her son. One had to see both of them together to realize that the mother had bound her son to herself with an invisible, yet unbreakable bond. She cursed him and praised him and demanded that he take care of her forever. Like a small boy, he did not know how to respond.

Parents who care too much and who become overly involved and intrusive, tend to enmesh their offspring in the crossfire of their own emotional problems and bind their children unto themselves in a manner that makes it difficult for the children to gain independence. When such parents grow older and become more dependent upon their children, an impossible situation is created for everyone involved.

> When neither a nurse nor a spouse was available, a daughter had to take care of her frail Holocaust survivor mother who had become ill. Because of the daughter's earlier ambivalent feelings toward her mother, she had great difficulties taking such a role upon herself, feeling both angry and guilty toward her mother who had endured so much during the war. Occasionally open expression of hostility toward her mother led to self-reproach, and she tried unsuccessfully to resolve the conflict by taking care of her mother even more, neglecting her own children for a long period. She said: "I could not stand being with her, but I kept nursing her until she died. I had no choice. My mother had lost her mother in the war and I had to make it up to her!"

Children like these take upon themselves the role of being parents to their own parents. Helen Motro (1996) explains: "We are older now than our parents were when they survived. And yet they in their old age still feel like orphans, and we often feel like their parents. It is our duty to fill all voids." This kind of role reversal with the traumatized parent may be conceptualized as *defensive caretaking* (Metzger-Brown, 1998), *narcissistic parenting* (Rosenberger, 1973), *enmeshment* (Zlotogorski, 1985; Seifter-Abrams, 1999), *engagement* (Podietz et al., 1984), or *parent-child role diffusion* (Zilberfein, 1996). Through *invisible loyalties* (Boszormenyi-Nagi & Spark, 1973), children adopt the role of parental and/or parentified child, and they thus sadly become orphans themselves with unfulfilled dependency needs of their own.

A specific kind of *double-bind* family communication may also account for trauma transmission. The child is fixed in an intense emotional relationship with a parent who, by the contradictions between the parent's verbal remarks and behavior, makes it impossible for the child to respond adequately. For example, a son may be encouraged by his mother to use initiative in his schoolwork. Yet when he wants to go to the library, his mother says: "Why do you leave me? I need you here and will become ill if you leave me alone." Such a double-bind restricts the emotional development of the child and further confuses the communication that is already very complicated. In fact, much of the family influence of trauma transmission may be explained as occurring through nonverbal, ambiguous, and guilt-inducing communication (Lichtman, 1984; Klein-Parker, 1988) and especially through the widespread *conspiracy of silence* (Danieli, 1998). The subliminal mediating influence of parental communication style, through either oversilence or overpreoccupation (Sorscher & Cohen, 1997), may be a major reason for the difficulty many children of Holocaust survivors have when trying to connect their vague sensations of fear, sadness, and vulnerability with actual memories of the experience of growing up with Holocaust survivor parents.

In a study on Holocaust survivors as parents, Kellermann (2001a) found that Israeli children of Holocaust survivors generally view their parents in a positive light and that difference in childrearing practices between Holocaust survivors and other Israeli parents on such major parenting behaviors as affection, punishing and over-protection, seem to be small, if taken as a whole. However, despite their devotion and largely successful childrearing behavior, Holocaust survivor parents were perceived as unable to prevent the Holocaust from having a significant impact upon their offspring. According to the findings of this study, their parents' past continued to have a strong influence on the lives of the offspring who felt that they had absorbed the inner pain of their parents. It was as if they had taken upon themselves a kind of emotional burden from their parents that had a major influence on their lives.

An *anniversary syndrome* can also appear in which offspring might reexperience a trauma of their parents or even grandparents at a similar age, or at the same date as the original trauma. In her paper on the "Ancestor Syndrome," Schützenberger (1998; 2000) explores how symptoms might appear in the descendants when they are at the age when a trauma occurred in an ancestor's life. With the use of genosociograms and psychodramatic enactments, she provides many examples of how life scripts may be seen in the light of a person's family heritage.

4. Biological or Genetic Models of Transmission

Some of the disorders detected in children of survivors may be simply explained by the fact that parents were not yet sufficiently healthy to give birth at the end of the war. This view is supported by a relatively unknown study of newborn children of concentration camp survivors that was conducted by a gynecologist in Munich as early as 1948 and which was first reported by Eitinger (1993). He found that of the 1,430 Jewish newborns at his department, one out of twenty-five (4 percent) had congenital malformations, while the average percentage of malformations at the same department earlier had been only one in one hundred (1 percent). More recently, Hazani & Shasha (2008) reiterated the idea that the physical health of offspring must have been severely affected by the difficult conditions that their mothers endured during pregnancy. For example, they postulated that maternal hunger and stress-induced high levels of maternal steroids during crucial stages of fetal development might have exposed the unborn child to risks of increased cardiovascular morbidity and mortality in adult life: "The epigenetic changes brought about by fetal programming are not limited to the fetal period. There is ample proof that they are permanent, last throughout life, and can be passed on to future generations" (p. 254).

Biological models of trauma transmission are based on the assumption that there may be a genetic and/or a biochemical predisposition to the etiology of a person's illness. Genes transmit constitutional elements from parent to child and some mental illnesses seem to have a clear hereditary etiology. For example, studies indicate that children of schizophrenic parents are much more likely to develop the disorder than the general population and children of parents with mental illness experience significantly more secondary trauma than children of non-ill parents, regardless of parental traumatization, according to Lombardo & Motta (2008). Holocaust traumatization may be similarly passed on "almost as if psychological DNA were planted in the personality of the younger generation through its relationships with the previous one" (Volkan, 1997, p. 44). Memories of fear can thus be carried across generations through physiological processes and get *picked up* by another mind, and elements of the collective experience of the species are thus reflected in the genome (Perry, 1999).

Such a direct *transposition* (Kestenberg, 1982; 1989) of trauma was thought to have been inherited, absorbed, or contracted by the child, as if the persecution complex of the parents was contagious, infecting offspring across generational lines. As carryovers from the past, this traumatization was perhaps denied or "forgotten," but was assumed to find expression in some emotional distress or irrational behavior. Thus, when children learned to behave in disordered ways similar to those of their parents, there was a direct transposition of a distinct disorder (such as PTSD, depression, or general anxiety disorder) from the parents to the children.

Although the genetic model of transmission may evoke resistance because of its similarity with the Nazi ideology of purifying the gene pool of the German race, it provides a clear theoretical basis for future research. Primarily, it suggests that parental traumatization may be transmitted in the same manner as some hereditary diseases are passed on from one generation to another. Genetic memory code of a traumatized parent may thus be transmitted to the child through some electrochemical processes in the brain. The neural organization of various memory systems in the parent (e.g., hyperalertness) would lead to a similar organization and constitution in the child. Given that psychic trauma is assumed to have long-term effects on the neurochemical responses to stress in traumatized parents (Van der Kolk, McFarlane, & Weisaeth, 1996), it may also lead to the same enduring characterological deficiencies and to a kind of biological vulnerability in the child. Children of Holocaust survivors, who are born to severely traumatized Holocaust survivor parents, would then be *predisposed* to PTSD. In other words, adult children of Holocaust survivors, regardless of whether they themselves ever had PTSD, seemed to demonstrate similar biological alterations to trauma survivors with PTSD. This provocative finding suggested that what may have been transmitted to the children of Holocaust survivors is not necessarily PTSD in itself, but a certain degree of vulnerability to stressful life events (Yehuda, 1999), which would appear only under difficult situations.

In an attempt to investigate these assumptions, Yehuda and colleagues (2000) found that low cortisol levels were significantly associated with both PTSD in parents and lifetime PTSD in offspring, whereas having a current psychiatric diagnosis other than PTSD was relatively, but nonsignificantly, associated with higher cortisol levels. Offspring with both parental PTSD and lifetime PTSD had the lowest cortisol levels of all study groups. They concluded: "Parental PTSD, a putative risk factor for PTSD, appears to be associated with low cortisol levels in offspring, even in the absence of lifetime PTSD in the offspring. The findings suggest that low cortisol levels in PTSD may constitute a vulnerability marker related to parental PTSD as well as a state-related characteristic associated with acute or chronic PTSD symptoms" (p. 1252).

Aggravating and Mitigating Factors

The above four theories of trauma transmission suggest that trauma transmission occurs when there are unconscious displaced emotions, inadequate parenting, family enmeshment, and/or a hereditary predisposition or vulnerability to PTSD. Such aggravating factors are assumed to increase the likelihood of developing psychopathology as a result of parental traumatization. In addition, clinical experience suggests that trauma transmission is more likely to occur when: (a) offspring were born early after the parents' trauma and sometimes in a DP-camp (between 1945 and 1955); (b) offspring were either the only or the first-born child; (c) both parents were survivors (Yehuda et al., 1998b), rather than only one of them; (d) offspring were *replacement children* to children who had perished in the war; (e) parents had endured extraordinary mental suffering and significant loss of close family members and were highly depressed as a result; (f) symbiotic relations were dominant between parents and children, and family relations were characterized by enmeshment without sufficient corrective periods of disengagement and without a supportive peer group; and (g) the trauma was talked about too little or too much (Wiseman et al., 2002; Wiseman, Metzl & Barber, 2006). In addition, maternal, not paternal, PTSD may be related to increased risk for PTSD in offspring of survivors, according to a recent study by Yehuda et al. (2008).

An additional aggravating circumstance for the development of psychopathology in the children of survivors was pointed out by Bar-On et al. (1998) in their multigenerational study on coping with the Holocaust. They emphasized that the lack of resolution of traumatic grief on behalf of the parent, rather than the trauma in itself, would contribute to the attachment problems in the child. In addition, they pointed out that children who themselves were directly exposed to parents who had nightmares, panic attacks, psychotic breakdowns, and depressions and who were overly preoccupied with the Holocaust, would be more at risk than others who had no such direct personal experiences. To directly witness such extreme suffering in a mother or father would obviously be a very overwhelming experience that most children could not handle.

Clearly, however, because many children of Holocaust survivors adjusted well despite having grown up in a dysfunctional family in which there was a major risk for the development of psychopathology, several other circumstances may be assumed to influence the process of trauma transmission except the ones described above. For example, Keinan, Mikulincer, and Rybnicki (1988) have suggested that some children of Holocaust survivors developed unique coping mechanisms that better enabled them to deal with their parents' psychological burden. Similarly, Sagi-Schwartz et al. (2003) found that Holocaust survivors seemed to have been able to protect their daughters from their war experiences, although they themselves still suffered from the effects of the Holocaust. Even if the parents were deeply traumatized, these children might not have absorbed the trauma because of certain *mitigating effects* that may have helped them to withstand the stress despite everything. According to Sorscher & Cohen (1997):

> Numerous studies of these children have reported a wide
> spectrum of reactions, both detrimental and adaptive, to the

Holocaust. The variety of responses suggests the presence of mediating factors that may mitigate the transgenerational impact of trauma. Parental communication style, in particular, has been identified as a crucial determinant in the adaptation of families beset by catastrophe (p. 493).

Similarly, Axelrod, Schnipper, & Rau (1980) observed that a major difference between functional children and their hospitalized patients seemed to be that the better adjusted (functional) children, while growing up, were exposed to fairly open discussion of parents' camp experiences in *nonfrightening* ways. In addition, far from being socially isolated, better-adjusted families were involved in survivor organizations that may have provided support and a sense of extended community that gave perspective to the close-knit Holocaust survivor family. The acceptance of a Jewish or a specific immigrant identity in such close sympathetic communities, as well as the lack of renewed anti-Semitism may also have played a mitigating role.

Furthermore, reparative periods in school, youth movements, summer camps, and in other social support systems (Heller, 1982) might have helped the offspring to differentiate from their parents and to alleviate some of their detrimental influence. Indeed, for many such children of survivors, the phase of adolescence became a time for age-appropriate separation and individuation that helped them move away from home and what it represented. The importance of such *outside-the-home* socialization in the peer groups of childhood and adolescence has been amply emphasized by Harris (1995): "Many psychologists have marveled at the robustness of development; despite vast differences in the way their parents treat them, most children turn out all right ... Children usually turn out all right because the environment that does have important and lasting effects is found with little variation in every society: the children's play group" (p. 458). Those children of Holocaust survivors who failed to experience such *nonfamilial* support during childhood may be assumed to have been more affected by the detrimental effects of parental traumatization than others. They are at higher risk of absorbing the trauma of their parents and of developing mental distress as a result.

In an effort to understand more clearly some of these aggravating and mitigating factors, Kellermann (2008b) recently conducted a demographic study of a clinical subpopulation of the *Second Generation*. This population consisted of a self-selected sample of 273 children of Holocaust survivors who applied for counseling in Amcha and, as such, they may be assumed to represent the more gravely affected children of survivors. Results indicated that most of this clinical population was indeed born soon after the war ended, to parents who were both Holocaust survivors, and that they were mostly female, married, highly educated, working as teachers or in the helping professions, were the first or the second child, and had parents who were inclined not to share their Holocaust experiences with their children. Parents were mostly rated as fully functioning, without severe mental and physical disease and as not overly preoccupied with the Holocaust.

An Integrative View of Trauma Transmission

We are now in a position to more precisely define the various factors that influence the process of trauma transmission and to answer the question posed about which kinds of Holocaust survivor parents influence which kinds of children under which circumstances. According to the above theories, trauma transmission in a child of Holocaust survivors is a function of unconsciously displaced parental emotions, inadequate parenting behavior, family enmeshment, and/or a hereditary predisposition in combination with specific aggravating and mitigating circumstances.

Such an integrative view of trauma transmission (Kellermann, 2001d) takes into account the intricate interplay among different levels of transgenerational influence, suggesting that trauma transmission is caused by a complex of multiple related factors, including biological predisposition, individual developmental history, family influences, and social situation. Whether hereditary or environmentally inflicted, specific manifestations of trauma transmission can thus be explained as being determined by any or all of the above mentioned psychodynamic, sociocultural, family system, and biological factors or by an *ecological* combination of these. For example, the recurrent Holocaust nightmares reported by the child of survivors in the first paragraph of this chapter may be understood, first as a manifestation of the displaced unconscious fears of the parents. The child is experiencing what the parents themselves cannot perceive and express. Second, it may be explained as the result of a specific kind of social learning and parenting. The child responds to the anxieties indirectly expressed in deleterious childrearing behavior. Third, it may be the result of family enmeshment and tacit communication. The child is trapped in a closed environment in which the shadows of the past are ever present. Finally, the disorder of the parent may be biologically transferred to the child who also becomes more vulnerable to stress.

The film *Shine* (1997) tells the story of David Helfgott, the Australian piano prodigy who disappeared into mental health institutions and reemerged fifteen years later to become an international star. We see how too much affection by a tormented survivor parent can destroy a vulnerable and sensitive child who is unable to defend himself against the detrimental parental influence. David's dominant father, a Polish-Jewish refugee who emigrated before World War II but who lost most of his family in the Holocaust, drives David literally crazy by holding him close and pushing him away at the same time. On the one hand, the father wants his boy to have everything that he himself was denied as a child. On the other hand, the father is resentful, even envious, of the opportunities that the child enjoys that he could not. This ambivalent situation is common for many children of Holocaust survivors and it may illustrate the multidetermination of mental disorders in this population. Although such a sensitive child might have been biologically predisposed to mental illness, the emotional abuse inflicted by his disturbed father and the dysfunctional family environment in which he grew up, certainly acted as triggers that produced the actual outbreak of the mental disorder.

Although this example probably represents an extreme case, it does illustrate how genetic inheritance and psychosocial influences usually co-occur to increase or decrease susceptibility to trauma transmission. Biological predisposition seems to be a necessary but not a sufficient condition for the development of trauma transmission. None of the factors by themselves can produce the traumatic effect.

Signs of biological vulnerabilities in the offspring of Holocaust survivors have been found in a number of empirical studies during the last decade (summarized in Kellermann 2001b). Despite these empirical resarch reports, however, the complex etiology of transgenerational transmission of Holocaust trauma remains allusive and difficult to investigate with empirical research. Studies that address secondary transmission of PTSD from major trauma to their offspring are sparse (Baranowsky et al., 1998) and no studies were found that investigated the interaction of various components of transmission. Usually psychoanalytic and relational models were substantiated with descriptive reports from the clinical setting, whereas the biological models were studied with comparative research. Thus, because of the multitude of variables involved, we still have insufficient empirical data to show how the components described above *work together* to produce trauma transmission.

Children of Child Survivors

Most accounts of the Second Generation have described children of survivors born during the first decade after the Second World War, during the baby-boom years between 1946 and 1956. They were born to adult survivors who had lost their original families and who were eager to create new ones as fast as possible. However, many of the survivors who were children during the war (child survivors = CSs), created families (if at all) much later, and their children were usually born in the 1960s and later. For many years, these CSs remained almost forgotten and it is only during the last two decades that they have come into sharper relief as a special subgroup. Despite the fact that this younger Second Generation (2G) of child survivors (2GCSs) already has reached middle age, they are still almost invisible and have only recently received any professional attention at all.

However, because of their experiences of having grown up with child survivor parents, they deserve our special professional attention. While they were born a long time after the war, they were born to *orphan parents* who had lost their own parents under terrible circumstances. We may therefore assume that some of these early survival experiences of the parents in some ways have influenced these 2GCSs. It would, for example, be interesting to investigate if there are any specific differences between "ordinary" 2Gs and 2GCSs and if so, how they influence the functioning of the 2GCSs as parents to the third generation (c.f. Kellermann, 2008a).

As far as I know, there are no specific empirical studies investigating the clinical population of children of the child survivors and I did not find any studies comparing the older and the younger 2Gs. Because of the multitude of variables involved, perhaps such a study would be difficult to design. A qualitative study, with interviews, would probably be a good start to map the characteristics of this population. The following observations may be an initial overview. It is based on clinical impressions of more or less disturbed CSs and their 2G offspring clients in individual and group therapy in Amcha, and with discussions with the staff of Amcha in Israel, and it cannot be generalized to a nonclinical population.

The most obvious and apparent observation seems to be that these 2GCSs *children of children* took the role of becoming parents to their own (earlier orphaned) parents. This was naturally no simple task, as it in effect made them parentless as well. A female client said: "I had to take care of my mother ever since I was a young girl because she was unable to take care of herself. I did everything for her, and for the family, and I was in effect the only mother present for everybody." This specific client could not marry and create a family of her own, and after the death of her mother, she felt a strange sense of relief, together with all the resentment and feelings of guilt for not being able to be a *good enough* mother (for her mother). This may in fact be a more common situation than what we expect because such CS mothers become so very demanding toward their children that they live in a relative state of reclusion and seldom ask for help.

A sad aspect of such CS parenting is that they frequently compare the childhood that they themselves had with the childhood of their own children (and even with their grandchildren). "I never had those things," they might say, and then go on to complain about the spoiled children of today. In secret, I have even heard such CS grandmothers express hidden feelings of jealousy against their own grandchildren.

As a response to such demanding behavior from the CS parent, many 2GCSs unconsciously internalize the suffering of their parents, minimize their own suffering as compared with that of their parents, and constantly attempt to find a suitable distance and closeness, which is almost impossible to establish. There will always be complaints of being either too close or too far and that nothing is *good enough*. One such mother told her daughter: "You are worse than the Nazis! You will bring me to my early death!" Some such 2GCSs decide to immigrate to another country to start a life of their own, and others continue to live in the same apartments all through life. In terms of separation-individuation, there is very little understanding in CS parents of this need in their children, because they themselves often suffered from the lack of any parenting at all. Apparently, if there are emotional and mental problems, these will be more severe than in the corresponding *older* 2G groups.

In addition to the above-mentioned characteristics, Amcha therapists shared that such 2GCSs often have difficulties with physical touch, and that communication between family members is often very complicated. There will be frequent misunderstandings and long-standing conflicts that often make the family atmosphere unbearable. Some family therapists who are called upon to make some order in these entangled relations feel that the best remedy is to find some kind of actual separation and physical distance between the parties that respect the individual needs of each person.

Treatment of the Second Generation

A wide range of treatment procedures are presented in the literature to alleviate the mental difficulties of children of Holocaust survivors. Most of these include ways to encourage free expression of feelings, thoughts, and associations that were hitherto largely covered up. Being vaguely aware of the impact of the Holocaust on their lives, many children of survivors are unable to find a suitable expression to their seemingly unwarranted anger, anxiety, and depression. Frequently, psychoanalytically oriented psychotherapy is therefore offered to help them become more aware of the unconscious or preconscious processes that continue to propel the transmission of trauma from one generation to another.

Sometimes such individual therapy is combined with analytic group psychotherapy, or group therapy as a single modality is suggested with various orientations, including expressive forms of music, art, psychodrama (Kellermann, 1992), and bibliotherapy. The common aspect of these approaches is to provide the children of survivors with opportunities to gain some insight into the roots of their problems, followed by a gradual process of working through and reintegration. Group therapy approaches provide a suitable setting for children of survivors to compare experiences and to develop a unique *second-generation identity* (Fogelman & Savran, 1979; Wardi, 1992; Weiss & Weiss, 2000).

Given that so much of the second-generation problems are centered on conflicts of enmeshment, it is a major task of family therapy to help them break away and separate from their parents and to find their own identities. If the relationship between parents and children is so close that it is impossible to tell the feelings of one from the other, some help in differentiation is required. In short, if children feel that their original Holocaust survivor family environment is too much to handle, they need to be helped to "leave home" both in reality and in fantasy. As we have already pointed out, this is easier said than done in families that have suffered so many traumatic losses and put so much hope and expectations on the offspring. Many second-generation clients, therefore, need a lot of support and encouragement to work through such an individuation process step-by-step. At the same time, they will also try to rid themselves from the burdensome dark influences of the Holocaust trauma that often come with being the children of Holocaust survivors.

Conclusion

An important milestone in this long journey of coming to terms with the past is when we succeed in transforming our initial sense of handicap into an important human resource that gives purpose and meaning in life. At that time, the trauma of our parents will not only be perceived as a curse, but also as a powerful legacy. When this occurs, we can start to come to terms with the fact that the contradictory forces of vulnerability and resilience will always continue to be a part of us.

While the *transmitted trauma* that we have inherited from our parents might increase our suffering, the very fact that we have vicariously experienced so much tragedy, may also provide us with some adaptive coping ability and with survival skills (described in chapter 2), which usually are insufficiently developed in other people. If any or all of these skills were predominant in the survivors, we may assume that they were also passed on to the offspring. In addition, because of our close affinity with the tragedy of our parents, traits such as compassion, empathy, and a deep understanding of human suffering may be assumed to be highly developed in the Second Generation, giving us a special predisposition to work in the helping and teaching professions.

It would be a simplification, however, to describe vulnerability and resilience as two separate forces struggling to take hold of the inner person of the Second Generation. Rather, offspring of Holocaust survivors seem to simultaneously struggle with both forces at one and the same time, and will have periods when one or the other is more dominant. Some of us might suffer from lifelong debilitating psychopathology with periods of tranquility, while others may function excellently most of the time with shorter periods of severe anxiety and depression. It is important, therefore, not to view this client population as a homogenous group, which either suffers from specific psychopathology or which manifests posttraumatic growth, but to see them as simultaneously struggling with both forces throughout life.

CHAPTER 5

Holocaust Trauma in Grandchildren of Survivors

Your sons weren't made to like you. That's what grandchildren are for.

—Jane Smiley

The last remaining Holocaust survivors have reached the twilight years of their lives; their children are in midlife or beyond, and their grandchildren— already in their earlier twenties—have begun to take center stage.

Who are these grandchildren, and what is their legacy?

What will they bring with them from the past to the future? Will they continue to carry the heavy burden and vicarious traumatization described in earlier chapters, or will they leave the past behind and emerge unscarred from this half-century-old drama with a sense of accomplishment and pride for what has been achieved, despite everything?

Throughout this book, we have argued that major trauma such as the Holocaust leaves its indelible scars upon subsequent generations. So, it's not strange to expect a continuation of this trauma transmission into the third generation—and perhaps beyond. But with the passage of time, the transmission of Holocaust trauma upon the third generation clearly becomes less pronounced and more difficult to recognize than it was for previous generations.

The Third Generation

These grandchildren of Holocaust survivors—or the "Third Generation," as they are sometimes called—may be deeply affected by the tragic history of their ancestors (Fogelman, 1998). But how, and to what extent, is still unclear. It probably depends on many things. The most obvious variables affecting their inclination to absorb the sediments of history include who they are, who their parents and grandparents are, and how their relations with them are or were. For example, if they had a lot of contact with their Holocaust-survivor grandparents, we can expect that their grandparents' influence was much greater than if they lived in another country and only saw one another occasionally, even if they might have been exposed to the Holocaust indirectly through the Internet and/or films, such as *Schindler's List*, *Shoah*, *Life is Beautiful*, or *The Pianist*.

Thus, we may expect grandchildren who regularly celebrated festive occasions with their entire families to have absorbed more of the specific Holocaust radioactivity than others. On such occasions as bar/bat mitzvahs, weddings, funerals, or birthday parties, grandparents may have remembered their losses, cried, and openly shared their Holocaust memories.

In addition, we would expect grandchildren who interviewed their grandparents for their school projects, who took part in the *March of the Living* journey, or who visited *Yad Vashem* or any other Holocaust memorial museum, to be more affected than those who never met their grandparents and never heard about their Holocaust experiences firsthand. Personal encounters have a profound and often lifelong effect on the way these grandchildren view their own connection to the Holocaust. Dzieza (2004) explained:

> Sol had always been simply "Grandpa," a kindly, helpful man who would make me omelets when I visited and play ping-pong with me by the pool. I had always been aware that my grandfather was different from those of my friends, his halting accent, the numbers tattooed on his arm, for example. But it wasn't until I was thirteen, when he thought I was ready, that I truly understood his story.

Close encounters between the first and the third generations were not only important for children. They also opened doors to the inner lives of elderly Holocaust survivors that had been closed many years. Often keeping their tragic memories hidden from their own children, many elderly Holocaust survivors found it easier to open up to their grandchildren and share details with them that had previously been avoided. As a result, we frequently hear about Holocaust survivors who started to speak about their traumatic pasts for the first time only after their grandchildren interviewed them for a school project. Such events functioned as a trigger for survivors to finally deal with their pasts.

Having children and grandchildren was not always something simple, natural, and self-evident for the survivors, especially for those who had witnessed the starvation and murder of infants during the war—some of whom were their own brothers and sisters. Such experiences made them apprehensive about having children or overly anxious about something happening to them. As a result, newly born children were sometimes treated ambivalently by their grandparents. However, this attitude often disappeared as the children grew up and their relationships with grandparents became closer and more mutual.

Naturally, elderly Holocaust survivors yearned for their grandchildren to grow up without fear of another Holocaust. This was beautifully illustrated by the following story, retold by Greenberg (2006):

> While visiting Israel, a teacher of mine encountered an American minister who started badgering him with hostile questions and comments about Israel, and finally asked him, "What is it that you Jews really want?" My teacher responded with the following story: at Stolpce, Poland, on September 23, 1942, the ghetto was surrounded by German soldiers. Pits had been prepared outside a nearby village where the Jews would be led and then shot. The Germans entered the ghetto, searching for the Jews. A survivor by the name of Eliezer Melamed later recalled how he and his girlfriend found a room where they hid behind sacks of flour. A mother and her three children had followed them into the house. The mother hid in one corner of the room, the three children in another. The Germans entered the room and discovered the children. One of the children, a young boy, began to scream, "*Mama! Mama!*" as the Germans dragged the three of them away. But another of them, only four years old, shouted to his brother in Yiddish, "*Zog nit Mameh. Men vet ir oich zunemen*" (Don't say Mama. They'll take her, too). The boy stopped screaming. The mother remained silent. Her children were dragged away. The mother was saved. "I will always hear that," Melamed recalled, "especially at night; *Zog nit Mameh*—Don't say Mama. And I will always remember the sight of the mother. Her children were

dragged away by the Germans. She was hitting her head against the wall, as if to punish herself for remaining silent, for wanting to live." After concluding the story, my teacher told the minister, "What do we Jews really want? Well, I'll tell you what I want. All I want is that our grandchildren should be able to call out *Mama* without fear. All we want is that the world leaves us alone" (p. 3).

Because of such fears, survivors constantly think about possible future dangers, sharing with their families where it would be more or less safe to live (in Israel or abroad?).

Research

The research on the effects of the Holocaust upon the third generation is scarce. Taking into consideration that it is hard to study the influence of the Holocaust on the first generation, and even more so upon the second generation, the studies on the third generation become very challenging, indeed.

Such studies may be regarded as highly speculative, because a multitude of variables are involved. It is even difficult to clearly define the investigated population itself. For example, a grandchild of Holocaust survivors may have had one, two, three, or four grandparents who were persecuted during World War II. In addition, these grandparents may have had very different war experiences, from imprisonment in concentration or labor camps, to living in ghettos, going into hiding, joining the partisans, or any other hardships, all with or without the crisis that comes with immigrating to a new country.

The number of years that a grandchild knew his or her grandparent also seems to be an important factor, as well as how much—and in which words—he was told about the Holocaust. We know from such narratives that many grandparents retold their stories in ways that would be less disturbing for the grandchild, sometimes censoring what they said to avoid burdening their grandchildren with too many gruesome details. Finally, the country of immigration also plays an important role in grandchildren's internalization process, as many of them struggle with their own Jewish identities and the long-term meaning of the Holocaust for the Jewish people. For example, a grandchild who grew up in the United States or Canada would be differently influenced than someone growing up in Israel, Europe, Australia, or a small village in Hungary.

As a result of such speculative connections between the mental state of the grandchild and the Holocaust past of the grandparent, very few grandchildren of survivors turn to mental health counseling because of what their grandparents endured during the Holocaust. Nevertheless, a number of studies have been done on this issue.

One of the first studies investigated Holocaust survivors' grandchildren's ability to express their anger. In a comparative study, Bachar et al. (1994) found that grandchildren of Holocaust survivors did not differ in their expression of aggression from the control groups. A year later, Hogman (1995) interviewed a small group of Holocaust survivors' grandchildren who were old enough to articulate their feelings. While not observing any general Holocaust effects, Hogman found some specific signs of children's identification with their grandparents in the studied population, such as frequent thoughts about death and fears of not being able to stand up and die for what they believe in. Other nonspecific cultural, religious, and historical manifestations of Holocaust trauma could also be observed in the offspring. Most importantly, however, the children seemed to glorify the lives and achievements of their grandparents, who were seen as "bigger than life" and as role models to emulate. After all that they had gone through, grandparents were thought to possess some extraordinary survival abilities that had helped them to overcome the most difficult ordeals.

Fossion et al. (2003) presented some clinical observations from therapy sessions with Holocaust survivor families in which the third generation's symptoms appeared to be a consequence of transgenerational transmission of Holocaust trauma. In a more controlled study, Kassai and Motta (2006) investigated whether grandchildren of concentration camp survivors were more prone to PTSD symptoms than others. Results indicated that the residual impact of Holocaust-induced secondary trauma diminished to such an extent by the third generation that the differences between grandchildren of Holocaust survivors and the overall population were statistically nonsignificant.

Zohar, Giladi, & Givati (2007) tried to find out if disordered eating in second- and third-generation women would be related to their levels of Holocaust exposure and family dysfunction. They found that the disordered eating of women of the third generation was only partially predicted by their mothers' disordered eating and by their mothers' Holocaust exposure. The second generation reported more maternal overprotection and emotional overinvolvement than did the third generation. Contrary to expectation, however, the third-generation women reported being more exposed to the Holocaust than their parents.

Observing Holocaust survivors' grandchildren who enlisted in the army, Scharf (2007) examined the long-term effects of extreme war-related trauma on the second and the third generations of Holocaust survivors in eighty-eight middle-class families. As expected, she found that parenting variables mediated the association across generations between the degree of Holocaust experience in the parents' families of origin and ambivalent attachment style and self-perception of the adolescents. In other words, the more exposure parents had to the Holocaust, the more problems the children displayed. When only one parent was a survivor, the children showed little effect, but when both parents were survivors, problems seemed to increase.

As there are no clear-cut trauma findings among the children of survivors, Sagi-Schwartz et al. (2008) tried to find out if intergenerational transmission of trauma might have "skipped a generation," therefore manifesting in the grandchildren rather than the children of survivors. However, a meta-analytic study of 1,012 participants in thirteen nonclinical samples did not provide sufficient evidence of such "tertiary traumatization."

When summarizing this preliminary research, it seems that the mental states of survivors' grandchildren are similar to the second-generation group: that is, that there are no clear signs of trauma transmission in this group, but specific aggravating and mitigating variables are present that make it more or less probable that a survivor's grandchild would be detrimentally affected by Holocaust trauma. For example, if a child grew up in a highly dysfunctional family, with depressed and suicidal parents and grandparents, the probability of him or her absorbing some of their problems would be greater than if he or she grew up in a well-balanced and harmonious family. To verify that such an effect was actually caused by the Holocaust trauma of the grandparents, however, remains almost impossible, because such an influence may be assumed to be highly diluted after half a century.

But even though such tertiary traumatization cannot be clearly demonstrated, it seems to me that all grandchildren of survivors still carry within themselves a vague trace of the Holocaust that will become visible only in certain situations. Even if not fully aware of it, they may have inherited an *existential angst* from the Holocaust in which the themes of death and survival are always present. Some of them might become aware of this only when they are in danger or in moments of crisis, while others might sense this quality in everyday life and as a part of their ordinary experiences. This existential angst has become a part of their destiny because their lives cannot be taken for granted after the Holocaust. Simply put, if their grandparents had not miraculously survived, they would not exist, either.

Some of these vague characteristics cannot be easily described and may not be suitable for scientific investigations. They lend themselves better to qualitative studies, which emphasize narrative reports, emotional nuances, or nonverbal expression. For example, when asked about the *meaning* of having a Holocaust survivor grandmother, a young boy said, "It makes me a more compassionate human being, as I am more aware of the enormous losses that she experienced in her life, and that she nevertheless decided to continue to live. I owe my life to her."

In fact, many grandchildren emphasize the value of having grandparents tell their stories in a way that inspired them and gave them a deep sense of meaning in life. Their heroic efforts to survive during the war, and then to build up their lives again after the war, has made a great impression on their grandchildren. Mark Yoslow, a grandchild of survivors who has also initiated an investigation on this issue, assumed that what the third generation has absorbed is not a classical trauma transmission—as their parents may have absorbed—but a profound, transformative experience that gives meaning to life.

I have also observed some of these phenomena in my own family. As a child of survivors with a tendency for Holocaust imagery, I suspect that I have passed some of my own unconscious Holocaust baggage on to my own children. Unfortunately, there are many signs of such trauma transmission in my own children. For example, before my sixteen-year-old daughter went to Poland with her class, she interviewed my mother about the Holocaust. She visited the concentration camps and the memorials, including Auschwitz, where my mother had lost almost her entire family when she was also sixteen years old. She read the names of relatives who had been killed and lit candles in their memory. Throughout the journey, she felt as if she was revisiting my mother's Holocaust past, trying to re-actualize it as best as she could, and she cried for almost the entire week.

After her return to Israel, she had a long talk with my mother and then reported having further Holocaust nightmares for some time. Having previously been a cheerful and outgoing girl, she now felt anxious and upset about things that reminded her of the Holocaust. She dreamt that she was "in hiding" and taken away by soldiers, but she survived miraculously— while her friends perished. Obviously, she identified closely with the Holocaust experiences of my mother. She had "taken in" the deep layers of emotions from her grandmother, even though her grandmother was careful not to share the worst parts of her experiences with her.

Most importantly, my daughter's visit to Poland was unconsciously experienced in a way that resembled a "real visit" to the Holocaust, and it therefore became very traumatic for her. Naturally, this makes us question not only the educational value of such trips, but also their viability in terms of the emotional price paid for understanding what it was all about, and if it is at all recommended to expose young people to such an ordeal. My daughter insisted that the trip had been very meaningful for her, and my mother said that it had also been important to her that my daughter had done the trip. "But now," she added, "let's return to the present, and let's leave the past behind for a while."

Two Families

Around *Yom HaShoah* in 2007, I facilitated two intergenerational encounters that were filmed and later broadcasted on Israel's First Channel Television Network. Both included members of three generations of two Holocaust-survivor families, and focused on how the Holocaust legacy had passed on from one generation to the next. We first listened to the personal Holocaust narrative as remembered by the first generation family member, then asked the children to specify what the Holocaust trauma of their parents had meant for them. Finally, we explored the tacit messages understood by the grandchildren and their emotional responses to the family tragedy. Issues focused on the conspiracy of silence, overt and covert communication, on the "sender" or "transmitter" of Holocaust trauma and the "receiver" or "absorber" of Holocaust trauma, and on the "legacy" conveyed as well as the inevitable process of transgenerational transmission of trauma.

The first "fighter family" (Danieli, 1981a) depicted a survivor who had readily and frequently talked about his experiences in the Kovno Ghetto and in several concentration camps, as well as his participation in the death march at the end of the war and his miraculous escape. His three grown children had each absorbed different emotions from his Holocaust trauma: anger, pride, pain, and grief. They had also taken upon themselves some of the roles—and the names—of the perished family members. At the end of the film, the seventeen-year-old grandson, who was waiting to enlist in the Israel Defense Forces (IDF), sat next to his proud grandfather and looked very troubled, as if he was taking upon himself the heavy burden of defending the entire Jewish people.

The second family described a child survivor from Transnistria, which is located in a strip between the Dniester River and Ukraine. The survivor had never talked about his war experiences until his granddaughter had interviewed him for her school project. As a result of talking about his tragic past, a deep wound in him was opened up, and he started to cry uninterrupted for weeks until he received therapy through Amcha. In the film, he told his son, daughter, and granddaughter how he had lost one member of his immediate family after the other, all under the most difficult circumstances during the war. Afterwards, he had been left alone as a small boy to care for himself. When he shared the experience of lying next to his mother who had frozen to death, the entire family was in tears. Soon after having heard this story for the first time, his daughter and granddaughter revealed that they had also started having nightmares about the Holocaust. The courageous family worked hard to face and contain their grandfather's traumatic past, emerging as a close-knit family with enormous strength and mutual affection.

Intergenerational Programs

Such magic moments of intergenerational intimacy are often created when elderly survivors of the Holocaust share their war memories with youth, whether the youngsters belong to the third generation or not. As a result, intergenerational programs are established in Israel and elsewhere in which survivors are encouraged to share their Holocaust experiences with youth. Such programs have a two-fold benefit: the elderly survivors get an opportunity to talk about the past, and the young learn Holocaust history firsthand. This helps the children improve their school performance, boost their self-esteem, connect with their community, engage with positive role models, learn new cultural and historical perspectives, and better appreciate the profound legacy of senior citizens. For the elderly, the program reduces their isolation, reinforces the sense that they are still able to contribute to the community, stimulates their mental capacity, promotes continued learning, introduces them to new experiences with youth from diverse backgrounds, and rekindles their joy of living. What can be more therapeutic than that?

We have already mentioned that many Holocaust survivors found it difficult to talk about their experiences immediately after the war, leading them to silence for many years. Some of these survivors learned to open up only as a result of being invited to talk in schools and youth clubs about their war experiences. Only later did they slowly start to overcome their fear of being in touch with their most traumatic personal experiences.

One of the survivors who took part in such an intergenerational program said, "I talk with the youth about my experiences with the clear intention that the youth and future generations should know what happened then and there. It is my responsibility to talk and to share this tragic part of our people's history. The meetings are important, not only to them, but also to me. I feel when I share with them that all my suffering gets a new meaning, as if it was meant that I should survive and let others know what happened. So that those who were killed did not die without anyone knowing about it ..."

Many intergenerational programs, however, should not end with the survivor sharing her Holocaust past. It is very important that children are asked to do something creative on the basis of what they have heard, such as write a story, paint a picture, build a sculpture, or enact a play because it gives them an opportunity to process what they have heard on a very personal and deep nonverbal level. In addition, it gives the elderly Holocaust survivors a chance to get an outside reflection of what others have perceived from their narrative. This very dialogue makes the entire experience much more meaningful than if it had remained only a one-way communication with a passive audience.

As the relationships develop and become closer, additional intergenerational activities may be arranged that include any or all of the following:

- *Theme-centered cultural events (such as music performances, concerts, readings, drama rehearsals, excursions, and lecture-demonstrations on a variety of subjects);*

- *Meetings around memories of the Holocaust in which the elderly survivors talk about their experiences and the youth document these experiences in an artistic and creative manner, helping to promote the emotional processing of Holocaust stories by youth;*

- *Computer courses, Internet clubs and multimedia events provided by volunteer youth to the elderly (not necessarily Holocaust related);*

- *House visits by volunteer youth to homebound elderly survivors on a regular basis;*

- *Social gatherings, birthday parties, and festive occasions arranged by both generations;*

- *Special preparation meetings before and debriefing after school trips to Poland;*

- *Letters and drawings from younger children sent to homebound and/or hospitalized Holocaust survivors;*
- *Opportunities for child survivors of the Holocaust to join ordinary school classes to study general subjects they were unable to study during the war when they were children.*

Such intergenerational programs enhance elderly Holocaust survivors' ability to continue to live in dignity and integrity within the community. As a result, their most traumatic memories may be transformed into something to be proud of, a life experience that others can learn from. Indirectly or directly, the younger generation can see for themselves that it is possible to overcome personal difficulties, even when everything looks utterly hopeless.

CHAPTER 6

Holocaust Trauma in Israel

State apologizes to Holocaust survivors in special Knesset session.

—*Jerusalem Post* headline, August 21, 2007

On July 7, 2001, when conductor Daniel Barenboim led the Berlin *Staatskapelle Orchestra* in a performance of Richard Wagner's *Overture to Tristan und Isolde* in Israel, it provoked outrage from the audience, and denunciations across the Israeli political spectrum, because Wagner is still *persona non grata* in Israel. Apart from his notorious anti-Semitic opinions, his music was played on ceremonial state occasions of the Nazi regime, during book-burning ceremonies, and when concentration camp prisoners were marching to their deaths. As a result, the tones of *Tristan und Isolde* are still a powerful trigger for the reactivation of collective Holocaust trauma in Israel.

Like the characteristic pattern of Wagner's musical ornamentations, such repressed Holocaust themes seem to be a *Leitmotif* (leading motive) in the collective unconscious of the Jewish People. As overt manifestations of such hidden scenarios, the roles of victim, perpetrator, bystander, and savior are continually played out within the texture of the Israeli society. As Israel marked the sixtieth anniversary of the end of the Second World War in 2004, it was apparent that understanding the national Israeli psyche without viewing it through the prism of the Holocaust is impossible.

Naturally, this hidden *Leitmotif* has been heard (and sometimes expressed)—*loud and clear*—for over sixty years by the many thousands of Holocaust survivors who are still alive in Israel today and they recognize every note of it. For them, this is a continual companion melody that defines their every mood and daily existence. For others, however, it is felt only as an almost inaudible background noise that causes concern only in certain moments, such as when there is a national crisis or when a Nazi war criminal is captured. And while there may be a small minority of people who have grown up with a different narrative and cannot understand what the whole Holocaust fuss is all about, most informed Israelis today recognize the repeated and almost mythical characteristic of this historical echo from the *Shoah*.

Thus we observe that the trauma of the Holocaust has not only left its indelible mark on the survivors who themselves experienced the persecution, or on their descendants who were vicariously affected, but on the entire Jewish people who have never recovered from this tragedy. In the words of the former speaker of the Israeli Parliament, Shevach Weiss: "Auschwitz is a part of our daily life, not our past. In our society, our souls, our national spirit, everything is connected with the memory of the dark period of Auschwitz." Similarly, Shalev (2002), the director of *Yad Vashem*, described the Holocaust as a living catastrophe for the entire nation: "It's in the air, you can feel it," he said. "The wound is there still. We are still mourning; we are still processing and trying to cope. The trauma is so deep and so painful, it is still going on."

These individual and collective psychological effects of the Holocaust upon the Israeli society were also described by psychiatrists, such as Dasberg (1987b), Gampel (2000), and many others. They emphasized that, even if these effects cannot always be easily detected, there will always remain a trace of the tragedy imprinted upon the collective unconscious in the Jewish people.

A major traumatic event such as the Holocaust will obviously have an enduring impact upon any society. Unable to free itself from the constraints of such a tragic past, such a society will continue to get stuck in this psychological trauma for a long time and, if the trauma is not properly *remembered, processed, and worked through*, the society will be compelled to repeat it in a compulsive manner. Such a traumatized society would thus be thrown into a kind of "hypnotic spell" in which the trauma keeps re-igniting in new cycles of trauma reenactments, which lead to new violence, self-destructiveness, and revictimization (cf. Foa, 2009). This analysis of the collective psychological effects of the Holocaust upon Israeli society would postulate that Israel keeps exposing itself to situations reminiscent of its original Holocaust trauma in order to gain mastery. Indeed, Volkan (1997) called a collective trauma that is utilized by the state for specific purposes a *chosen* trauma. In the case of Israel, he suggested that their chosen trauma on the one hand helps build group cohesion and a sense of *we*. But on the other hand, it might also justify aggression against the Palestinians who would then be seen as *them*. Throughout this "displaced expression of hostility," Israelis refrain from really working through their actual feelings of grief, shame, and fear emanating from the Holocaust.

Similarly, Witztum, & Malkinson (2009) recently underscored the importance of understanding how individual and collective mourning processes are interwoven with one another: "The trauma of the Holocaust stamped itself indelibly on the national psychology. The timing of the realization of the scope of the Holocaust may have served as an additional incentive to invest all available resources in the furthering of the emerging state. But the result was more than fifty years of silence bypassing the agony and pain of grief while the survivors were forced to remain silent and mute. Thus, the avoidance of the bereavement and suffering experienced by those who were exposed to the reality of the Holocaust was the price paid by the survivors in the process of integrating into the new, emerging society" (p. 130).

Contrary to these points of view, however, there are those who feel that the ancient persecution and genocide of European Jewry during World War II has little impact upon the Israeli society of today. They hold that Israeli citizens finally and effectively have put their past behind them and that they instead have created a new Israeli-Jewish identity, which is fully detached from its tragic European past and which, through its short history, also has become largely resilient to such old traumatic influences. If at all important, they say that the effects of the Holocaust may be as significant as any other historic event of the Jewish People, but that it has a negligible impact of their lives today.

Wishful thinking?

Perhaps.

Because as years go by, the long-term influence of the Holocaust upon Israeli society is as relevant as ever. In fact, the effect of the Holocaust on Israel's collective consciousness seems to have increased over time. Its meaning for the early settlers and founders of the state was certainly different than it is for the citizens of Israel today (Ne'eman-Arad, 1997; Kenan, 2003).

Terror in the Past and Terror in the Present

For some Israelis, it seems as if *that war* never really ended; there continually are new major crises evolving, which (again) threaten the fragile existence of the Jewish state. Like a traumatized person, who jumps at every loud noise, the Israeli society seems to be constantly living on the edge, as if it was sitting on a sack of dynamite waiting to explode at any time. For example, when Israelis made some progress in the peace-talks with their neighbors, and people started to hope that things would finally become better, a new catastrophe occurred when Prime Minister Yitzchak Rabin was assassinated on November 4, 1995. And when Prime Minister Ariel Sharon showed some willingness to compromise with the Palestinians, he suffered a stroke on January 4, 2006. Most urgently however, while the former threat climaxed in the Nazi Holocaust's attempt at total annihilation of the Jewish people, the recent threat may lead to "wiping Israel off the map" as recently declared by Iran's president Mahmoud Ahmadinejad.

As a result of such frequent stressful national events, Israelis have internalized a distinct sense of catastrophic expectancy. In such a world, bad things can happen at any time and we need to be prepared for when they happen all the time. For Jews in Israel, it means that they have to be prepared for the next annihilation attempt by their enemies. Such an attitude may range from a vague sense of suspicion that we are not the most popular kids on the block, to a paranoid conviction that there are vicious anti-Semites out there who harbor *unconditional hate* (see chapter 8) against Israelis and who plan their next steps to annihilate the Jewish people. As a response to these undercurrents of malicious intent, Israeli Jews feel that they are in constant danger and that they live on *borrowed time*. With the words of Bartov (1996): "Since the Holocaust 'belongs' to the state, the victims are potential Israelis, and the Israelis potential victims. Hence the historical link is projected into the future, and Israelis are perceived as survivors of a catastrophe still living on the brink of an abyss." Such catastrophic expectancy brings with it a need for strong (military) leaders who can provide protection and a sense of safety.

Thus, past Holocaust trauma in Israel is triggered, not only by the sound of Wagner's music, but also by every new military emergency, and especially during terrorist bombings or when bombs are falling. At these times, the new trauma re-actualizes the old one.

At the age of eighty-two, Sara is sitting next to the window in her small apartment in the town of Sderot in southern Israel, looking at the passers-by running for shelter when the Red Alert warning is heard. She holds her breath waiting for the Qassam-rocket to fall, and then she relaxes as it explodes in the distance. It makes her remember the bombardment of the Second World War when she was a child in Europe, before she was transported to

Auschwitz and later to Bergen-Belsen. "Not much has changed," she says with a trembling voice. "My entire life has been a long struggle for survival ..."

In a country that has bombproof wastebaskets, it is always difficult to separate remnants of past Holocaust trauma from the present consequences of terrorism. But I have the distinct feeling that many of the present emotional responses to security politics have hidden roots in the Holocaust. Terrorist attacks, suicide bombings, or shooting rampages target innocent civilians at home, on buses, on city streets, at weddings, in discos or pizzerias in busy marketplaces, or quiet neighborhoods. They may strike at any place and at any time. For Israelis, the fear and pain of terrorism have become part of daily life. Though people still move about their daily lives, the impact of the attacks is slowly taking its toll.

Indeed, Israel has become a place where "death is a way of life" and where its citizens are "slipping back into the psychological stance that is most dangerous for it—the stance of the victim, of the persecuted Jew" (Grossman, 2001). Such sentiments are especially felt on memorial days, when the country remembers and mourns its many losses from its wars. For example, during the Memorial Day on May 2, 2006, the state of Israel commemorated its 22,123 soldiers who had fallen during their duty to the state, and its 1,358 victims of terrorist attacks. In addition, it also commemorated the approximately 200 Jews that were killed in terrorist or anti-Semitic attacks abroad since 1968.

The Palestinian *Intifada* caused Israelis to become agoraphobic, to be afraid of public spaces and of crowds and therefore to build a security wall for protection. This wall makes some citizens feel as if they were hiding in a large ghetto. People are worried and jumpy and there is a high level of interpersonal violence everywhere.

The fact is that there are chilling similarities between the scenes of the terrorist bombings of today and the Holocaust events from the past. A mother sat with her daughter on her lap in a pizza restaurant in Jerusalem at the time of the explosion and she was found burned to death in this same position. Later, the surviving family pointed out that her Dutch grandmother probably had been similarly killed with her daughter on her lap in the gas chambers and later burned in the crematoria some sixty years earlier. During this onslaught, children were killed in front of their mothers in kibbutz bedrooms, guests at a Passover celebration were suddenly blown to pieces, dancers at a wedding were murdered like in a pogrom, and young people who travelled by bus were suddenly mutilated, and so on. How can Israelis be exposed to such events and not think of the Holocaust?

On a collective level, Israelis respond to their multiple tragedies in two contrasting ways. On the one hand, the prior Holocaust trauma renders them clearly more vulnerable to extreme stress. But on the other hand, the successful coping with the initial Holocaust trauma has strengthened their resistance and made them more resilient to the effects of present and future trauma. On the background of the Holocaust, there are a wide variety of emotional and cognitive responses to the military tension in Israel that range from catastrophic expectancy and fear, to calculating defiance and an urge to strike back. Such Israelis would say that "we should have learned by now, not to trust our Gentile neighbors," while others would rather take a dovish political stance, refusing to strike out at (and revenge?) innocent victims, so as "not to do to them, what the Nazis did to us."

Political influence

Any of these responses naturally mold the Israeli public into one or the other political bias and it is a main reason for the fact that the Holocaust has been and still is utilized for political purposes in every quarter of the political spectrum. It has been used both by hard-liners and doves to score political points and is often a reference point for cultural debates (Nessman, 2005). In her book *Israel's Holocaust and the Politics of Nationhood*, Zertal (2005) criticized such a recruitment of the Holocaust for constructing Israeli collective memory and for the way this archetypal catastrophe has been invoked in the name of security and survival. But actual and imagined Holocaust narratives have kept on influencing policymaking and policy reasoning ever since the State was founded (Naor, 2003) and it is still an effective emotional persuader for any politician who wants to talk to the heart of the Jewish people. The master of such inspirational speech was the late Prime Minister Menachem Begin. Avner (2006) tells the following anecdote about Begin's first day of his premiership in 1977, dealing with the question of winning recognition by the PLO for the right of Israel to exist. At the podium of the Knesset, Begin warmed to this theme.

> "Our right to exist—have you ever heard of such a thing?" he declared, passion creeping into his voice. "Would it enter the mind of any Briton or Frenchman, Belgian or Dutchman, Hungarian or Bulgarian, Russian or American, to request for its people recognition of its right to exist?" He glared at his audience and wagged a finger, stilling every chattering voice in the

Knesset chamber. And now, using his voice like a cello, sonorous and vibrant, he drove on: "Mr. Speaker: We were granted our right to exist by the God of our fathers at the glimmer of the dawn of human civilization four thousand years ago. Hence, the Jewish people have an historic, eternal, and inalienable right to exist in this land, Eretz Yisrael, the land of our forefathers. We need nobody's recognition in asserting this inalienable right. And for this inalienable right, which has been sanctified in Jewish blood from generation to generation, we have paid a price unexampled in the annals of nations." Then he rose up on his toes, his shoulders squared, thumped the podium, and perorated in a voice that was thunder. "Mr. Speaker: From the Knesset of Israel, I say to the world, our very existence per se is our right to exist!" A spontaneous applause rose from the benches. Many got to their feet in full-throated acclaim. It was a stirring Knesset moment—a moment of instinctive self-recognition affirming that though the State of Israel was then but twenty-nine years old, its roots in *Eretz Yisrael* ran four thousand years deep.

During its entire history, the Holocaust became a political football game in the hands of the various factions that fought for power in Israeli politics (Segev, 1986). This included frequent reminders of essential Holocaust lessons to justify one or the other political position. In addition, the tendency of many Israelis to ignore the views of the outside hostile world may also have been an indirect way of showing distrust and alienation. In fact, this might explain the arrogant and self-righteous behavior of the classical Israeli *Sabra* who wanted to be the exact opposite of the helpless and persecuted (despised) *Diaspora Jew* during World War II. For example, when right-wing hard-liners wanted to evoke negative sentiments against Prime Ministers Rabin and Sharon, who were willing to make concessions to the Palestinian people, they depicted them in Nazi SS uniform to evoke hatred and repulsion. Similarly, left-wing peace-activists equated Israel's occupation of the West Bank and Gaza, and its treatment of the Palestinians, to *Nazi* behavior. Such utilization of symbols from World War II was most frequent when Israel left Gaza in 2005. On that occasion, the settlers' opposition to the withdrawal utilized a multitude of Holocaust symbols, including wearing a yellow/orange star with the word *Jude*, and calling Israeli soldiers *Nazis* and accusing them of carrying out a *pogrom*. On posters around Israel, they accused the government of wanting to make this geographic area of Israel *Judenrein* (clean of Jews).

Naturally, Holocaust survivors find such political abuse of the memory of the Holocaust detestable and unacceptable.

Periods of Post-Holocaust Adaptation to the Israeli Society

The European Holocaust refugees' absorption in Israeli society was a long and arduous journey. In the early days of the Jewish state, the image of the helpless and persecuted Jewish victim from Europe was a shameful contrast to the emerging national mythology of the strong and heroic new Israeli Jews who "would have fought back." Even though they accounted for about half of the wave of immigration to Israel in the aftermath of World War II (Yablonka, 1999), Israelis looked at the survivors with a mixture of suspicion ("How did they survive?"), contempt ("They went like sheep to the slaughter!"), and/or pity ("God help you poor things!"). None of these attitudes helped the survivor to feel welcome in the Jewish homeland, nor would their personal experiences be understood if they shared them. The survivors were even given the nickname *soaps*, implying that they were weak people who could easily be washed away. It was only years later that a hidden meaning of the nickname became publicly known: Nazis used to make soap out of the bodies of the victims (Moses & Cohen, 1993, p. 130; Volkan, 1997, p. 45). Most disturbing, however, was the fact that the elderly and sick survivors encountered particular difficulties in absorption given that the available medical, psychological, and welfare resources were largely inadequate (Solomon, Neria, & Ram, 1998).

As described by Almog (2000), the Zionist myth of the zealous pioneering *Sabra* represented the alternative to the ghetto mentality of Diaspora Jews and everything that they represented. The Holocaust narrative had no place in this *Zionist Revolution* and survivors quickly understood that they should not reveal too much about their tragic memories in this environment. In addition, survivors who immigrated to Israel were immediately confronted with the hard reality of a state that fought for its existence, and there was no room for any reminiscences. Unable to cope with their own suffering, and told to "forget the past and to suppress their traumatic memories," many survivors kept their scars hidden for half a century or more.

But at the same time as the individual Holocaust narrative was kept locked in, the collective lessons of persecution underscored the urgency and vital necessity of a Jewish homeland. Thus, it provided a justification for creating a Jewish state in the first place. Holocaust survivors immigrated to Israel in a steady flow and created new families and joined the *Yishuv* in building the country and safeguarding it from its enemies. For many, the State of Israel symbolically served as the ultimate failure of the "Final Solution" of the Nazis (Solomon, 1998; Sagi-Schwartz et al. 2008). Indirectly, survivors also brought with them large sums of collective compensation payments that strengthened the general economy of Israel (cf. Sikron, 1957; Porat, 1986; Segev, 2000; Sheleg, 2001).

By placing the Holocaust as the significant event leading to the creation of the state, however, Friedländer (1990) argued that the myth of catastrophe and redemption was created, which was broken only at the Eichmann trial.

The lack of empathy for the tragic experiences of Holocaust survivors began to change in 1961 when the trial of Adolf Eichmann was broadcast on national radio, and the testimonies were brought out into the open. In her book *The State of Israel vs. Adolf Eichmann*, Yablonka (2004) examined the enormous impact of this historic trial on the Israeli psyche. But why did it take more than forty years after the end of the war to give a voice to the survivors? Many reasons have been suggested. First, a new social awareness of the Holocaust began to develop during these years. Having been silent for decades, more survivors than ever were ready to speak out and openly share their memories and their mental suffering. As a result, the Second Generation grew increasingly curious about their parents' past, asking questions and seeking answers and perhaps as a result, the psychological effects of transgenerational transmission of trauma upon the offspring also became more widely acknowledged (see chapter 4). Second, the legacy of guilt and shame that was (unjustly) bequeathed to the Holocaust generation was reevaluated and slowly disappeared. Finally, with time running out for the aging survivor community, many felt the responsibility of bearing witness and preserving memory before it would be too late. In sum, these periods of postwar Holocaust survivor adaptation, and specifically the interplay between individual and collective *trauma pattern norms,* which developed in Israeli society and the formation of a collective memory in the Jewish state, were delineated by Nadler's (2001) three distinct periods of Holocaust survivor acceptance in the Israeli society: (1) 1945–60 simplistic and judgmental; (2) 1960–80; willingness to listen to the survivors' life stories; and (3) attention also to the effects of the Holocaust upon the survivors' families and upon the society at large.

The significant change in the attitude of the Israeli state toward the Holocaust and its survivors, however, occurred only in the 1980s. During the 1973 *Yom Kippur* War, when there was an actual threat of the destruction of the country, many Israelis further started to grasp the deeper significance of the Holocaust. In the 1980s, the Holocaust became a part of the high school matriculation exams and an annual Holocaust Memorial Day (*Yom HaShoah* in Hebrew) was instituted to commemorate the martyrs and heroes who died under the Nazis. Each year in the spring, a special ceremony was (and still is) held at *Yad Vashem*, the Jerusalem Holocaust Museum. A siren is sounded in Israel and everyone stands for one minute of silence in memory of those murdered. On that day, all Jewish places of entertainment are closed in Israel and many people attend public events of Holocaust commemoration. In addition, an ever-increasing number of Israeli high school pupils travel to Auschwitz and other Nazi death camps, as well as to abandoned synagogues and old Jewish cemeteries in Eastern Europe, to see for themselves where the atrocities occurred. Finally, the IDF bring many of its officers to *Yad Vashem* and to Auschwitz to keep them informed of the past and perhaps to motivate them to protect the nation from any such future horrors.

All these events together contributed to transforming the Holocaust from a *hidden trauma* that was kept away from the public, to an event that could be talked about openly and everywhere. As a result, the attitude of Israelis in general toward the Holocaust and its survivors has become much more accommodating and understanding. As a climax to this long process of acceptance, certain financial demands that the elderly survivors had on the Jewish state were also accepted. It took the Jewish state almost sixty years to admit that it had neglected to provide sufficiently for its Holocaust survivors. "During a special Knesset session in August of 2007, Speaker Dalia Itzik strongly condemned the state's treatment of Holocaust survivors over the decades: 'Israeli society must make amends for its wrongdoings,' she said" (Hoffman, 2007, p. 6). Even if it was coming so very late, this recognition might be seen as the last chapter of the long journey of absorption of the survivors in the Jewish homeland.

Holocaust Lessons for the Future

As a result of this long journey and of the various educational programs instituted, the Israeli society today is perhaps able to deal with its Holocaust past in a more differentiated manner than before. Perhaps it is more widely accepted that this Holocaust past is not only a story of either genocide and persecution, or heroism and martyrdom. Nor is it only a confrontation with the forceful presence of the ultimate evil and the cruelty of human beings to each other, or the great manifestations of compassion and courage under the worst of conditions.

The Israeli Holocaust narrative of today includes both of these two opposing and paradoxical learning experiences; both *posttraumatic stress*, and *posttraumatic growth*. The first kind of learning makes us more vulnerable to stress, while the second makes us more resilient. The Holocaust teaches that the world can be evil and meaningless, that life is terminal, and that people are cruel. But the Holocaust may also teach that there may be hope even in the worst of conditions. As Israelis start to listen carefully to the stories of the Holocaust survivors, they have slowly come to appreciate this profound lesson and it has provided them with strength and hope and courage for the future.

It is my hope that, as Israelis become more accustomed to this dual reality, they will come to realize that this duality does not only include the assumptive world of the victims, but also of the perpetrators (who may not be only cruel), the rescuers (who may not be only saints), and the bystanders (who may not be only indifferent). While many still have a tendency to look at these main actors of the Second World War in *black-and-white* terms, it is my hope that they will be seen as ordinary people of flesh and blood, like everybody else. Whatever the results of such a learning experience, it is my hope that being confronted with the history of the Holocaust in depth, means that we will be also helped to face ourselves today. This might be the main thing to digest.

CHAPTER 7

Holocaust Trauma
in Germany and Austria

*The legacy of the Hitler regime still haunts us, causing many
of us Germans to feel frustrated or even angry at anybody who
mentions the Holocaust.*

—Ursula Duba (1997)

Earlier chapters of this book discussed the obvious long-term emotional
effects of Holocaust traumatization upon the survivors and their families.
The traumatic impact on those who belong(ed) to the "other side," however,
remains more obscure. But the fact is that many Germans and Austrians
also may suffer from one or the other traumatic effects of the war, even
if some of them have chosen to put a lid on their wartime experiences.
Apparently, there has been insufficient psychological working through
(German: *Bewältigung, Auseinandersetzung*) of this tragic legacy, both on
an individual and a collective level.

> The tall man was born in 1927 and had served in the German
> *Wehrmacht*. He told us that at one occasion, he had stood face-
> to-face with Adolf Hitler during a general inspection of the
> troops at a train station. As the former soldier showed us the
> situation in action and looked the man playing Hitler deep in the
> eyes, I asked: "What would you have done if you had met Hitler
> today?" The question obviously shook him, and he became pale

in his face, but he declined to respond and backed off. It was unclear if he would have embraced the *Führer*, or if he would have shot him.

The scene is taken from a group session held in Vorarlberg in the autumn of 2004 in which Austrian participants of various ages were looking at their National Socialistic past and themselves today. The situation symbolically represents the essence of the German-Austrian discourse, in which its Nazi past is neither embraced, nor rejected, but largely avoided. For very many years, it was left out of consideration; the first generation of Nazi collaborators and bystanders refused to talk about it at home, neither was it taught properly in schools, nor dealt with in a straightforward manner on a sociopolitical level. World War II (German: *Der Zweiter Weltkrieg*) remained a *taboo* subject in many circles of society for almost half a century.

During the last decade, however, this situation has started to change, but slowly. Now, the Holocaust is moving from being avoided to becoming a focal point of contemporary interest. The younger generation has started to confront its National Socialist past and to also admit its own people's responsibility for the Holocaust. However, while the collective responsibility of Germany-Austria became more acknowledged, the working through of individual family histories remained difficult. In addition, there was a substantial lack of knowledge among the younger generation of the genocide committed during World War II. As a remedy for this, it was decided to improve the quality of Holocaust education. In conjunction with the *Yad Vashem's* International School for Holocaust studies in Jerusalem, various educational projects were initiated for teachers at German and Austrian schools.

The goals of these projects were to make the history education of National Socialism and the Holocaust more relevant for students today and to connect this tragic period of history with the present. As a psychologist and group therapist with experience from the treatment of Holocaust survivors and their children I was invited to facilitate self-reflection sessions within these seminars for more than ten years. In addition, I conducted a series of workshop seminars when traveling through Germany and Austria during the last decade. All together, there must have been more than a thousand participants in these events.

The present chapter is an attempt to summarize some impressions from these group sessions. After an overview of the Second Generation literature in Germany and Austria and a description of the methods used in my experiential investigations, I will discuss secondary war traumatization among descendants of victims, collaborators, perpetrators, bystanders, rescuers, and resistance fighters, or a combination of these.

As it is not immediately obvious why a subject like this is presented in a book on Jewish Holocaust trauma, I would like to make a few comments on my personal interest in this matter. Being a child of Holocaust survivors who grew up in a German-speaking family of emigrants from Vienna, this was a highly personal issue for me. As with many Jews of German/Austrian heritage, I have ambiguous and complicated feelings toward the former homeland (German: *Heimat*) of my family. A deep affection for everything Austrian is mixed with the bitter memories of Nazi persecution. Often, the Viennese *Gemütlichkeit* still reverberated in my blood and phrases like *Guten Morgen, Guten Abend, Auf Wiedersehen, Grüss Gott,* and *Servus* make me immediately feel at home. However, this affection is overshadowed by also hearing the rough sounds of German commands and curses like *Juden raus! ("Out with the Jews!")*, while learning about the systematic persecution of Austrian Jews before and during the Second World War that reduced the Jewish population of Austria from about 300,000 in the 1920s, to less than 15,000 today. Returning to the land of my family's dispossession, I cannot refrain from being highly disturbed by this tragic history as well as by the observation that there presently is an upsurge in "new" anti-Semitism in many parts of Europe. It is therefore with great curiosity that I take a peek "on the other side" to try to understand how our former neighbors live with their memories and daily concerns.

Second Generation Literature in Germany and Austria

Ever since the end of the Second World War, German/Austrian literature has continually been discussing the consequences of the Holocaust and the question of individual and/or collective guilt.

Already in 1946, Karl Jaspers wrote about *The Question of Guilt* (German: *Die Schuldfrage*) and called for individual war criminals to be held responsible, rather than promoting collective guilt which would be regarded as more anonymous. In the early 1960s, the Eichmann trial in Jerusalem and Hannah Arendt's subsequent book (*Eichmann in Jerusalem: A Report on the Banality of Evil*, 1963/1977), reopened questions about individual and collective guilt in Germany and Austria.

The notion of a collective burden of responsibility upon an entire nation is unique to the Holocaust. Collective guilt meant that all Germans and Austrians shared the blame, not only for the war, but for Nazi atrocities as well, and that they should take responsibility for its consequences. But as years have passed, such guilt has begun to fade out, while the responsibility has taken its place. This was clearly expressed by West German chancellor Helmut Kohl, during his visit to Israel on January 24, 1984:

> The young German generation does not regard Germany's history as a burden but as a challenge for the future. They are prepared to shoulder their responsibility. But they refuse to acknowledge a collective guilt for the deeds of their fathers. We should welcome this development.

But the Holocaust continued to disturb authors of all types and descent. The most prominent were perhaps the following four Nobel Prize-winning authors who attempted to come to grips with the Holocaust in their writing: (1) Thomas Mann strongly denounced National Socialism and encouraged resistance by the working class; (2) Heinrich Böll, the leader of the postwar *rubble-literature* (German: *Trümmerliteratur*) in his books kept returning to the painful memories of the war, the Nazis, and the guilt that came with them; (3) Günter Grass (who recently disclosed his service in the *Waffen-SS*) described the ambiguous attitudes in postwar Germany in his famous 1959 novel *The Tin Drum*. But only in his 2002 book *Crabwalk* (German: *Im Krebsgang*), did he also describe the emotional suffering of German civilians during the war; and (4) Elfriede Jelinek, in her critical novel *The Children of the Dead* (1995), focused on the repressed Nazi past and how the new Austrian republic rested upon the precarious foundation of millions of disavowed murder victims. The following paragraph from *Wonderful, Wonderful Times* (1980) is particularly colorful and sums it all up very succinctly:

> Presently there are, however, still numerous innocent perpetrators. Full of war memories, their friendly faces look at the public from windowsills decorated with flowers, they wave or hold high posts. In between geraniums. Everything should finally be forgiven and forgotten so they can make an entirely new beginning (p. 7).

These are all parts of the general postwar German literature. However, among the first specific accounts of children of perpetrators was an article in *Die Zeit* and, in 1965, a critical book, *Children of the Perpetrators* (German: *Kinder der Täter*) by Dörte von Westernhagen, a daughter of an SS-commander who committed suicide before she was born. In an attempt to come to terms with her conflicting roots, she researched the past and accused her father of participating in the crimes of the Third Reich.

A second early description of children of perpetrators was Sichrovsky's (1987) book *Born Guilty: Children of Nazi Families*. Born in postwar Vienna by Jewish survivors, Sichrovsky grew up with children of former Nazis. After becoming a journalist, he asked them what their fathers had done during and after the war. In fourteen tape-recorded case studies he presented portraits of deeply complex people with various kinds of conflicts and psychopathology. The contents of this book have been dramatized and are presently being shown in a theatre in Tel Aviv.

A third early investigator of the children of Nazis was Norbert Lebert, a German journalist who, in 1959, set out to interview infamous Nazi leaders' children. But for some reason, he himself never published his findings. After his death, his son Stephan discovered the interviews and reinterviewed some of those children of perpetrators, including the daughters of Himmler and Göring, and published their accounts in the year 2000.

Subsequently, many other accounts of children of perpetrators, and the issues raised with German and Austrian attempts to work through their Nazi past, were published, including Wolf (1989), Heimannsberg & Schmidth (1989), Halbmayr (1995), Merten (1995), Krondorfer (1995), Rosenthal (1997), Ziegler & Kannonier-Finster (1997), Staffa & Klinger (1998), Staffa & Spielmann (1998), Kranz (1999), Neumann (1999), Munn (2001a), and Berger & Berger (2001).

The pioneering field research of Dan Bar-On from the mid-1980s received wide attention. His book on the *Legacy of Silence* (1989b) contains reports on interviews conducted in Germany with the children and grandchildren of Nazi perpetrators. Later publications (Bar-On, 1989a; 1990; 1995; 1996; 2000) described additional issues regarding this population, and defined specific characteristics such as the *double wall* that prevented the generations from communicating with one another.

Ursula Duba, a non-Jewish German-American writer shared her observations from meetings and discussions with German youth in her book *Tales from a Child of the Enemy* (1997). Her poetic descriptions of the massive silence are both telling and moving and explain some of the ignorance and lack of empathy that the German people feel for the victims of the Holocaust. For example, she pointed out that most German children know from a very early age not to ask as to what grandpa did during the Third Reich.

Müller-Hohagen, a psychotherapist and son of a cooperating family who settled in Dachau, worked for more than twenty years with perpetrator families. In his books *History in Us* (1994) and *Denied, Repressed, Silenced* (2005), he presented actual case studies and suggested enlightening analyses about the dynamics of their massive repression. In a conference proceeding on this theme, Staffa (1998) concluded that "The perpetrator generation tacitly or explicitly transmitted their guilt or hate, their views of the enemies, their biases, or their anxieties upon the children or grandchildren" (p. 72). Jurgovsky (1998) suggested the term *subsequent effects* to describe such transgenerational phenomena.

But it took many years for ordinary Germans and Austrians to realize that their Nazi past indeed continued to have an effect on subsequent generations, and even on the grandchildren of Nazis. This wider awareness was to a large extent created as a result of the publication of the book with the pertinent title *My Grandfather Was Not a Nazi* (German: *Opa war kein Nazi*) based on the study by Welzer, Moller, & Tschuggnall (2002). From interviews with 142 grandchildren of German soldiers, they found that most of the forty families tended to construct a positive picture of their grandparents who were seen either as victims or as heroes, or as unknowing passive bystanders, but not as Nazis, even though they clearly were Nazis. This book showed more than all the previous studies the extent to which personal family involvement in the crimes committed had been massively repressed or silenced, making it very difficult for the subsequent generation to really grasp what had actually happened and to acknowledge their painful past. However, in subsequent discussions of the above study, someone cynically suggested that the above title may have had some truth in it after all: "Grandfather *was* not a Nazi, he *is still* one!"

Didactic and Methodological Remarks

The method used in the group sessions I conducted in Israel, Germany, and Austria was a combination of lecture demonstrations, workshop-seminars, sociodramatic explorations, and open-ended discussions with a high level of participation by the group members. After a brief overview of the long-term psychological effects and treatment of Holocaust trauma, the focus was put on the personal experiences of the German and Austrian participants themselves, asking: "How does all this affect you?" Common history from the war was thus shared in action and memories from the past were brought to the surface. The following elements were frequently utilized as *warm-ups* to facilitate a process of individual and collective working through:

- *Holocaust survivors and war witnesses were invited to give testimony in front of the group, who would ask them personal questions;*

- *Year-of-birth spectogram;*

- *Role play (various roles from the first generation in Germany and Austria) with a reversal of roles within the same person;*

- *Sociodrama: experiential process for the investigation of social phenomena in action from then and now (Kellermann, 2007);*

- *Role play demonstration of communication problems between parents of the first generation and children of the second generation with action alternatives;*

- *Dialogue between children and grandchildren of survivors and of perpetrators;*

- *Screening and discussion of the film 2 or 3 Things I Know About Him (German: 2 oder 3 Dinge, die ich von ihm weiß). This is a provocative documentary film from 2005 in which German director Malte Ludin examines the impact of Nazism in his family;*

- *Discussion of the study My Grandfather Was Not a Nazi (German: Opa war kein Nazi) by Welzer, Moller, & Tschuggnall (2002).*

An exercise frequently used was the *year-of-birth spectogram* which makes some of the more unconscious processes more visible and hopefully also easier to comprehend and to digest emotionally. This is a group demographic investigation tool in which participants place themselves on an imaginary continuum in a room according to their year of birth, thus focusing on the various generations after the war. At the beginning of the line were those from the first generation (who were born before the war and who had experienced it *firsthand*); then came the child survivors and *war children* (who were born during the war); then the *postwar* children (born between 1945–49); then the often numerous subgroup of *baby-boom* children of these first groups (born between 1950–60); and finally came the grandchildren of those who experienced the war (usually in their early twenties or younger). Going around the group, and focusing on each person at a time, the participants were encouraged to share how the war had influenced them.

At a later stage of the group process, during various active role-playing simulations, some of the communication difficulties between parents of the first generation and children of the second generation were demonstrated and improvised. Thus, the concept of *transgenerational transmission of trauma* was introduced and made more visible. These group explorations made it repeatedly obvious that while each and every person somehow has his or her own personal relation to the NS-time, they all together form a microcosm of collective consciousness (or collective repression) that may be representative for the German/Austrian population as a whole.

Facing the history of World War II means that we are also facing ourselves. The following points were used for further working through and discussion:

1. A self-critical look at our own NS-past. How does the Holocaust history affect me personally? What is my own personal connection with the NS-past in Germany and/or Austria?

2. Was there a "conspiracy of silence" in my family? Was there a taboo against talking about what my parents or grandparents did during the war? Did they remain silent and did I refrain from asking them?

3. Who was guilty? Individual and collective guilt. Inherited guilt (German: *Erbsünde*).

4. What meaning does the Holocaust have for the first generation, the war children (*Kriegskinder*), the second generation, and the grandchildren of the war generation?

5. What were the different roles of the war generation? How did these roles interact within the same person?

6. What was transmitted upon the second generation? Shame, guilt, responsibility, and/or perpetratorship?

7. What can we learn from the Holocaust? To fight against racism? To be more tolerant? Not to follow orders blindly? To be more politically aware and active?

8. How could it have happened in the first place and why in Germany and Austria? If students ask: "Were these Nazis human beings?" what can we respond with? (see chapter 8).

Primary and Secondary War Traumatization

Raising issues about the Second World War inevitably evoked strong emotions in participants. In addition to breaking the conspiracy of silence from the past, it also brought to the surface the heavy burden of years of concealment. When the past had been so massively repressed, it was not easy to suddenly acknowledge and digest painful emotions that suddenly were revealed, such as shame, guilt, anger, sadness and anxiety. These appeared in a confusing combination; compassion with the pain of the victims, shame of the bystanders, guilt of the perpetrators, ethical questions about possible personal or collective responsibility and the urgent need for reconciliation and normalization. Depending on what they themselves, or their parents and grandparents had endured during the war, participants expressed such painful emotions, which had a profound impact on their entire lives.

Whatever influence, the groups gave an opportunity for participants to face history in the context of facing themselves. This led them to variously describe themselves or their parents and grandparents as taking the roles of:

1. the victim;
2. the collaborator and/or the perpetrator;
3. the bystander; and
4. the rescuer and/or the resistance fighter.

These roles (or archetypes) were then utilized to look at any war scenario. But it immediately became obvious that none of them were easily delineated and that they should not be used in a simplistic and *either-or* fashion. Hence, more than one role may have been present in one and the same person at the same time. During the extraordinary chaotic times of World War II, a *Wehrmacht* soldier may, for example, have been first a perpetrator and then a victim, as well as a bystander and possibly also a helper in certain situations. I will clarify these war roles further in the following sections.

1. The Victim

While we (Israeli Jews) have come to retain the *victim* designation for those who perished, and the word *survivor* for those who lived through it all, the word victim (German: *Opfer*) will be retained here, as it has become commonly utilized in German and Austrian vocabulary and because it seems to bring additional underlying meanings in German-speaking countries. Hence, *victims of the Nazi-regime* refer to all kinds of people who were more or less detrimentally affected by the war and who may be therefore eligible for some kind of compensation. Such a broad definition of *victimhood* may thus include additional groups of citizens who were either for or against the NS-regime, whether they initially suffered from it or not.

Because people preferred to see themselves as (innocent) victims instead of (guilty) perpetrators after the war—according to Müller-Hohagen (2008), "Perpetrators were the others!" (p. 155)—this created various kinds of *victim-myths* (German: *Opfer-mythos*) both in Austria and in Germany. And the more they focus on their own victimhood, the less they are able to face their own responsibility for the war. Urban (2004) even observed that "Holocaust education in Germany is being slowly but steadily undermined by the new trend of seeing Germans themselves as victims, with many people feeling that they are fed up with the Shoah."

The most famous one was perhaps the Austrian victim-myth (Pollak, 2005), which claimed that Austria had been the first Nazi-victim when occupied by Germany on March 12, 1938 and that it therefore was not responsible for the Holocaust. It is now more widely accepted that, while there were Austrians who opposed Hitler, the German NS-regime was enthusiastically welcomed by the Austrian people, who cooperated willingly with the persecution of its Jews.

A similar myth was created by the communist regime of the former East Germany. Instead of recognizing their own part in the implementation of the NS-policies, East Germany blamed the "anti-Semitic and fascistic West" for having initiated the Holocaust while the East was portrayed as taking part in the resistance movement and were the sole heir of antifascism (Wolffsohn, 1995; Völter & Dasberg, 1998).

But West Germany was not immune to such myths either. Urban (2008) explained how some of these modern myths originated by subtle rationalizations: "Historian Guido Knopp, who is director for the public station ZDF of a large number of TV series on aspects of World War II, the Holocaust, the Third Reich, and its leaders, does much to promote this trend of rationalizing one's own behavior. His documentaries often deny that there was any possibility to act against the Nazis. He and many other historians often distinguish sharply between Nazis and Germans. Thus, those who lost their homes or even families in the Allied bombing or were expelled after 1945 are *Germans*. The Nazis are such as Adolf Eichmann or ghetto administrators. Indeed, history requires distinctions and not every German was a Nazi; some were persecuted or executed for political reasons. The Nazis, however, clearly were Germans (and Austrians, as well as collaborators from all over Europe). Knopp presents in one of his numerous productions, a six-part series on the Holocaust, a former female camp guard from Bergen-Belsen named Helga Bothe who justifies her actions. She says she was not guilty because she only obeyed orders, and otherwise she would have been sent to a camp as well (part 6 of the serial *Holokaust*, ZDF, 21 November 2000). Her statement is shown without comment or contrast—such as a guard who helped inmates, a bystander who chose to help, a story of a Bergen-Belsen inmate, and so on. This fosters an impression of a National Socialism without National Socialists, a Holocaust without or nearly without perpetrators. Such narratives can be viewed as modern German myths."

The classical German victim-myth, however, is best expressed during the yearly memorial march of the allied bombing of the town of Dresden on February 13, 1945, in which the population mourns the victims (Friedrich, 2002). The problem is that neo-Nazis utilize this event to declare that this "mass murder" was the *real* Holocaust of innocent German civilians and refugees who perished as a result of the British and American "genocide." Contrary groups, including anti-fascist, leftist, and Green party groups, vehemently protest against such a revision of history, and arrange contra-demonstrations under the slogan *Geh Denken!* ("Go think," which is a paraphrase also for a memorial). I was impressed by the intense emotional energy both groups of anti-fascist demonstrators, as well as the police, invested in the event during a personal visit to Dresden in 2007.

Undoubtedly, however, there were also many *real* German and Austrian war-victims. But they were mostly silenced because it was not politically correct to openly talk about them. Given that the Germans and Austrians were the war-villains, the public tended to focus on blame rather than sympathy and understanding. More than sixty years after the war, Radebold (2005)—a psychiatry professor treating elderly German war children—hesitantly asked: "Are we allowed *as Germans* to deal with this part of our history? Are we allowed to call ourselves *victims*?" (pp. 25–26).

And he answered in the affirmative: "The surviving younger elderly must become aware of how painful their childhood was and that they still suffer from these effects until today.... We must become aware that: *We have a history, we are history, and we embody history*" (p. 27).

But acknowledging human suffering and victimization in the very same people that committed crimes during the war remains a controversial subject. One may ask if this is another attempt to transform the perpetrators into victims, and thus to minimize their responsibility. This is not my intention. What I want to emphasize is simply that war traumatization is present in this population and that it must be illuminated parallel to an acknowledgment of personal and/or collective guilt.

Perhaps it is easier today for everybody to recognize that the German and Austrian peoples suffered millions of civilian victims during the war and to allow them to grieve for their losses. For example, the German historian Friedrich (2002) noted in his book, *The Fire: Germany in the Bombing War 1940–1945* that over half a million German citizens, including eighty thousand children, were killed in the bombings on German cities. Even though some of his characterizations of the allied bombing falsely equalized the events with the systematic and intentional annihilation of the persecuted Holocaust victims, the truth is that innocent civilians accidentally perished and that their surviving relatives naturally responded with grief. Perhaps it is now easier to share such victimization because the collective guilt and responsibility of Germany and Austria has been more openly admitted. From a psychological point of view, perhaps the time has also finally come to recognize the need of the German people to mourn their losses and to express their suffering?

Because clearly, the civilian population did endure extraordinary hardships and suffered a multitude of traumatic experiences that left their indelible marks. As a result, some of them still continue to hoard food, express fears of renewed occupation, and mourn family and friends who perished in the war.

In a series of publications, Radebold (2000; 2003; 2004; 2005) described such late effects of the war on the elderly German population who suffered a multitude of losses, violence, flight, and expulsion. In his book, *The Dark Shadows of the Past,* Radebold (2005) pointed out that there were two million children and youth among Germany's refugees, and about a third of these had experienced traumatized experiences. Many of them still feel the effects of these late in life, even if they do not like to speak about them: "The fallen left more than 1.7 million widows, almost 2.5 million half-orphans and about 100,000 full-orphans (Dörr, 1998, p. 323, 563) and about a quarter of all German children grew up without a father" (Radebold, 2005, p. 23). Many of these war children (German: *Kriegskinder*) suffered from emotional scars similar to the Jewish Child Survivors described in chapter 3.

Another effort to investigate the suffering of such war-children was initiated by Ermann (2004) and colleagues. One of their studies found that 10.8 percent of former German children of the war still suffered from PTSD symptoms sixty years later (Kuwert et al., 2006).

As I have already pointed out, the first generation of German/Austrian war survivors were suffering alone without anywhere to turn for help.

Concepts such as a *conspiracy of silence*, a failure of society to accept and understand traumatized individuals, while first utilized in connection to Holocaust survivors, made perfect sense also for the description of the first generation of German and Austrian individuals afflicted by war trauma. Similarly, the massive repression of all emotions, including the inability to mourn (Mitscherlich & Mitscherlich, 1967) and anxiety-provoking triggers from the war were relevant also for such war survivors (cf. chapter 2). However, despite such profound personal scars from the war, these had been left almost untouched, or totally repressed (or diagnosed as a "psychosomatic ailment" by the mental health establishment). It was as if some kind of collective consensus had tried to conceal anything that would admit individual vulnerability in connection to war trauma. A reason for this silence might have been the overwhelming feelings of guilt and shame felt by many when they realized the scope of the destruction that their own people had inflicted on others. According to Kahn (2006), however, many younger Germans now feel shame for their parents' deeds and accept a responsibility for rectifying the damage that was done. For example, one woman commented: "I think my guilty conscience has to do with the fact that fundamentally, in my heart of hearts, I can't comprehend that a people can intend to totally negate another people, to wipe them out, along with everything that belongs and is connected to them. I must be missing a link. I don't get it. And I don't understand where this set of ideas comes from" (p. 88).

The workshop seminars sometimes gave a first opportunity to hesitantly share such painful emotions with others and to realize that they were not alone. In fact, such sharing revealed that most participants (or their parents) had experienced some primary or secondary traumatic experiences during World War II. They shared accounts of personal pain and suffering from the war and/or immediately after (during the occupation of the allied forces). This included the terror of the Hitler regime, the fear of bombs, long periods of starvation, painful war injuries, years of imprisonment, contemptuous foreign occupation, the rape of German/Austrian women, the loss of close family members, the debilitating grief of orphans and widows, etc.

Most participants initially talked about their parents' (primary trauma) experiences: "My father was a soldier who lost a leg and two brothers in the war. But he never talked much about it, and he never shared his feelings with us. I saw that he was suffering and I heard him shout during the night as if he was still in the midst of battle. But he took it all into his grave ..." Only later did participants also share their own (secondary trauma) feelings of having grown up in these severely dysfunctional families, and how they carried within themselves their heavy burdens (Bar-On, 1989).

In addition to these disclosures, it became clear that the participants also carried within themselves a kind of collective trauma of the German/ Austrian people as a whole. Even if they had been born many years after the war, they had somehow absorbed the feeling of having been born into a *despised people* and they felt unjustly victimized as a result. German and Austrian youth had indeed inherited a legacy of guilt, shame, and blame. Duba (1997) put the responsibility of such feelings on the German society, which did not help the young generation to properly acknowledge the suffering inflicted by their grandparents. Instead, the youth were burdened with the impossible task of defending the "innocent perpetrators," who continued to exert enormous powers upon them even from their graves.

2. The Perpetrator and Collaborator

The perpetrators and the collaborators were directly responsible for orchestrating the atrocities against civilians during the war.

After the war, however, most criminals did not readily want to admit their involvement in the Holocaust. The gradual process of acknowledging personal responsibility seemed to proceed through various stages of rationalization, from blaming others to the admission of personal guilt. When asked by their children about why they had participated in the war, the parents responded in any of the following ways. (It sounds so much more convincing in the German language):

- *"Hitler war Schuld. Die Nazis waren es."*
- *"Die Totalität des Führerstaates erlaubte keine andere Möglichkeit."*
- *"Ich habe nur Befehle befolgt."*
- *"Wir waren besetzt. Ich wäre erschossen worden, wenn ich mich geweigert hätte."*
- *"Ich habe nur in die Luft geschossen."*
- *"Wir wurden in die Irre geführt. Sie haben uns mit ihrer Propaganda einer Gehirnwäsche unterzogen."*
- *"Wir glaubten, dass uns Hitler ein besseres Leben ermöglichen würde. Jeder glaubte an ihn. Er war unsere Hoffnung!"*

Translated: "Hitler was to blame. The Nazis did it. I was only following orders. We were occupied. I would have been shot if I refused to enlist. I shot only in the air. I didn't kill anyone. I was so young. We were misled. They had brainwashed us with their propaganda. We believed that Hitler would make life easier for us. Everyone believed in him. He was our hope!" Only in exceptional cases was there a realization of disillusionment, an admission of guilt, and the ensuing remorse and a search for reconciliation.

Thus, participants who were more informed about the historical facts were understandably skeptical when learning that their fathers had served "only in the *Wehrmacht*," implying that, unlike the SS, they were innocent of crimes against the Jews, that they had done only their duty and served their country and that they had treated civilians with respect.

In fact, many of the loyal followers of Hitler and devoted members of the NS-party, the *Bund Deutscher Mädel* (BDM)—The League of German Girls, or *Hitler Jugend* (HJ)—The Hitler Youth, never felt any remorse. After the war, they found it very difficult to adjust to the new social reality. Upon returning to their homes and towns, they had not only lost the war, but were also reprimanded by society and (sometimes) by their families for having enlisted in the first place. Similar to returning Vietnam War veterans, they felt that society had let them down twice; first, when they were recruited to a mission without purpose, and secondly, when they returned home broken and defeated. Before they had been told (or forced) to love and serve Hitler. Now they were treated as war criminals.

Therefore, they were invariably unable to take individual responsibility for the war crimes even though they admitted that "bad things had happened." In order to cope with this cognitive dissonance, they found it easier to take upon themselves the role of the victim of circumstances, saying: "I only did what I was told. I had nothing to do with the decisions. In fact, I did not shoot anybody. I shot only in the air." Secretly, however, some admitted that the first years of Hitler-rule "were the happiest in my life!"

Immediately after the war, former soldiers of the Third Reich were first imprisoned for a short time or for many years and then "de-Nazified," which was a process of resocialization and admission that they had given up their NS-ideology and their loyalty to the *Führer*. During this first period after the war, there was an official effort to erase the outer signs and symbols of the former regime. A participant remembered: "After the war, everything suddenly changed. Pictures of Hitler were taken down from the walls. We were no longer supposed to greet one another with *Heil Hitler!* Defeated soldiers came home from years of imprisonment with physical and emotional injuries. The Russian and other occupying armies did terrible things to us."

Fathers who returned from the war had lost face in their families and there was an enormous void between them and their children. They became *absent men* even if they were physically present. Many were struggling with pent-up aggression and became addicted to alcohol in order to repress their feelings. As a result, many of the children who were born immediately after the war had the feeling of growing up without fathers. For reasons of their own, mothers remained depressive, anxious, and largely detached, unable to show affection to their children.

Perhaps it was possible within the closed circles of the various veterans clubs (*Kameradschaftsbund*) to talk about the war, but not with remorse or regret. The study by Welzer, Moller, and Tschuggnall (2002) confirms that it was easier to talk about the victorious moments and happy occasions, rather than sharing the painful experiences. The sweet taste of heroism was probably a more popular subject than the fact that they had lost the war, their beloved *Führer* (and all the hopes that he had evoked), their comrades-in-arms, and many years of their youth and young adulthood (for nothing). In closed circles, a call for revenge possibly took the place of mourning and old anti-Semitic sentiments were again expressed.

But this first period of postwar adjustment was soon transformed into the next period of rebuilding and renewal. Citizens tried to put the past behind them and look to the future, to forget and to close this chapter of history forever. Rapidly, they learned to present themselves, not as aggressors, but as victims of the NS-regime and/or of the Allied Forces. Memories from the war were repressed and family secrets were created (Padover, 2001; Rommelspacher, 1995).

This massive repression had a detrimental effect on family communication. When children grew up and asked their parents about the war, they received no answers. As a result, the children developed all kinds of fantasies about the "real" identities of their parents: "Where did he serve? Who did he kill? Was he a war criminal and a Nazi? Why does he have to conceal everything? What does he have to hide?" Intergenerational conflicts arose between children and their fathers.

In the extraordinary film document that we have already mentioned above, Malte Ludin tells the *typical German* story of his father who was a war criminal and of his mother, sisters, and other relatives who didn't want to talk about the past. Malte grew up without knowing much about his father because most facts had been carefully hidden from him; old photos and memorabilia were put in a closed wooden box in the cellar and his father was described only as a hero and as a martyr. After the death of

Malte's mother, the box was opened and its contents investigated, and the truth was finally revealed. Malte's father had indeed been a real Nazi war criminal. When asking his older sisters about this, they refused to describe him as such, even though Hanns Ludin, a devoted NS-supporter and Hitler's envoy to Slovakia, had clearly been one, and he had been sentenced to death for his crime. The sisters tried everything to prevent the truth from being revealed: "No, he didn't do anything. He didn't know what happened to the Jews in Slovakia. He was a lovable person. Why do you destroy his memory?" Like most Germans, facing the fact that the father had been a "bad person" created a cognitive dissonance that apparently would have been too much for them to digest.

During one of our public debates after the screening of his film, I asked Malte Ludin if it would have helped if his father had acknowledged his guilt. I suspected that if the *content* of the transgenerational transmission was out in the open, perhaps the children would have suffered less. And he immediately affirmed that this would indeed have been very helpful.

Similar to Malte Ludin, the (19)68 generation (Götz, 2008) loudly deplored the Nazi past of their fathers and proclaimed symbolic Patricide. Many processed their paternal relations in a series of books (e.g., Henisch, 1975; Frank, 1987; von Schirach, 2005; Weiss, 2005; Botz, 2005; Pollack, 2004/2006) in which they openly confronted their parents with their complicity in the Nazi regime. As a result of such confrontations, parents and children often clashed in violent and painful conflicts around such or similar subjects during the 1970s and 1980s. In some families, it resulted in a total split that could not be bridged for decades. It was much more than a generation gap. It was a vast desert of conflict and misunderstanding. One participant who had broken up with his father explained: "How can I continue to have anything to do with my father, who was a former Nazi (and who might still be one)?"

Instead, children left home early and distanced themselves from their (unreformed) parents. Many developed extreme left-wing opinions, in which their disgust for any totalitarian system could be expressed. The parents, in turn, responded with an equally massive rejection of their children, who they felt were accusing them unfairly. And as the intra-family conflicts intensified, any honest discussion of what had actually happened during the war was even further pushed out of the common frame of reference.

This situation was further intensified during various public events in Germany and Austria, which also reignited the family conflicts and actualized the unfinished business of the past. The Eichmann trial in Israel was perhaps the most obvious, as well as the screening of the TV series

The Holocaust in 1979 (Märthesheimer & Frenzel, 1979). In addition, the controversial 1995 exhibition on the war crimes of the *Wehrmacht* (Heer & Naumann, 1995) made it common knowledge that ordinary *Wehrmacht* soldiers, not just Nazi hard-core *Waffen-SS*, had participated in the atrocities against civilians during the war. Similarly, the publication in 1996 of Goldhagen's book *Hitler's Willing Executioners* also became a powerful trigger for opening the old wounds of German conscience. Lately, the heated discussions around the Holocaust memorials erected on the *Judenplatz* in Wien (2000), and on a block south of the *Brandenburg Gate* in Berlin (2005), also created major political and aesthetic controversies and public debate.

As they recounted these public events, participants shared the moral dilemma of being descendants of fathers who had committed horrendous acts of crime against humanity during the war, but who still were their (biological) fathers. The processing of this dilemma took different forms in different people, but inevitably created an inner conflict that demanded some kind of resolution. The conflicts were frequently resolved, according to Simenauer (1978), by "a depreciation of the father figure, with the resulting negative identification" (p. 412).

While learning the facts about the Holocaust, such children of perpetrators tried to work through (sort out, or in German: *Auseinandersetzung*) some of the issues that their parents had been unable to even acknowledge. This German concept of *sorting out* is in fact a very suitable one in this context, because it indicates that there is a healthy *differentiation* process (cf. separation-individuation) between parents and children, which is sometimes overlooked on account of the more commonly described process of *identification*.

In the process of identification, it became apparent that the second generation of German perpetrators had inherited not only guilt and shame, but also a kind of predisposition to become perpetrators themselves. "If my father could do it," they ask, "Could I?" Müller-Hohagen (2008) suggested that such an absorbed trait could become a kind of *perpetratorship* (German: *Täterschaftigkeit*); a potential scary disposition of becoming a murderer. Through identification with the aggressor-father (who was a former Nazi), the child would unconsciously internalize a (potentially) abusive and violent parent-representation in themselves, which they have to struggle with all through life. For example, during a psychoanalytic session, the son of a sadistic SS officer exclaimed: "Ich kann nicht zurück, aber ich kann auch nicht vorwärts. Ich bin ein Deutscher, ein Glied in einer Kette, wenn auch die Kette fatal war. Aber wie kann ich mich von meinen Wurzeln abschneiden? Also bin ich dazu verurteilt, das zu bleiben was ich bin. Ich bin ein Sohn, ich habe keine anderen Väter, auch wenn sie mir Gift vererbt haben."

> I cannot go back, nor can I go forward. I am a German, a link in a chain, even if the chain was a fatal one. But how can I cut myself loose from my roots? So I am condemned to remain what I am. I am a son; I have no other fathers, even though they bequeathed me poison (Jokl, 1998, p. 99, as reported in Kahn, 2006, p. 89).

Because such internalized self-representations are largely unacceptable in the present day society, a German *underworld* has been created in which anti-Semitism, racism, and xenophobia continue to flourish.

As a result of this identification with the aggressor, the assumed content of transmission of children of the war generation of Germans and Austrians (2GGA) will be decidedly different from the kinds of trauma transmission found in children of Holocaust survivors (2GHS). If the 2GHS absorbed vicarious traumatization, the 2GGA got secondary perpetratorship. On a collective level, while the Israeli Jews absorbed the consequences of catastrophic anxiety, the German and Austrian people got collective guilt. Both have a vague sense that there is something wrong with them: the 2GHS because they continually feel persecuted and the 2GGA because they feel seen as potential villains. The lesson of persecution for the 2GHS was to create their own Jewish homeland, while the lesson for the 2GGA was to merge within a global European Union, which somewhat erased their national heritage.

3. The Bystander

According to the stories told by group members, however, most Germans and Austrians seem to have been "neutral" or "passive" bystanders, who preferred to "mind their own business" while the Holocaust occurred. The German word for bystander is *Zuschauer*—someone who *watches*, but is not actively involved. For example, people would say: "We saw that they took the Jews away, but we didn't know what would happen to them ..." The more correct German word for this behavior, however, would be *Wegschauer*—someone who *looks away*, in order not to see what was happening and in order not to have to take personal responsibility for it (Latane & Darley, 1970; Gellately, 2002).

There is an important lesson to be learned from bystander behavior. Ervin Staub (1989) from Hungary was saved during the war by a courageous Christian woman who was not a bystander, but an active rescuer. This personal experience evoked his curiosity in understanding why some people became active rescuers, while others remained passive bystanders. Many years later, as a psychologist, he conducted some psychological experiments, which further investigated this phenomenon. In one such study, for example, volunteers heard a loud crash from the next room, followed by sobbing and groans. When the confederate said, "That probably has nothing to do with us," only about 25 percent of the volunteers investigated the source. But when the confederate said, "Let us see what is happening," every volunteer went to see what was wrong. The study showed the power of bystanders to prevent crime, brutality, and acts of violence. By simply being witnesses (and not *looking away*), bystanders can empower the victims and possibly prevent further injustice.

Most Germans still feel that bystanders were powerless and largely free from any responsibility. For example, in a Spiegel-survey (1992) of three thousand (East and West) German citizens, most respondents (45 percent) felt that "only those Germans who were involved in the persecution" were guilty, as were "only the Germans who knew about it" (32 percent).

But it is still unclear as to how much ordinary Germans and Austrians really knew about the Holocaust: about the deportations, about the extermination camps, and the systematic annihilation of the Jews. In their retrospective study of three thousand German respondents in the 1990s, Johnson & Reuband (2005) found that a little more than a third of those asked at the end of the war had *known, heard,* or *suspected* that the Jews were annihilated en masse (p. 369). In his suspicious manner, Welzer commented that it remains unclear what was behind the "open secret" of the *other 62 percent* of the respondents who said that they had known nothing about it at all. "Unfortunately, all historic, social-psychological evidence indicate that this is not true.... [They did know.]... It is even more tragic that so many of them not only knew about the persecution of the Jews, but that they were in favor of it" (Welzer, 2009, p. 74).

Historians, such as Bankier (1992), Kulka & Jäckel (2004) and Longerich (2006), summarized various studies on what the Germans in general felt about the persecution of the Jews. While most public opinion reports confirmed that the German society was saturated with anti-Semitic views, they also concluded that on the whole, it was impossible to definitely answer the question whether the attitude toward the persecution of the Jews among the non-Jewish Germans was marked more by indifference or by agreement.

Whether they knew or not, many bystanders expressed feeling *shame* for what the Nazis had done during the war. In fact, Brendler (1997) found that 65 percent of German youth still felt ashamed when they heard of the mass murder perpetrated by their ancestors during the war. Many also felt guilty, paralyzed, and afraid of punishment when thinking about the Holocaust. Brendler (1995) concluded that "the enormous guilt of the ancestors was combined, in these young people's concept of themselves, with their own identity as Germans" (p. 260). According to Marks (2009), the Germans felt ashamed after 1945 because: (1) they had lost the war; (2) they had endured many traumatic war experiences; and (3) they had a bad conscience because of the Holocaust. Various defenses against such shame continue to poison interpersonal relations within and between such families and they are such a normal part of the German culture that people seem not to notice anymore.

Emphasizing such more general issues of bystander mentality, shame, and social responsibility makes history teaching of the Holocaust even more relevant for students today. For example, during a sociodrama on the effects of the Holocaust in Austria, a Kurdish immigrant shared with the group an incident in which he had been called a "filthy Turk." Though people around had clearly heard the comment, nobody had reacted. It was immediately obvious how the earlier anti-Semitism had been presently transformed into the hate of immigrants (xenophobia). Thus, Holocaust history can be looked at and learned from, not as a distant thing from the past, but as a relevant universal lesson for the present. More specifically, students can examine, not only the responses of victims, victimizers and bystanders during World War II, but also discuss moral and ethical issues, such as acceptable and unacceptable behavior, prejudice, conflict, power, leadership, and obedience that are relevant in their lives today.

4. The Rescuer and the Resistance Fighter

Apparently, not everybody did as they were told during the war. There were also those who resisted Hitler. As an illustration, a participant proudly told the following story about his socialist father: as a small boy, he had come home from school one day wearing a Hitler Jugend uniform, and proudly showed his parents how he had learned to pronounce the Hitler greeting correctly. Instead of praise, however, he received a slap on his face for his behavior and was severely reprimanded. His socialist parents explained that Hitler's ideology was dangerous and repulsive to them and that they were strongly opposed to it. The son adopted this worldview of his parents and he soon found himself in a prison with other opponents of the NS-regime who were treated as criminals, ridiculed, ousted from the community, or murdered to set an example.

Some of these opponents to the NS-regime continue to feel ousted from society until this day. For example, a non-Jewish Austrian former political prisoner who had spent many years in Dachau because of his opposition against Hitler, and who joined me in sharing his experiences in an Austrian school, told me that he still felt intense animosity around him in the small town where he lived. People seemed to be unable to forgive him for his betrayal of the "Fatherland." When walking past a tree, he stopped to describe how the leaves change colors during the various seasons of the year. He said: "First they are green, and then they become red (socialist or even communist), and then finally, they become brown (NS)." For him, nothing much had changed in Austria since the war.

There are plenty of historical accounts of German opposition to Hitler (e.g., Balfour, 1988; Thomsett, 1997). In fact, more than half a million non-Jewish German civilians were imprisoned for such resistance, which was classified as a *political crime*. Such resistance was found within the religious, political, civilian, and even military communities. Several church and political leaders, as well as ordinary citizens protested against the National Socialistic regime before and during the war, and were severely punished for this. For example, at the Memorial of German Resistance in Berlin, a documentary film was shown about a priest with the name Lichtenberg who openly resisted Nazi persecution policy, was imprisoned, and died in 1943 on his way to Dachau.

Other active rescuers risked their lives to save Jews by providing them with shelter, food, and clothes or by helping to bring them to safety over the borders (Oliner & Oliner, 1988). Many of these conscientious *Righteous Gentiles among the Nations* are honored in *Yad Vashem* for their brave behavior during these dangerous times. Such non-Jews who risked their lives during the Holocaust in order to save Jews from extermination by the Nazis are awarded a medal bearing their name, a certificate of honor, and the privilege of having a tree planted or their name added to those on the Wall of Honor at *Yad Vashem*. In addition, the law also authorized *Yad Vashem* to provide them with honorary Israeli citizenship in recognition of their brave acts. Recipients who choose to live in the state of Israel are entitled to a pension, free health care, as well as assistance with housing and nursing care. At the beginning of January 2008, over twenty-two thousand individuals from forty-five countries have been recognized as such, most of whom are of Polish, Dutch, French, or Ukrainian origin.

When Pope John Paul II visited Israel's national Holocaust memorial *Yad Vashem* on March 23, 2000, it did not only initiate the old controversy of the role of the Vatican in the Holocaust. More importantly, it focused on the incredible stories of courage that had saved many Jewish lives. Most remarkable was the story of Edithera, who, aged eleven, had fled through the sewers of Krakow but was later interned in a Polish labor camp. On the day of liberation by the Soviets, she was near death when a young priest named Karol Wojtyla fed her and carried her three kilometers on his back to join other survivors. Now she stood with tears streaming down her cheeks before that same man, now Pope John Paul II.

Conclusion

At the end of a seminar, a participant spontaneously commented: "I am surprised that you still are occupied with all this Holocaust stuff. I thought it was already finished/completed (German: *erledigt*) a long time ago!" He was visibly shaken by the fact that people still were upset about the Holocaust and that it was such a loaded subject even after so many years. His comment bothered me and after some thought I realized that his use of the German word *erledigt* had offended me. The meaning of this word could be interpreted both as the final solution of the Jewish problem and as something being finally settled and finished with forever, indicating that "we have provided compensation and now have nothing more to do with this issue." I suspect that his words expressed a common desire in Germany and Austria that their NS past would be finally settled and forgotten once-and-for-all, that they should stop being reminded of it all the time and that there finally would be an end-line (German: *Schlußstrich*) over the Holocaust past.

Evidently, the present project did exactly the opposite.

It recommended a very personal kind of Holocaust education, both as a way to work through and confront a past that was massively avoided for years, and as a springboard for learning for the future. Such a process would help Germans and Austrians to become aware of the various traumatic events that formed them, both those that they inherited from their parents and grandparents and the collective responsibility of their country that they may identify with.

It is their moral obligation not to forget so that it will not be repeated. Otherwise, they will be guilty of the *second guilt*, described by Giordano (1987), that of trying to cover up that it ever happened.

However, in addition to learning about what happened to the *others*, the present project also tried to provide a setting in which it would be possible to talk about themselves in connection to the Second World War. From my experiences in these groups, it seems that there is a real need among Germans and Austrians to work through, both on an individual and on a collective level, their feelings about the war. But to the best of my knowledge, there is no institution that deals specifically with this issue in Europe today.

Because the issues raised are complex and multifaceted without any clear-cut answers, this would include the sharing of ambivalent feelings and thoughts that evolve during a long process of personal and collective working through taking place over many years. The ultimate goal would be to help remember and mourn the victims on both sides, and to motivate German and Austrian communities to start to come to grips with their empty or burned-down synagogues and destroyed cemeteries. In addition, it would encourage teachers to include the history of the expulsion, persecution, and annihilation of the Jews in their school curriculum and to initiate youth visits to former working and extermination camps in Europe so that they can see for themselves what happened. Holocaust survivors and other witnesses from the war would be invited to give personal accounts of their experiences and relevant questions about how all this could have happened could then be discussed.

Then, we could start to listen also to the former soldiers of the Third Reich and try to understand why they behaved as they did, and learn important lessons about social behavior and group pressure, about the danger of propaganda and totalitarian regimes and about large groups who blindly follow a strong leader. As a result, the value of free speech and democracy would be appreciated and, possibly, we would be able to empower one another to have the courage to make a difference if we *do not* look away when we see injustice done.

Most importantly, however, such a process would make it easier for children and grandchildren of the German and Austrian victims, perpetrators, bystanders, and helpers to meet with one another and to share their common burdensome legacy. In addition, children and grandchildren of perpetrators and of Holocaust survivors would be able to discuss their common tragic history, as reported in various such encounters around the world (e.g., Bar-On, 1993; Krondorfer, 1995; Krondorfer et al. 1998).

One by One dialogue groups, for example, are open for Holocaust survivors and their descendants, as well as for perpetrators, bystanders, resisters, and their descendants, and are led by professionally trained facilitators from both sides of the war experience. Another program is called *To Reflect and Trust* and it has conducted annual encounters amongst descendants of Holocaust survivors and descendants of convicted Nazi war criminals ever since 1992. Similarly, a specific *Austrian Encounter* was convened by Samson Munn (2001b) and, finally, Yaacov Naor (1999) from Israel, together with colleagues from Germany, utilized psychodrama and expressive therapy methods in such groups.

Because both the German/Austrian and the Jewish participants are more or less vicariously traumatized, the Holocaust falls like a heavy shadow on these encounters. Although seldom verbalized, each group approaches the other with a certain amount of apprehension, to detect some potential trigger that might remind them of their Holocaust trauma. A hidden scenario is played out in which the child of a survivor initially wants to know the war history of the German or Austrian participants: "What did your parents do during the war? Were they actively involved in the killing of Jews? Were they Nazis?" On the other side, German or Austrian children of war participants try to find out if the Jew still holds a grudge toward them, and if there is a place for reconciliation: They frequently ask: "Can you forgive our people for what we did to your people?"

Simply put, both tend to project their own internalized representations of the victim and the perpetrator upon the other. Germans and Austrians tend to look upon children of survivors as potential victims and children of Holocaust survivors tend to look upon the Germans and Austrians as potential perpetrators. During this process, both sides try to conceal their different painful emotions that arise from these projections: the Germans and Austrians cover up their sense of guilt and shame while the children of survivors try to cover up their fear and anger. Only after some mutual *testing of the limits* will the relation become more relaxed and open for further exploration and deeper working through.

The situation described in the beginning of this chapter, in which a German soldier is standing in front of Hitler, seems to remain the prototype scene of Holocaust trauma in Germany and Austria, as well as among Jews in Israel and elsewhere.

Will the soldier embrace or kill the dictator?

Will he raise his hand in a *Heil Hitler!* salute, or will he protest?

Will he follow the command or will he follow his inner human voice?

We do not know.

But we will certainly be watching.

CHAPTER 8

Unconditional Hate

I took part in the murder of many people. I often asked myself after the war whether I had become a criminal because, being a dedicated National Socialist, I had murdered men, and I found no answer. I believed in the Führer; I wanted to serve my people.

—Hans Stark (1978, p. 128)

The present chapter (some of which has been previously published in Kellermann, 2005; and Halasz & Kellermann, 2005) is an immediate continuation of the previous ones, although this might not be immediately obvious at first glance. Having described the individual and collective effects of Holocaust trauma, we have become witnesses to the ultimate evil. As a result, we are left with a burning question that demands some kind of answer: "How was it all humanly possible?"

How were people able to exterminate millions of human beings like vermin, not in a sudden act of violent outburst, or in self-defense, but in a planned, orderly, and premeditated fashion? The persecution and mass murders were not carried out at random, or accidentally inflicted upon bystander war casualties. The "final" solution of the Jewish question (German: "*Die Endlösung der Judenfrage*") was a process of intentional, systematic, and state-sponsored industrial killing that required highly trained and motivated personnel for its implementation. In addition, and besides its principal task of annihilation, it relentlessly applied what Primo Levi (1988) called "useless violence": the brutal cruelty that the murderers used to torture innocent men, women, and children before actually killing them.

These perpetrators were not only recruited in Germany and Austria, but also in all the occupied Axis countries. In fact, there was no lack of volunteers who collaborated with the Nazis in the persecution of Europe's Jews; citizens of Lithuania, Latvia, Estonia, Belarus, and Ukraine spontaneously formed groups that committed some of the worst atrocities of the Holocaust. Many of these pro-Nazi collaborators even voluntarily enlisted in the Waffen-SS, while others simply helped enforce the anti-Jewish legislation by rounding up and deporting Jews to the extermination camps or elsewhere. Members of fascist paramilitary organizations such as the *Hlinka Guard* (Slovak: *Hlinkova garda*), the Iron Guard (Romanian: *Garda de fier*), the *Ustaša* Croatian Revolutionary Movement (Croatian: *Ustaša—Hrvatski Revolucionarni Pokret*), and the Arrow Cross Party (Hungarian: *Nyilaskeresztes Párt—Hungarista Mozgalom*) actively terrorized, robbed, and murdered local Jews, either under German guidance or on their own initiative. How did the NS-regime succeed in recruiting such personnel and persuade them to freely join the SS, the Gestapo, and/or the special task forces (German: *Einsatzgruppen*), all of which had as their principal task the slaughter of innocent civilians?

I have not found any satisfactory answer to this question, even though there are many attempts in the literature to explain how ordinary people became perpetrators during the Holocaust (e.g., Kelley, 1947; Adorno et al., 1950; Allport, 1954; Huxley, 1958; Hillberg, 1961; Dicks, 1972; Langer, 1972; Bandura, 1973; Fromm, 1973; Milgram, 1974; Arendt, 1963/1977; Waite, 1977; Sabini & Silver, 1980; Lifton, 1986; Bullock, 1990; Charny, 1991; Browning, 1992; Gellately, 1993; Rosenberg, 1998; Staub, 1999; Bauer, 2001; Welzer, 2005). These authors have described the cruel behavior of Nazi perpetrators from a variety of theories and list any or all of the following possible reasons for why perfectly normal men turned into mass murderers:

1. They were "brainwashed" and indoctrinated (and almost hypnotized) by the Third Reich's many years of powerful NS propaganda.

2. They had blind faith in their authoritarian and charismatic leadership and a sense of duty and obedience to their *Führer*.

3. They would profit personally from the extermination of the Jews, and they desired their property after years of poverty.

4. There was a strict division in the bureaucratic administrative process between those who gave the orders

and those who followed them. That relieved both parties from personal responsibility for the criminal acts committed. Such compartmentalized thinking further helped them focus only on small tasks, without taking the larger picture into consideration.

5. Some of the perpetrators actually enjoyed their work, deriving sadistic satisfaction from feeling total power over the destiny of their captives.

6. Dedicated Nazis and members of the SS were convinced that the Jews were the root of all evil and felt that they were only doing what was best for German society and for the world.

7. Jews could be easily eradicated because they had been gradually demonized for many years. To finally exterminate them was only the natural consequence and culmination of a generally accepted and well established public opinion.

8. Jews could be easily singled out as the scapegoats of everything detrimental in German society, and they were easy targets for mass extermination.

9. German and Austrian culture was a fertile ground for Nazi ideology, which emphasized discipline, a strict upbringing of children, and severe punishments for misbehavior. People feared disobeying authority.

At first glance, these explanations may make a lot of sense. But even after understanding that people might have been in such a state of indoctrination, we are still left with a sense of bewilderment as to what other basic motives these people might have had. Before suggesting what these motives could have been, however, I would like to make the following preliminary comments.

When trying to understand perpetrator behavior, we must decide if it is morally correct to paint a diverse and colorful picture of the Nazis or if they should be viewed in the uniform colors of black and white. If we choose the former way of presenting them, they become "ordinary people" of flesh and blood who were misled and who can possibly be forgiven. If we choose the latter way of presenting them, they will be depicted as dangerous monsters and as criminals who must be punished.

In his book *Ordinary Men: Reserve Police Battalion 101 and the Final*

Solution in Poland, Christopher Robert Browning (1992) adopted the first point of view and concluded that the men of Unit 101 were not demons or Nazi fanatics, but ordinary, middle-aged men of working-class background who killed out of a basic obedience to authority and peer pressure, not bloodlust or primal hatred. These men were ordered to round up Jews— and, if there was not enough room for them on the trains, to shoot them. The commander of the unit gave his men the choice of opting out of this duty if they found it too unpleasant, but the majority chose not to exercise that option. This point of view underscores the similarities between the Jewish Holocaust and other acts of genocide, bringing us to the conclusion Max Picard (1946) reached: that "there might be a Hitler in each of us."

Ordinary Men achieved much acclaim, but Daniel Goldhagen denounced it for omitting the role German culture played in causing the Holocaust. Goldhagen's own controversial 1996 book, *Hitler's Willing Executioners,* was largely written to rebut Browning's book. The differences between them reflect the two different approaches to explaining the Nazi behavior mentioned above. Browning emphasized that the murder of the Jews was gradually developed and became functional to the general intentions of the war, while Goldhagen insisted that it was a premeditated and intentional act of Hitler's Nazi regime.

Browning (2006) explained why it is important to examine the perpetrators' history:

> I think what we must avoid is to look at the Holocaust as some kind of natural disaster. The Holocaust was not a tsunami. It was not an earthquake. The Holocaust was a manmade event. People made decisions and people acted. And if we treat it as some kind of supernatural event, we are simply removing the Holocaust from history and turning it into a kind of mystified or mystical event. I think we have to preserve the human dimensions of it, and to do that, we have to look closely at the perpetrators, both in terms of those who shaped policy and made decisions and in terms of those who implemented those decisions, who carried out the murder day after day, face to face, with their victims. And to treat them as human beings. Never losing sight that the whole purpose of this is to capture the horror of what all of this means. Because, of course, once you start treating the perpetrators as human beings, then you are faced with that uncomfortable [question of]: Are they fundamentally different than I am? And, in that situation, what would I have done?

The official position of *Yad Vashem* largely supports this approach. The curriculum on Nazi behavior within the International School of Holocaust Studies (Imber et al., 2006) emphasizes that students must understand that the mass murderers were ordinary human beings who made their own choices and that these choices created the conditions for murdering six million Jews and millions of other victims. According to them, the history of the Holocaust should therefore be viewed from the point of view of human behavior and psychology. They state: "How people reach the point of shooting and gassing thousands of innocent human beings, that is the question that the Holocaust forces us to consider." But they also add that an effort to understand the Nazi perpetrator as a human being does not mean that we accept these actions or that we justify them in any way. To understand the perpetrators' personal motives only means that we want to learn from history.

The Holocaust obviously did not occur "on another planet." The perpetrators were human beings of flesh and blood, and their behavior can be understood within the spectrum of (ab)normal human behavior. Some individuals, however, did not subscribe to a complete and confident Nazi ideology but changed their positions several times during the war, having first been opposed to the Hitler regime, then cooperating with it for a time, only to switch again at the end of the war. These people often pointed out that anyone who did not live through these times cannot really understand the kind of societal pressures that faced the population, and that one should not be too quick to judge them: "How would you have behaved in a similar situation?" they ask. "Would you really have been willing to sacrifice yourself and your family for this cause?" This is especially true as experiments have shown that very few people have the personal integrity and moral stamina to withstand strong authority and peer pressure from a majority of the population.

But we still remain unable to comprehend fully how it all developed into such an enormous climax of premeditated butchery. The roots of evil seem to be as incomprehensible as the Holocaust itself.

Responding to the question of how it was humanly possible with the answer that the Nazis were merely ordinary men, like you and me, is of course insufficient. In my opinion, there have to be additional elements to any convincing explanation. I would like to suggest that the kind of cruel Nazi behavior that was perpetrated must have also been driven by a strong sense of *unconditional hate*. If such an emotion was present, benign bias could be converted first into "malignant prejudice" (Parens et al. 2007) and then into sporadic harassments and finally into systematic mass murder. In the following sections, I will try to explain this concept in more detail, and also relate it to the new anti-Semitism of today—which is apparently still permeated by a sense of unconditional hate.

Can it Happen Again Today?

I was traveling in the Berlin *U-ban* (subway) in the middle of the night. A teenage couple entered the train and sat opposite me. The girl was in tears, telling her boyfriend about what she had just seen.

"It was terrible," she exclaimed, "a right-wing extremist was fighting with a Turkish man, and when the Turkish man turned his back, he was stabbed with a knife." She sobbed heavily. "How can a person do such a thing? What kinds of parents gave birth to such a monster? What *kinds of people* could do such a thing?" Her boyfriend didn't say much. He just held her and wiped hear tears. After a few minutes, she calmed down and they left the train.

I was left with her question ringing in my ears: "What *kinds of people* could do such a thing?" Are these extremists the same Germans who committed the crimes of the Holocaust? What had happened *then-and-there* was obviously happening again *here-and-now*. Nazi ideology evolved into a hatred of foreigners in general. Indeed, according to a recent opinion poll, 50 percent of Germans do not want more foreigners in Germany (or in Europe). Those who do accept them do so because they believe the immigrants will be of use to Germany, not because "the foreigners" might need to come to Germany for work, asylum or to start a new life.

A little later, in a *Bierstube* (pub), I observed some hooligan sports fans all dressed in red, singing their football club anthem while loudly denigrating the opponent's club. Their need to feel "*we against them*" was so palpable that I was again thrown back to the past, when *they* were against *us*. It triggered images in my mind of the riots of November 9–10, 1938, also known as the *Night of Broken Glass* (German: *Kristallnacht*). Scores of Nazis, armed with sledgehammers and axes, destroyed Jewish property and attempted to murder and deport Jews.

The Jews Are Guilty!

During a visit to Vienna a few years later, I walked through the *Graben* in the middle of the town. As I strolled through the open square in front of the St. Stefan Cathedral, I saw some Palestinian activists demonstrating for their self-determination, handing out pamphlets describing their mission and presenting large signs with the well-known slogans of "*Free Palestine!*"

What struck me was not the demonstration in itself, but a large picture that was displayed for everyone to see. The picture depicted the corpse of a Palestinian infant with a bullet hole in its chest.

The whole scene made me feel sick. Here I was in the middle of Vienna, some fifty-five years after the Second World War, realizing that again, Jews were being accused of killing children. The underlying message of the picture was loud and clear: "Israelis are killing children. The Israelis = the Jews; they are doing it again." The passers-by had been used to hearing similar opinions for centuries, within churches all over Europe: that the Jews kill children. After all, Jews had killed the child of God, Jesus Christ. Now, they were also killing Palestinian children. It made perfect sense.

In my imagination, I could see dozens of Nazi flags all around, a large portrait of Hitler, and a hundred German soldiers in precise, unbroken ranks, holding out their arms in the familiar salute: "*Sieg Heil!*" The *Führer* would have been very pleased with the whole spectacle. His mission was not forgotten.

I was trembling, trying to control my outrage and despair. It hit me like a punch in the stomach that hatred of the Jews was still abundant in Europe, as if people had learned nothing from Auschwitz. The Austrian population was again passively allowing all this to happen before their eyes, and in front of the church, doing nothing to stop it.

I suspect that my emotional response was intensified by the fact that, more than sixty years earlier, my father and his family had barely escaped Vienna. While he was among the lucky few to survive, the Nazis had murdered the majority of European Jews. Jewish children were torn to pieces by dogs or left to starve in ghettos and in hiding places, or were thrown alive into Birkenau's burning pits. More than 1.2 million Jewish children were murdered in Europe during World War II. And now, half a century after the war, in the middle of Vienna, everything was turned upside down. They were accusing *us* of killing children! The victims were made into criminals, and the criminals into victims. The eternal justification of anti-Semites for killing Jews reverberated in my head: "*Die Juden sind Schuld!* The Jews are guilty!"

All across Europe, people collaborated with the Nazis, but they have not yet acknowledged that. I would expect them at least to have a moral obligation to protect the surviving Jews, whether they live in Austria, in Israel, or elsewhere. Instead, they equate *us* with Nazis.

From the end of the Second World War until recently, people generally assumed that anti-Semitism had mostly disappeared from Western Europe. After the Holocaust, people had finally learned, we thought. We were wrong. Overt anti-Semitism has reappeared again. While the memory of the Nazi Holocaust was still fresh, anti-Semitism remained silent. But as that memory fades, a new anti-Semitism emerges.

We also thought that the creation of a homeland in Israel would eliminate anti-Semitism once and for all, that Israel would transform the Jews into "normal" people who lived among themselves as the majority rather than among the Gentiles as strangers and minorities.

However, while the State of Israel has given Jews a margin of physical safety, it has not erased anti-Semitism. Now, Jews are not only hated for what they do outside Israel, but especially for what they do in the Holy Land. Anti-Semitism is now being nurtured in a general climate of antagonism against the Jewish state and everything connected to it. Now, we are hated not despite having a homeland, but because we have it, and because of what we do in order to live in and defend it.

One would have to be blind, deaf, and dumb not to recognize that this hatred of Israel is profoundly anti-Semitic. Such hostile sentiments— sometimes disguised as a "legitimate" critique of Israeli politics—have been called the "new" anti-Semitism. I will here further describe its manifestations, explore its roots in the old hatred of Jews, and discuss some ways of responding to this alarming phenomenon.

New Anti-Semitism

The "new" anti-Semitism preaches hatred, not only against Jews, but also specifically against Israel.

It is therefore not surprising that its main proponents come from the Arab world. Inspired by Nazi propaganda, Arab media spreads the message that the "Zionist Jew" is trying to conquer not only Palestine, but the entire world. As a result, we can assume that over 300 million Arabs may harbor such an intense grudge that they are motivated to inflict harm upon Jews. Another billion Muslims might not become violent, but they certainly don't like us very much. Considering that there are only about fourteen million Jews worldwide and six million Jews in Israel, these proportions are astounding.

While the most intense hatred comes from the Arab world and Islam, this "new" anti-Semitism is also spreading rapidly in Europe. In recent opinion polls, the general populations of France, England, Holland, and other Eastern European countries have clearly expressed negative sentiments against Israelis and Jews. For example, in a 2003 survey with 7,515 citizens from fifteen EU member states, a majority of respondents from the Netherlands, Austria, and Germany perceived

Israel as the greatest threat to world peace. In addition, the European Union in itself has been biased in its treatment of the Middle East conflict, seeing Israel as the villain and Palestine as the victim of oppression.

As a result, Jews do not feel safe in Europe (again). This can be exemplified by the security instructions given to participants of the European Council of Jewish Communities meeting in Budapest in May 2004 titled, "We Are a Part of Europe." Under the heading about how to behave outside the well-guarded conference hotel, participants were recommended to hide that they were Jews. As a result of these sentiments, it has (again) become hazardous to walk around showing any overt sign of being Jewish in many parts of Central Europe.

As the hatred of Israel intensifies, so does the hatred of Jews. Memorials and tombstones are destroyed or desecrated; synagogues, schools, and community centers are attacked; and machine-gun-wielding police guard Jewish institutions at all times.

Anyone browsing the Internet can easily find Web sites and discussion groups such as stormfront.org and exterminance.org that function to spread lies about Jews and throw dirt on Israel. After having mentioned these Web sites in an earlier version of this paper (Kellermann, 2005), I received an e-mail from Mr. N., alias "Adolf Hitler," stating that I had gotten it all wrong:

From: Adolf Hitler (e-mail address).
Subject: Your article

Shalom. I am Exterminance. Earlier this year, you published an article which made reference to my Web site. I am writing this e-mail to share my observances upon your reference to my Web site. Your article: http://www. jewishmag.com/91mag/antisemitism/antisemitism.htm.

My article mentioning yours: http://www.stormfront.org/forum/ showthread.php?t=226687.

So how's the weather in Israel?

Heil Hitler,
B.N.

After some thought, I decided to answer his e-mail.

Re: Your article.
Dear Mr. N.,

Thank you for your e-mail.

Sorry if I offended you by implying that you have something against us Jews.

However, I would be curious to understand you better.

The weather here in Israel is fine.

Yours,
N.K.

Among many other things, he answered, "To be perfectly honest, I am somewhat prejudiced against Jews." We had an exchange of ten e-mails altogether in the fall of 2005. All of these were (and perhaps still are) listed on the URL mentioned above. I asked questions, and Mr. N. answered. He explained about white pride, white civil rights, and why people hate the Jews. It all boiled down to the fact that Jews themselves are responsible for being hated, because of their "repulsive" behavior: "People hate Jews because they live among other people and promote the extinction of the white race through promoting multiculturalism while preserving their own culture. As for what occurred in Europe sixty years ago, it was not unique. At one time or another, the Jews have been driven out of every land in Europe, sometimes more than once. Sooner or later, the alien presence makes itself unpleasantly known to the point where expulsion is inevitable."

When he described the Holocaust as a "myth" and I responded by mentioning that my mother had received a number in Auschwitz, he broke off the conversation. A final comment explained that such personal arguments apparently were "too emotional" for Mr. N., who found Holocaust claims "unsubstantiated and insane":

> As far as I'm concerned, "Holocaust" belief is a faith-based religion, a power-tripping cult of coercion, oppression, hatred, and deceit against my people. Mr. Kellermann has moved to tactics which will give him the excuse to employ emotion in his arguments, and I'm not interested in entertaining crocodile tears, so I'm dropping the correspondence.

For me, however, there was an important lesson to be learned from this interchange. What it taught me was that there are really individuals with views like Mr. N. out there and that we must take them seriously, even if they are highly offensive.

A strange mixture of people and organizations are involved in this "new" anti-Semitism. They do not come only from the pro-Palestinian camp and from Islam, but also from the radical left and extreme right. Radical leftist groups who protest against U.S. colonialism, globalization, and the Western capitalist civilization in general have joined up with extreme rightist groups of neo-Nazis, Holocaust deniers, skinhead activists, racists, and xenophobes who all share the common bond of Jew hatred. These "new" anti-Semites make no differentiation between Jews in general and Israelis in particular. For them, Jews and Israelis all represent the ultimate Zionist threat, which should be destroyed at all costs.

Much of such anti-Israeli sentiments came to a violent eruption during the *First World Conference Against Racism* in Durban, South Africa, in September 2001. The conference attempted to de-legitimatize Israel by equating Zionism with racism. A few years later, the Second Durban Conference took place in Geneva on April 21, 2009, coinciding with Israel's yearly Holocaust Remembrance Day (Hebrew: *Yom HaShoah*). At this UN-sponsored global summit on racism, Iranian President Mahmoud Ahmadinejad opened the agenda by condemning Israel as a *racist state*. Later, one hundred countries unanimously approved an official declaration in which the state of Israel was indeed characterized as such.

It seems to have taken the world only seventy years (1939–2009) to reproduce the kind of violent, anti-Jewish atmosphere that allowed a "new Hitler" (Ahmadinejad) to condemn the Jews for their very existence. Both Hitler and Ahmadinejad stated clearly that they wanted to wipe the Jews and Israel "from the face of the earth." The world again looks on in silence and complacency, as if it has learned nothing from the Holocaust.

The fanatic, pro-Palestinian terrorist camp certainly does not make any distinction between Zionists and anti-Zionists or between the right and the left in Israel. People from all such political fractions travel in buses, and they are all exposed to the same threat of being blown up in terrorist attacks. What is most surprising, however, is that such terrorists also attack Jewish institutions outside Israel. One would think that Jewish institutions outside of Israel would comply with the Palestinian preference of a Palestine without Jews. This nondifferentiation between hating Jews in Israel (either in central Israel or in the occupied territories), or hating Jews who live outside Israel is the main evidence of the blurring of anti-Zionism and anti-Semitism.

According to Natan Sharansky (2004), the former Soviet dissident and prisoner of Zion, anti-Zionism becomes *de facto* new anti-Semitism and not legitimate criticism of Israel if it contains the following characteristics, described as the "3D test":

1. If Israelis are seen as Nazis and Palestinian refugee camps as concentration camps (*demonization*);

2. If Israel is criticized for human rights abuses while other nations with similar actions are not (*discrimination* and *double standards*); and

3. If the right of Israel to exist is denied (delegitimization).

Thus, the difference between a leftist pro-Palestinian activist who wants to get rid of the Jews in Israel, and a neo-Nazi who wants to get rid of the Jews everywhere else, is purely academic. Both think Jews should be deprived of certain rights, be kept out of certain economic, social, and political positions, be expelled from their country, and, finally, be eliminated. Such views have deep roots in the "classical" hatred of Jews that has been the destiny of the Chosen People for centuries.

The Old Anti-Semitism

The old anti-Semitism, with its pervasive animosity toward Jews, seems to be more than a personal opinion or an attitude. It also involves a strong emotional and physiological arousal, similar to its opposite, love. But instead of attraction, anti-Semites feel repulsion and disgust, almost as if they have an allergic reaction to Jews. In such a "Judeo-phobic" response, the anti-Semite would say: "I do not really know why, but I detest the Jews and everything that has to do with Judaism and Israel!" If nurtured, this repulsion may develop into a complete worldview and a persistent belief system about Jews' "evil nature."

No reasoning persuades the anti-Semite about his or her biased conceptions of Jews. Like a religious faith that cannot be argued rationally, anti-Semites do not question their prejudices. Even though they might have never had any direct contact with Jews, they are convinced of the correctness of their perceptions, assuming others will perceive Jews in the same way.

Public-opinion surveys conducted since the early postwar years have shown that anti-Semitism remains stronger in Austria than in Germany, France, or the United States (Pauley, 1996). For example, in polls conducted in 1986, 63 percent of the Austrians surveyed said that they would not want to live next to a Jew, compared with 48 percent of Germans. The surveys have also shown that about 75 percent of all Austrians privately articulate at least some anti-Semitic views, and about 20–25 percent have strong anti-Semitic opinions. About 7–10 percent can be described as extreme anti-Semites.

For example, the grandmother of a group member from Austria was convinced that Jews have green blood. Logic could not persuade her that this was incorrect. The group member therefore introduced her to a Jew, and to disprove her preconception, the Jew stuck himself in the finger. When red blood came forth, she exclaimed, "Yes, I see that you have red blood like everybody else. But then, you cannot be a real Jew!"

Reasons for Anti-Semitism

Various theories have been suggested to explain such persistent antipathy against Jews. Here, five of the most common reasons for anti-Semitism that surfaced in different guises throughout history will be mentioned. Jews are hated because:

1. They cause all misfortunes (scapegoat theory);
2. They possess too much wealth and power (economic theory);
3. They claim supremacy over other peoples (conspiracy theory);
4. They killed Jesus (deicide theory); and
5. They are different and inferior (xenophobic theory).

The first reason concerns blaming Jews for all that is bad in society (crises, wars, famines, upheavals, revolts, etc.). According to Sartre (1946), the anti-Semite is convinced that "all or part of his own misfortune and those of his country are due to *Jewish elements* in the community." This *scapegoat theory* is a central element in all anti-Semitic belief systems: Jews are responsible for everything bad. In 1348, German Jews were put on trial, accused of poisoning the wells that caused the Black Plague. Between the First and Second World Wars, Jews were blamed for World War I, the Treaty of Versailles, the Soviet takeover in Russia, the economic depression, the emergence of a black market, and the unpredictable weather. More recently, Jews and/or Israel were viewed as guilty for global terrorism, 9/11, and all the recent wars in the Middle East. "Without the Jews, things would have been better," anti-Semites say. "It is common wisdom. Everybody knows that this is so." In fact, some anti-Semites went so far as to blame the Jews for the tsunami in Southeast Asia in 2004.

The second reason states that the Jews possess too much wealth and power. This *economic theory* of anti-Semitism postulates that Jewish wealth and power arouse the envy of other people, leading to anti-Semitism. Ever since the laws that barred Jews from almost all activity besides finance, the Jews have been stereotyped as avaricious, greedy, and obsessed with money and power. Shakespeare's Shylock, the Jewish moneylender in the *Merchant of Venice*, is perhaps the most well known archetype of the "rich Jew." However, media still reinforces this idea all over the world.

The third reason is a reaction to the Jews' claim of being the "Chosen People." In this *conspiracy theory*, anti-Semites say that Jews claim supremacy over other peoples and that the Jews are conspiring to destroy the "white race." The anti-Semites who hold this view believe that organized Jewry has pursued a vicious agenda to get incredible power to dominate the world, especially by being in control of the news and entertainment media. Such anti-Semites frequently quote from the fictional *Protocols of the Elders of Zion* to give credibility to their lies.

The fourth reason refers to the age-old biblical account of Jews killing Jesus Christ. For centuries, children in Europe shouted "God-killer!" at the Jews, for that was what they'd been taught. This accusation lies at the heart of the Jewish history of Europe from the day Jews first set foot there. This *deicide theory* fuelled two millennia of European anti-Semitism. Recently, Mel Gibson's film *The Passion of the Christ* has reawakened this type of anti-Semitism. Such sentiments are buried deep within the collective unconscious of many Christians, even though Vatican II (1962–65) stopped teaching this narrative, and Pope John XXIII wrote a prayer of atonement for all the suffering caused to Jews in the name of Jesus: "Forgive us the curse that we unjustly laid on the name of the Jews." Nevertheless, some Christian congregations continue to preach this narrative, including the preposterous lie that Jews use Christian blood for their religious rituals.

The fifth and final reason for hating Jews is that they are seen as different. This *xenophobic theory* argues that Jews do not belong in Western society because they are foreigners. This kind of hatred is not only focused on Jews, but is based on general racism and prejudice, present in various degrees in all societies; anybody who is different is also inferior and should be driven out, including foreign workers, immigrants, and other minorities. In order to withstand this last form of prejudice, Theodore Herzl (1896) observed Jews unsuccessfully trying to blend in and become more assimilated in the societies in which they lived.

Jews try to do so much not to be hated, but it doesn't matter what they do. We have honestly endeavored everywhere to merge ourselves in the social life of surrounding communities and to preserve the faith of our fathers. We are not permitted to do so. In vain are we loyal patriots, our loyalty in some places running to extremes; in vain do we make the same sacrifices of life and property as our fellow citizens; in vain do we strive to increase the fame of our native land in science and art, or her wealth by trade and commerce. In countries where we have lived for centuries, we are still cried down as strangers—and often by those whose ancestors were not yet domiciled in the land where Jews had already had experience of suffering. The majority may decide who the strangers are; for this, as indeed every point that arises in the relations between nations, is a question of might. If we could only be left in peace. But I think we shall not be left in peace.

Unconditional Hate

Many of the above-mentioned reasons for anti-Semitism are no longer relevant in today's Europe. First of all, fewer than two million Jews live in Europe, and most Gentiles simply have no personal contact with them. Second, the secular trend has made religious anti-Semitism irrelevant. Third, people are better educated and too aware of the history of the Second World War to believe the lies about the Jews. Fourth, there is less competition from Jewish intellectuals than before; because of the improved financial situation in Europe, Jews are no longer a privileged group. Finally, racial prejudice is more strongly focused upon immigrants, who are seen as more different and strange than assimilated Jews—who look, speak, and behave like everybody else. What remain are the stereotypes about alleged Jewish control of mass media, lately reinforced by anti-Zionism.

While these theories seem to be sufficient justification for many people hating the Jews, they do not withstand logical reasoning. Some of them are even preposterous in light of common sense and facts. For example, why would Jews initiate misfortunes that hurt themselves as much as anybody else? How can the Jews be ascribed with a bewildering variety of diametrically opposed and even contradictory roles at the same time— both as egotistical capitalists and as altruistic socialists, both as nationalists and as internationalists, and both as religious fanatics and as atheists? And if Jews had so much power, would they not have prevented the Holocaust and all the recent condemnations of Israel? And what kind of biblical or historical legal system can accuse today's Jews for the crucifixion of Jesus of Nazareth over two thousand years ago? Finally, if Jews are hated because of being strangers, why were assimilated Jews not spared Nazi persecution?

The truth is that none of these reasons really make any difference for the anti-Semite.

Jews could be good or bad, behave like everybody else or behave differently, and be assimilated or traditional. It didn't matter. Whatever they did was beside the point as far as Jew-haters were concerned. Jewish efforts to adapt to the cultures and norms of their host societies did not make them more accepted and welcome. No amount of Jewish charity would erase the charge of Jewish greed. This is hatred *per se* (in itself), or "generic" hatred (cf. Fineberg, Samuels, & Weitzman, 2007).

When hatred is present with such intensity, but without reason, I suggest that it is named *unconditional hate.* As in unconditional love, there are no strings attached to such an emotion, and nothing is expected in return. It is not dependent on what the other person *does,* but what he or she *is.* As a mother who loves her child unconditionally, even if the child misbehaves, the anti-Semite hates the Jew even if he or she behaves well. And as a mother who believes that there is something inherently good in her child worth loving, the anti-Semite is convinced that there is something inherently bad in the Jew. Unconditional hate is a dangerous phenomenon, because it may lead to what we call a "hate crime": violence based on extreme aversion toward someone because of race, religion, sexual orientation, ethnicity, national origin, or any other inherent trait.

The Ultimate Evil

In the minds of anti-Semites throughout history, Jews represented the essence of everything evil. For Christians, the Jew became a unique, mythic creature similar to the anti-Christ. During the Middle Ages, superstitious people saw the presence of evil powers in all calamities, then created elaborate fabrications, claiming that the Jews were affiliated with witches and demons who brought death and destruction to the community. Thus, when a catastrophe actually occurred, the Jews were singled out as the cause of the destruction, and people would take revenge.

In addition, most societies saw Jews as wicked pariahs and social outcasts. Neo-Nazis and right-wing extremist groups in the Western world still perceive Jews in this way. For example, in a chat room at stormfront. org, one participant described the Jew as a *parasite,* "someone who is living within another organism, and is dependent on something else for his existence without being useful."

Another contributor associated the Jew to the legendary Dr. Frankenstein: "Jews don't necessarily *try* to do what they're doing. They are just genetically engineered that way. They can't help themselves. Their subculture is set up so that those who are the most paranoid and destructive have no contact with Gentiles at all, but are the advisors to those who go out and implement their destructive strategies. It's almost like a mad scientist who takes out his vengeance on the world via his various Frankenstein monsters (Dr. Frankenstein was a Jew, no doubt)."

Such derogatory conceptions of Jews as belonging to a subhuman race, would (again) justify their total extermination.

Paranoia?

Reflecting on all of this makes me wonder if I am exaggerating. Do people really hate us so much? Perhaps it is only a part of my fantasy? Or, even worse, have I become a little paranoid? Or is this heightened sensitivity to anti-Semitism another sign of me being the child of Holocaust survivors?

I wish it were so. I wish that I was only exaggerating and that the people who hate us—if they exist at all—are so few, and so deranged that they no longer pose any real threat to our existence. But I really do not know. We were wrong about how far anti-Semitism would go in the past, and even being paranoid does not exclude the possibility of people still wanting to hurt us. The signs of danger are all around, and I cannot close my eyes and look the other way.

Our history taught us that large-scale annihilation of the Jews really is possible. We were persecuted by the Crusaders, Cossacks, and the Nazis, who finally slaughtered us by the millions. We would pray, cry, and die and do as we were told, but this still did not save us from being killed. But this time it is different. Now, we refuse to accept this scenario. We resist. We feel that we have a right to exist—in Israel and elsewhere.

Never Again?

In January 2005, for the first time in its history, the United Nations marked the sixtieth anniversary of the liberation of Nazi death camps. Survivors and foreign dignitaries—including German and Israeli foreign ministers—addressed the United Nations General Assembly in an impressive official remembrance ceremony for the more than six million killed during the Holocaust. Nearly 150 of the world body's 191 members backed the motion to hold the observance. The United States, Israel, the European Union,

Russia, Canada, Australia, and New Zealand sponsored the observance, which took place three days before a state ceremony in Poland at the site of Auschwitz-Birkenau. Coming thirty years after the world body adopted a resolution branding Zionism as a "form of racism," the special session represents a significant event in Holocaust commemoration. Holocaust survivors generally felt it as an acknowledgment that the world had at last started to listen to them.

But for others, it was an insignificant gesture in the wake of the violent anti-Semitism that has targeted the Jewish people and the State of Israel during the course of the last years, which has reached an intensity that has not been seen since the end of World War II. Apparently, humankind is still far from absorbing the lessons from the Holocaust, and the civilized world still refuses to condone genocides in Bosnia, Rwanda, and Darfur. In addition, among the forty-one speeches delivered during the remembrance, only five mentioned Israel, the country that has provided a new home to most Holocaust survivors and that is the only homeland of the Jewish people. In my view, the Holocaust commemoration event lost much of its significance without affirming the right of the Jewish State of Israel to exist as a safe place for survivors.

Throughout the event, the words "never again" were repeated many times. German Chancellor Gerhard Schröder (in office 1998–2005) asserted that "never again should anti-Semites succeed in haunting and hurting Jewish citizens in Germany." But attacks and threats against Jews all over Europe occur on a regular basis, leading to Jewish institutions in Berlin having to be protected by armed guards. The words *never again* have become irrelevant, and it rather seems that it does happen "again and again and again." In fact, we live in more dangerous times than ever. There has been a significant increase in antagonism against Jews, which has reached proportions not seen for many years.

While these times obviously are very different from the 1930s, there are certain similarities to the pre-Holocaust era. For example, the first stage of the genocide of the Jews involved persistent agitation, mass communication and mobilization of the public opinion against Jews. Hitler was an expert in spreading lies about the Jews and communicating them in a way that reached the masses. He fed into the old Christian prejudice about Jews and played with the average citizen's primitive emotions of fear of evil powers.

Similarly, Muslims all over the world are fed Nazi propaganda about the evil intentions of Jews and Israel. For example, in a speech on February 6, 2004, Ahmad Nasser, Secretary of the Palestinian Authority's Legislative Council, insisted that Israel has no right to exist because it is *Satan's offspring*, founded on theft and racism:

Israel was established on the basis of theft. Israel, the State of Israel, is the Satan's offspring, a Satanic offspring. Israel was founded on theft from the first moment. It was founded on the basis of robbery, terror, killing, torture, assassination, death, stealing land, and killing people. On this basis, Israel was founded and will continue this way, never able to exist because its [Israel's] birth was unnatural, a Satanic offspring, and cannot exist among human beings … Only in this way can Israel exist. It is not capable of existing naturally as other nations in the world.

And, in the 2003 summit of Islamic leaders, Malaysian Prime Minister Mohammad said, "The Europeans killed six million Jews out of twelve million, but today the Jews rule the world by proxy. They get others to fight and die for them. They have now gained control of the most powerful countries, and this tiny community has become a world power." The audience stood up in vocal agreement.

The Iranian TV drama, *For You, Palestine*, or *Zahra's Blue Eyes* offers another example of this unconditional hatred. The fictional story describes how Israelis are stealing the blue eyes of Palestinian children to implant them into Jewish children. The vicious plot effectively stirs up primitive hatred against Jews. The characters in the drama do not allow such hatred to remain passive and indifferent. Indeed, the father of Zahra promises to take revenge not only for his daughter, but for the crimes instigated against the entire Palestinian people. A sad consequence of this TV series is that it has cast doubts over a humanitarian Israeli project that has provided poor infants from all over the world—including Arab countries—with acute heart surgery, saving many lives as a result. Instead of allowing such a project to become a "bridge builder" between ordinary people in the Middle East, the TV series has infected it with suspicion.

Such Arab propaganda against Israel and the Jews has lately become very intense and dangerous. The masses of *Hezbollah* soldiers who are marching together while shouting anti-Israel slogans remind us of the *Hitler Jugend's* public manifestations against Jews before World War II. The *Hitler Jugend* easily transformed into *Einsatzgruppen*—special Nazi mobile killing units—during the war. Any Jew who enters into the *Hezbollah's* midst would be immediately lynched. However, while the threat of anti-Semitism and terrorism are certainly serious, Iran's nuclear program is surely the most dangerous for Israel. Ahmadinejad has openly talked about Iran's intentions to develop sophisticated weapons of mass destruction, has test-fired missiles with sufficient range to hit Israel, and probably already has at least some nuclear warheads.

What to Do?

So, what can we do? How can we respond? Should we choose fight or flight?

For one thing, we should not take these threats lightly. While nobody can predict if we will experience another Holocaust, the signs are truly alarming. Today, there is no excuse for "not knowing" about the dangers of anti-Semitism. It is no secret that Jew-haters exist and that they have malicious intent. Anti-Semites, from *Haman* to *Hezbollah* or *Hamas*, were dangerous in the past, and they are still dangerous in the present.

Thus, we must continue monitoring anti-Semitism all over the world, from overt acts of violence to covert expressions of Jew-hatred in the media. With this knowledge, we can voice our protests and influence public opinion and policymakers, locally, regionally, and internationally. While we may not be able to reform the hard-core haters, we must inform ordinary and decent people that this is happening again, so that they do not remain passive bystanders this time around.

On June 21, 2004, UN Secretary-General Kofi Annan stated, "It is hard to believe that, sixty years after the tragedy of the Holocaust, anti-Semitism is once again rearing its head. But it is clear that we are witnessing an alarming resurgence of these phenomena in new forms and manifestations. This time the world must not—cannot—be silent." Annan then asked UN member states to adopt a resolution to fight anti-Semitism, stating that the UN's Commission on Human Rights must study and expose anti-Semitism in the same way that it fights bias against Muslims. Annan correctly asked, "Are not Jews entitled to the same degree of concern and protection?"

Less than a year later, at the commemoration ceremony of the liberation of Auschwitz in January 2005, Annan added that new generations must not grow up unaware of the lessons of the Holocaust: "The founding of this organization was a direct response to the Holocaust. Our charter and the words 'untold sorrow' were written as the world was learning the full horror of the death camps. The evil that destroyed six million Jews and others in those camps is one that still threatens all of us today. It is not something we can consign to the distant past and forget about. Every generation must be on its guard, to make sure that such a thing never happens again."

REFERENCES

Adorno, TW., Frenkel-Brunswik, E., Levinson, DJ., & Sanford, RN. (1950). *The authoritarian personality*. New York: Harper & Row.

Albeck, HJ. (1993). Intergenerational consequences of trauma: Reframing traps in treatment theory: A second generation perspective. In MO. Williams & JF. Sommer (Eds.), *Handbook of Post-Traumatic Therapy*. Westport, CT: Greenwood Press, 106–125.

Allport, GW. (1954). *The nature of prejudice*. Cambridge, MA: Addison-Wesley.

Almog, O. (2000). *The Sabra—A profile*. Tel Aviv: Am Oved.

American Psychiatric Association (1994). *Diagnostic and statistical manual of mental disorders: DSM-IV*. Washington, DC: AMA.

Amichai, Y. (2000). *Open Closed Open: Poems*. New York: Harcourt Brace. [Hebrew original: Patuach Sagur Patuach. Tel Aviv: Schocken, 1998].

Amir, M., & Lev-Wiesel, R. (2001). Does every person have a name? The relationship between unknown identity and posttraumatic symptoms, quality of life, psychological distress, and personal resources among child Holocaust survivors. *Journal of Traumatic Stress, 14(4)*, 859–869.

Amir, M., & Lev-Wiesel, R. (2003). Time does not heal all wounds: Quality of life and psychological distress of people who survived the Holocaust as children 55 years later. *Journal of Traumatic Stress, 16(3)*, 295–299.

Anthony, EJ. (1974). Introduction: The syndrome of the psychologically vulnerable child. In EJ. Anthony & C. Koupernik (Eds.), *The child in his family: children at psychiatric risk*. New York: Wiley, 3–10.

Anthony, EJ., & Cohler, BJ. (Eds.) (1987). *The invulnerable child*. New York: Guilford.

Antonovsky, A. (1979/1982). *Health, stress, and coping*. San Francisco: Jossey-Bass.

Antonovsky, A. (1987). *Unraveling the mystery of health. How people manage stress and stay well*. San Francisco: Jossey-Bass.

Antonovsky, A., Maoz, B., Dowty, N., & Wijsenbeek, H. (1971). Twenty-five years later: A limited study of the sequelae of the concentration camp experience. *Social Psychiatry, 6,* 186–193.

Arendt, H. (1963/1977). *Eichmann in Jerusalem: A report on the banality of evil* (Revised edition). New York: Penguin.

Audouard, A. (2004, May 7). The Roots of Abu Ghraib: When liberators become tyrants. *New York Times,* p. A31. Retrieved from: http://www.nytimes.com/2004/05/07/opinion/the-roots-of-abu-ghraib-when-liberators-become-tyrants.html.

Avner, Y. (2006, June 14). Israel does not need Palestinian recognition. *The Jerusalem Post*. Retrieved from: http://www.jpost.com/servlet/Satellite?cid=1150191575275&pagename=JPost/JPArticle/Printer.

Axelrod, S., Schnipper, OL., & Rau, JH. (1980). Hospitalised offspring of Holocaust survivors: Problems and dynamics. *Bulletin of the Menninger Clinic, 44,* 1–14.

Ayalon, L. (2005). Challenges associated with the study of resilience to trauma in Holocaust survivors. *Journal of Loss & Trauma, 10(4),* 347–358.

Bachar, E., Cale, M., Eisenberg, J., & Dasberg, H. (1994). Aggression expression in grandchildren of Holocaust survivors—A comparative study. *Israel Journal of Psychiatry and Related Sciences, 31(1),* 41-47.

Baider, L., Peretz, T., Hadani, PE. et al. (2000). Transmission of response to trauma? Second-generation Holocaust survivors' reaction to cancer. *American Journal of Psychiatry, 157,* 904–10.

Baider, L., & Sarell, M. (1984). Coping with cancer among Holocaust survivors in Israel: An exploratory study. *Journal of Human Stress, 10(3),* 121–127.

Baider, L., Goldzweig, G., Ever Hadani, P., & Peretz, T. (2006). Psychological distress and coping in breast cancer patients and healthy women whose parents survived the Holocaust. *Psycho-Oncology, 15,* 635–646.

Baider, L., Peretz, T., & Kaplan De-Nour, A. (1993). Holocaust cancer patients: A comparative study. *Psychiatry—Interpersonal and Biological Processes, 56(4)*, 349–355.

Balfour, MLG. (1988). *Withstanding Hitler in Germany, 1933–45.* London: Routledge.

Bandura, A. (1973). *Aggression: A social learning analysis.* Englewood Cliffs, NJ: Prentice-Hall.

Bandura, A. (1977). *Social learning theory.* Englewood Cliffs, NJ: Prentice-Hall.

Bankier, D. (1992). *The Germans and the final solution: Public opinion under Nazism.* Oxford and Boston: Basil Blackwell,

Barak, Y. (2007). The aging of Holocaust survivors: Myth and reality concerning suicide. *Israel Medical Association Journal, 9(3)*, 196–198.

Barak, Y., Aizenberg, D., Szor, H., Swartz, M., Maor, R., & Knobler, HY. (2005). Increased risk of attempted suicide among aging Holocaust survivors. *American Journal of Geriatric Psychiatry, 13*, 701–704.

Baranowsky, AB., Young, M., Johnson-Douglas, S., Williams-Keeler, L., & McCarrey, M. (1998). PTSD Transmission: A review of secondary traumatization in Holocaust survivor families. *Canadian Psychology, 39(4)*, 247-256.

Barel, E. (2009). Living in Israel helps survivors cope with trauma. In C. Liphshiz, *Haaretz*. Retrieved from: http://haaretz.com/hasen/spages/1079396.html.

Barocas, HA., & Barocas, C. (1980). Separation-individuation conflicts in children of Holocaust survivors. *Journal of Contemporary Psychotherapy, 11*, 6–14.

Bar-On, D. (1989a). Holocaust perpetrators and their children: A paradoxical morality. *Journal of Humanistic Psychology, 29(4)*, 424–443.

Bar-On, D. (1989b). *Legacy of silence: Encounters with children of the Third Reich.* Cambridge: Harvard University Press. (New German edition 2003 by Koerber Foundation: *Die Last des Schweigens*).

Bar-On, D. (1990). Children of perpetrators of the Holocaust: Working through one's moral self. *Psychiatry, 53*, 229–245. German version: *Integrative Therapie, 3*, 222–245.

Bar-On, D. (1993). First encounter between children of survivors and children of perpetrators of the Holocaust. *Journal of Humanistic Psychology, 33*(4), 6–14, 21.

Bar-On, D. (1995a). Encounters between descendants of Nazi perpetrators and descendants of Holocaust survivors. *Psychiatry, 58(3),* 225–245.

Bar-On, D. (1995b). *Fear and hope: Life-stories of five Israeli families of Holocaust survivors: Three generations in a family.* Cambridge, MA: Harvard University Press.

Bar-On, D. (1996). Studying the transgenerational after-effects of the Holocaust in Israel. *Journal of Personal & Interpersonal Loss, 1,* 215–247.

Bar-On, D. (1999). *The indescribable and the undiscussible: Reconstructing human discourse after trauma.* Budapest, Hungary: Central European University Press.

Bar-On, D. (2000). *Bridging the gap.* Hamburg: Koerber.

Bar-On, D., Eland, J., Kleber, RJ., Krell, R., Moore, Y., Sagi, A., Soriano, E., Suedfeld, P., Van der Velden, PG., & Van Ijzendoorn, MH. (1998). Multigenerational perspectives on coping with the Holocaust experience: An attachment perspective for understanding the developmental sequelae of trauma across generations. *International Journal of Behavioral Development, 22,* 315–338.

Bartov, O. (1996). *Murder in our midst: The Holocaust, industrial killing, and representation.* New York: Oxford University Press. Retrieved from: http://www.millersville.edu/~holo-con/bartov.html.

Bastiaans, J. (1974a). Het KZ-syndroom en de menselijke vrijheid. *Nederlands Tijdschrift voor Geneeskunde, 118,* 1173–1178. [The concentration camp syndrome and human freedom].

Bastiaans, J. (1974b). The KZ-syndrome: A thirty-year study of the effects on victims of Nazi concentration camps. *Revue Medico-Chirurgicale de Jassy, 78,* 573–578.

Bauer, Y. (2000). Speech at the ceremonial opening of the forum. Retrieved from:http://www.manskligarattigheter.gov.se/stockholmforum/2000/page898.html.

Bauer, Y. (2001). *Rethinking the Holocaust.* New Haven, CT: Yale University Press.

Ben-Zur, H., & Zimmerman, M. (2005). Aging Holocaust survivors' well-being and adjustment: associations with ambivalence over emotional expression. *Psychology and Aging, 20*(4), 710–713.

Berger, A., & Berger, N. (2001). *Second generation voices: Reflections by children of victims, perpetrators, and bystanders of the Shoah.* New York: Syracuse University Press.

Berger, AL. (1997). *Children of Job.* Albany: State University of New York Press.

Bettelheim, B. (1943). Individual and mass behavior in extreme situations. *Journal of Abnormal and Social Psychology, 38,* 417–452.

Bettelheim, B. (1979). *Surviving and other essays.* New York: Knopf.

Blumberg, ML. (1977). Treatment of the abused child and the child abuser. *American Journal of Psychotherapy, 31,* 204–215.

Boder, DP. (1949). *I did not interview the dead.* Champaign, IL: University of Illinois Press.

Boder, DP. (1952). *David Pablo Boder papers, 1938-1957.* University of California, Los Angeles Library. Department of Special Collections.

Bonanno, GA. (2004). Loss, trauma, and human resilience: Have we underestimated the human capacity to thrive after extremely aversive events? *American Psychology, 59(1),* 20-28.

Boszormenyi-Nagy, I., & Spark, GM. (1973). *Invisible loyalties.* New York: Harper & Row.

Botz, G. (Ed.) (2005). *Schweigen und Reden einer Generation.* Wien: Mandelbaum. [Silence and talking in a generation].

Bower, H. (1994). The concentration camp syndrome. *Australian and New Zealand Journal of Psychiatry, 28,* 391–397.

Brendler, K. (1995). Working through the Holocaust: Still a task for German youth. In R. Kleber, C. Figley, & B. Gersons (Eds.), *Beyond trauma: Cultural and societal dynamics.* New York: Plenum.

Brendler, K. (1997). Die NS-Geschichte als Sozialisationsfaktor und Identitätsballast der Enkelgeneration. In D. Bar-On, K. Brendler, & P. Hare (Eds.), *Da ist etwas kaputtgegangen an den Wurzeln. Identitätsformationen deutscher und israelischer Jugendlicher im Schatten des Holocaust.* Frankfurt a.M.: Campus, 53–104. [Something was broken in the roots: The identity formation in German and Israeli youth in the shadows of the Holocaust].

Brenner, I. (2004). *Psychic trauma: Dynamics, symptoms and treatment.* Lanham, MD: J. Aronson.

Breslau, N., Kessler, RC., Chilcoat, HD., Schultz, LR., Davis, GC., & Andreski, P. (1998). Trauma and posttraumatic stress disorder in the community: The 1996 Detroit area survey of trauma. *Archives of General Psychiatry, 55,* 626–632.

Brodsky, J. (2005). *Health problems and socioeconomic neediness among Jewish Shoah survivors in Israel.* Jerusalem: JDC-Brookdale Institute of Gerontology and Human Development.

Brom, D., Durst, N., & Aghassy, G. (2002). The phenomenology of posttraumatic distress in older adult Holocaust survivors. *Journal of Clinical Geropsychology, 8(3),* 189–195.

Brom, D., Kfir, R., & Dasberg, H. (2001). A controlled double-blind study on children of Holocaust survivors. *Israel Journal of Psychiatry and Related Sciences, 38,* 47–57.

Browning, C. (1992). *Ordinary men: Reserve police battalion 101 and the Final Solution in Poland.* New York: HarperCollins. [German translation: Ganz normale Männer. Das Reserve-Polizeibataillon 101 und die »Endlösung« in Polen. Reinbek: Rowohlt Taschenbuch, 1996].

Browning, C. (2006). Lecture at the U.S. Holocaust museum on December 21, 2006. Retrieved from: http://www.ushmm.org/museum/exhibit/focus/antisemitism/voices/transcript/index.php?content=20061221.

Bullock, A. (1990). *Hitler: A study in tyranny.* Harmondsworth, UK: Penguin.

Carmil, D., & Carel, RS. (1986). Emotional distress and satisfaction in life among Holocaust survivors. A community study of survivors and controls. *Psychological Medicine, 16,* 141–149.

Charny, IW. (1991). *Genocide: A critical bibliographic review.* London: Mansell Publishing Limited.

Chodoff, P. (1963). Late effects of the concentration camp syndrome. *Archives of General Psychiatry, 8,* 323–333.

Chodoff, P. (1980). Psychotherapy of the survivor: In JE. Dimsdale (Ed.), *Survivors, victims, and perpetrators: Essays on the Nazi Holocaust.* Washington: Hemisphere Publishing, 205–218.

Clarke, DE., Colantonio, A., Heslegrave, R., Rhodes, A., Links, P., & Conn, D. (2004). Holocaust experience and suicidal ideation in high-risk older adults. *American Journal of Geriatric Psychiatry, 12,* 65–74.

Cohen, M., Brom, D., & Dasberg, H. (2001). Child survivors of the Holocaust: Symptoms and coping after fifty years. *Israel Journal of Psychiatry & Related Sciences, 38(1),* 3–12.

Conn, D. (2000). Depression in Holocaust survivors: Profile and treatment outcome in a geriatric day hospital program. *International Journal of Geriatric Psychiatry, 15,* 331–337.

Cook, JM. (2002). Traumatic exposure and PTSD in older adults: Introduction to the special issue. *Journal of Clinical Geropsychology, 8(3),* 149–152.

Danieli, Y. (1985). The treatment and prevention of long-term effects and intergenerational transmission of victimization: A lesson from Holocaust survivors and their children. In CR. Figley (Ed.), *Trauma and its wake.* New York: Brunner/Mazel.

Danieli, Y. (1981a). Differing adaptational styles in families of survivors of the Nazi Holocaust. *Child Today, 10(5),* 6–10.

Danieli, Y. (1981b). The aging survivors of the Holocaust: Discussion on the achievement of integration in aging survivors of the Nazi Holocaust. *Journal of Geriatric Psychiatry, 14,* 191–210.

Danieli, Y. (Ed.).(1998). *International handbook of multigenerational legacies of trauma.* New York: Plenum.

Dasberg, H. (1987a). Psychological distress of Holocaust survivors and offspring in Israel: Forty years later. *Israel Journal of Psychiatry & Related Sciences, 24(4),* 245–256.

Dasberg, H. (1987b). Society facing trauma (or: Psychotherapists facing survivors). *Sihot, 1(2),* 98–104.

Dasberg, H. (1992). Child survivors of the Holocaust reach middle age: psychotherapy of late grief reactions. *Journal of Social Work and Policy in Israel, 5–6,* 71–83.

Dasberg, H. (2000). Personal communication.

Dasberg, H. (2001). Adult child survivor syndrome: On deprived childhoods of aging Holocaust survivors. *Israel Journal of Psychiatry & Related Sciences, 38(1),* 13–26.

Dasberg, H. (2003). Late-onset of post-traumatic reactions in Holocaust survivors at advanced age. In H. Rossberg & J. Lansen (Eds.), *Das Schweigen Brechen*. Berlin-New York: Peter Lang, 311–348.

Dasberg, H., Bartura, J., & Amit, Y. (2001). Narrative group therapy with aging child survivors of the Holocaust. *Israel Journal of Psychiatry & Related Sciences, 39(1)*, 27–35.

David, P. (2003). *Caring for aging Holocaust survivors: A practice manual*. Toronto: Baycrest Centre for Geriatric Care.

Davidovitch, N., & Zalashik, R. (2007). Recalling the survivors: Between memory and forgetfulness of hospitalized Holocaust survivors in Israel. *Israel Studies, 12(2)*, 145–163.

Davidson, S. (1992). *Holding on to humanity—the message of Holocaust survivors: The Shamai Davidson Papers*, edited by Israel W. Charny & D. Fromer. New York: New York University Press.

DellaPergola, S. (2003). *Review of relevant demographic information on world Jewry*. Jerusalem: The Hebrew University.

Dicks, HV. (1972). Licensed mass murder: A sociopsychological study of some SS killers. New York: Basic Books.

Dimsdale, JE. (Ed.). (1980). *Survivors, victims, and perpetrators: Essays on the Nazi Holocaust*. New York: Hemisphere Publishing.

Dörr, M. (1998). *"Wer die Zeit nicht miterlebt hat ..." Frauenerfahrungen im Zweiten Weltkrieg und in den Jahren danach*. Bd. 1-3. Frankfurt a.M.: Campus. ["Those who have not experienced the times ..." Experiences of women during the Second World War and the years after].

Duba, U. (1997). *Tales from a child of the enemy*. New York: Penguin.

Durst, N. (1995). Child survivors: A child survives ... and then what? In. J. Lemberger (Ed.), *A global perspective on working with Holocaust survivors and the second generation*. Jerusalem: Brookdale/Amcha.

Durst, N. (2008). Psychotherapy in child survivors of the Holocaust. *Sichot, 23(1)*, 25–35 (Hebrew).

Dwork, D. (1991). *Children with a star*. New Haven: Yale University Press.

Dzieza, J. (2004). *The meaning of B1317*. Recipient of the 2004 Holocaust remembrance project. Retrieved from: http://isurvived.org/Frameset4Essays/-Dzieza_Josh.html.

Eaton, WW., Sigal JJ., & Weinfeld M. (1982). Impairment in Holocaust survivors after 33 years: Data from an unbiased community sample. *American Journal of Psychiatry, 139,* 773–777.

Eitinger, L., & Strøm, A. (1973). *Mortality and morbidity after excessive stress: A follow-up investigation of Norwegian concentration camp survivors.* New York: Humanities Press.

Eitinger, L. (1964/1972). *Concentration camp survivors in Norway and Israel.* London: Allen & Urwin.

Eitinger, L. (1980). The concentration camp syndrome and its late sequelae. In JE. Dimsdale (Ed.), *Survivors, victims and perpetrators.* New York: Hemisphere, 127–162.

Eitinger, L. (1993). The aging Holocaust survivor. *Echoes of the Holocaust,* 2.

Erikson, E. (1959). Growth and crises of the healthy personality. In GS. Klein (Ed.), *Psychological issues.* New York: Norton, 50–100.

Erikson, E. (1962). *Childhood and society.* New York: Norton.

Ermann, M. (2004). Wir Kriegskinder. *Forum der Psychoanalyse, 20,* 226–239. [We war children].

Favaro, A., Rodella, FC., & Santonastaso, P. (2000). Binge eating and eating attitudes among Nazi concentration camp survivors. *Psychological Medicine, 30(2),* 463–466.

Favaro, A., Rodella, FC., Colombo, G., & Santonastaso, P. (1999). Post traumatic stress disorder and major depression among Italian Nazi concentration camp survivors: A controlled study 50 years later. *Psychological Medicine, 29(1),* 87–95.

Felsen, I. (1998). Transgenerational transmission of effects of the Holocaust: The North American research perspective. In Y. Danieli (Ed.), *International handbook of multigenerational legacies of trauma.* New York: Plenum, 43–68.

Fineberg, M., Samuels, S., & Weitzman, M. (Eds.).(2007). *Antisemitism: The generic hatred.* Edgware, UK: Vallentine Mitchell.

Foa, EB. (2009). *Effective treatments for PTSD:* Practice guidelines from the International Society for Traumatic Stress Studies. New York: Guilford. (2nd ed.).

Fogelman, E. (1998). Impact on the second and third generations. In JS. Kestenberg & C. Kahn (Eds.), *Children surviving persecution: An international study of healing and trauma.* Westport, CT and London: Praeger.

Fogelman, E., & Savran, B. (1979). Therapeutic groups for children of Holocaust survivors. *International Journal of Group Psychotherapy, 29,* 211–235.

Fossion, P., Rejas, MC., Servais, L., Pelc, I., & Hirsch, S. (2003). Family approach with grandchildren of Holocaust survivors. *American Journal of Psychotherapy, 57*(4), 519–527.

Frank, N. (1987). *Der Vater: Eine Abrechnung.* München: Bertelsmann. [The father: a setting of scores].

Frankl, V. (1947). *Ein Psycholog erlebt das Konzentrationslager,* (2nd ed.). Vienna: Verlag für Jugend und Volk. [The doctor and the soul: From psychotherapy to logotherapy. 1968. New York: Vintage.]

Frankl, V. (1959/1963). *Man's search for meaning.* Boston: Beacon.

Freud, A., & Burlingham, D. (1943). *Infants without families.* London: G. Allen & Unwin.

Freud, A., & Dann, S. (1951). An experiment in group upbringing. *Psychoanalytic Study of the Child, 6,* 127–169.

Freud, S. (1913). Totem and taboo. In *Standard Edition, 13.* London: Hogarth Press.

Freud, S. (1930). Civilization and its discontents. In *Standard Edition, 21.* London: Hogarth Press.

Freud, S. (1958). Remembering, repeating, and working-through. In *Standard Edition, 12.* London: Hogarth Press.

Frey, E. (2005). *The Hitler syndrome: Dealing with evil in world politics.* Frankfurt: Eichborn.

Freyberg, JT. (1980). Difficulties in separation-individuation as experienced by offspring of Nazi Holocaust survivors. *American Journal of Orthopsychiatry, 50*(1), 87–95.

Freyberger, HJ., & Freyberger, H. (2007). 60 years later: posttraumatic stress disorders, salutogenetic factors and medical expert assessment in Holocaust survivors in the long-term course. *Zeitschrift für Psychosomatische Medizin und Psychotherapie, 53*(4), 380–392.

Friedländer, S. (1990). The Shoah between memory and history. *The Jerusalem Quarterly*, 53, Winter.

Friedländer, S. (1992). Trauma, transference and working-through. *History and Memory, 4,* 39–55.

Friedrich, J. (2002). *Der Brand: Deutschland im Bombenkrieg 1940–1945.* München: Propyläen. [The Fire: Germany in the bombing war 1940–1945].

Fromm, E. (1973). *The anatomy of human destructiveness.* New York: Holt, Rinehart, and Winston.

Funkenstein, A. (1993). The incomprehensible catastrophe: Memory and narrative. In A. Lieblich & R. Josselson (Eds.), *The narrative study of lives,* volume 1. Newbury Park, CA: Sage Publications, 21–29.

Gampel, Y. (1988). Facing war, murder, torture, and death in latency. *Psychoanalytic Review, 75(4),* 500–509.

Gampel, Y. (2000). Reflections on the prevalence of the uncanny in social violence. In A. Robben & M. Suarez-Orozco (Eds.). *Cultures under siege: Collective violence and trauma.* New York: Cambridge University Press.

Gellately, R. (1993). *Die Gestapo und die deutsche Gesellschaft. Die Durchsetzung der Rassenpolitik 1933–1945.* Paderborn: Schöning. [Gestapo and the German society: The implementation of racist policy 1933–1945].

Gellately, R. (2002). *Hingeschaut und weggesehen: Hitler und sein Volk.* Stuttgart, München. [Looking on and looking away: Hitler and his people].

Getreu, E. (1952). Praktisk pedagogik i ett skolhem. *Pedagogisk Tidskift, 88(3–6),* 39–126. [Practical pedagogy in a boarding school].

Gilbert, M. (1996). *The boys: Triumph over adversity.* Toronto: Douglas and McIntyre.

Giordano, R. (1987). *Die zweite Schuld, oder Von der Last Deutscher zu sein.* Hamburg: Rasch & Rohring. [The second guilt, or the burden of being German].

Goldhagen, DJ. (1996). *Hitler's willing executioners: Ordinary Germans and the Holocaust.* New York: Alfred A. Knopf.

Gottschalk, S. (2000). Reli(e)ving the past: Emotion work in the Holocaust's second generation. Retrieved from: http://www.unlv.edu/Faculty/ gottschalk/SecondGen.htm.

Greber, D. (2000). Personal communication.

Greenberg, D. (2006). Israel and the Holocaust. *Together: Newsletter of the American Gathering of Jewish Holocaust Survivors and their Descendants, 20(1),* 3. Retrieved from: http://www.americangathering. com/issues/April2006Tog.pdf.

Greenspan, H. (1998). *On listening to Holocaust survivors: Recounting and life history.* Westport, CT: Praeger.

Grossman, D. (2001). Where death is a way of life. *The Guardian,* May 14.

Götz, A. (2008). *Unser Kampf: 1968—Ein irritierter Blick Zurück.* Franfurt am Main: Fischer. [Our Struggle: 1968—An Irritated Look Back].

Halasz, G., & Kellermann, N. (2005, November). Unconditional hate (Part 1). *Mifgashim, 5.* Also in G. Zygier (Ed.), *ADC Special Report: A periodic publication of the B'nai B'rith Anti-Defamation Commission, 30.*

Halasz, G. (2008, April). Reflections on Kellermann's trauma workshop. *JHC Centre News,* 17–18.

Halbmayr, B. (1995, August/September). *Belastete Begegnung: "Es liegt nicht an uns, unsere Eltern zu versöhnen."* Neue illustrierte Welt (Vienna), 17. [Weighty encounter: "It isn't up to us to reconcile our parents"].

Hantman, S., & Solomon, Z. (2007). Recurrent trauma: Holocaust survivors cope with aging and cancer. *Social Psychiatry and Psychiatric Epidemiology, 42(5),* 396–402.

Harel, Z. (1995). Serving Holocaust survivors and survivor families. *Marriage and Family Review, 21(1–2),* 29–49.

Harel, Z., Kahana, B., & Kahana, E. (1993). Social resource and the mental health of aging Nazi Holocaust survivors and immigrants. In JP. Wilson & B. Raphael (Eds.), *International handbook of traumatic stress syndromes,* 241–252.

Harris, JR. (1995). Where is the child's environment? A group socialisation theory of development. *Psychological Review, 102(3),* 458–489.

Hazani, E., & Shasha, SM. (2008). Effects of the Holocaust on the physical health of the offspring of survivors. *Israel Medical Association Journal, 10,* 251–255.

Heer, H., & Naumann, K. (Eds.).(1995). *Vernichtungskrieg: Verbrechen der Wehrmacht 1941–1944*. Hamburg: HIS. [The war of annihilation: The crime of the German defense forces 1941–1944].

Heimannsberg, B., & Schmidt, CJ. (1989). *Das kollektive Schweigen*. Heidelberg: Edition Humanistische Psychologie. [The Collective Silence].

Heller, D. (1982). Themes of culture and ancestry among children of concentration camp survivors. *Psychiatry, 45*, 247–261.

Helmreich, WB. (1992/1996). *Against all odds: Holocaust survivors and the successful lives they made in America*. New York: Simon & Schuster.

Hemmendinger, J., & Krell, R. (2000). *The Children of Buchenwald: Child survivors of the Holocaust and their adult lives*. Jerusalem: Gefen.

Henisch, P. (1975/2003). *Die kleine Figur meines Vaters*. Wien: Residenz. [The small figure of my father].

Herman, J. (1992). *Trauma and recovery*. New York: Basic Books.

Herman, K., & Thygesen, P. (1954). KZ-syndromet. *Ugeskrift for Læger, 116*, 825–836.

Hertz, DG. (1990). Trauma and nostalgia: New aspects on the coping of aging Holocaust survivors. *Israel Journal of Psychiatry and Related Sciences, 27*(4), 189–198.

Herzl, T. (1896). *The Jewish state: An attempt at a modern solution of the Jewish question*. Ed. JM. Alkow. New York: American Zionist Emergency Council.

Hill, B. (1991). Solomon Fry, survivor. *Anthropology & Humanism Quarterly, 16*(4), 120–128.

Hillberg, R. (1961). *The destruction of European Jews*. Chicago: Quadrangle Books.

HistCite (2008). *Holocaust title search*. Retrieved from: http://www.garfield.library.upenn.edu/histcomp/holocaust_ti/list/py-pubs.html.

Hoffman, G. (2007, August 21). State apologizes to Holocaust survivors. *Jerusalem Post*, p. 6.

Hogman, F. (1995). Memory of the Holocaust. *Echoes of the Holocaust, 4*. Retrieved from: http://www.holocaustechoes.com/4hogman.html.

Huttenbach, HR. (1996). Holocaust or genocide studies? The "apologia rationalis" of the Journal of Genocide Research. *Chronicle of Higher Education*, May 31.

Huxley, A. (1958). *Brave new world revisited*. New York: Harper & Row.

Imber, S., Mkayton, N., Urban, S., Kasten, M., & Hildisch, EM. (2006). Deportationen: Täter, Mitläufer, Opfer. Ein multiperspektivischer Workshop. *International School for Holocaust Studies*, Jerusalem: Yad Vashem. [Deportations: Perpetrators, Cooperators, Victims. A multiperspective workshop].

Janoff-Bulman, R. (1992). *Shattered assumptions: Towards a new psychology of trauma*. New York: The Free Press.

Jaspers, K. (1946). *Die Schuldfrage*. Heidelberg: Schneider. [The question of guilt].

Jelinek, E. (1980). *Die Ausgesperrten*. Reinbek bei Hamburg: Rowohlt.

Jelinek, E. (1995). *Die Kinder der Toten*. Reinbek bei Hamburg: Rowohlt..

Joffe, C., Brodaty, H., Luscombe, G., & Ehrlich, F. (2003). The Sydney Holocaust study: posttraumatic stress disorder and other psychosocial morbidity in an aged community sample. *Journal of Traumatic Stress, 16(1)*, 39–47.

Johnson, E., & Reuband, KH. (2005). *What we knew: Terror, mass murder and everyday life in Nazi Germany*. New York: Basic Books.

Jokl, AM. (1998). Zwei Fälle zum Thema "Bewältigung der Vergangenheit." *Bulletin des Leo Baeck Instituts, 81*, 82–102. [Two case studies to the theme "Mastery of the past"].

Jurgovsky, M. (1998). Nachträgliche Wirksamkeit. In C. Staffa & J. Spielmann (Eds.), *Nachträgliche Wirksamkeit: Vom Aufheben der Taten im Gedenken*. Berlin: Institut für Vergleichende Geschichtswissenschaften, 23–29. [Subsequent effect].

Kahana, B., Harel, Z., & Kahana, E. (2005). Holocaust survivors and immigrants: Late life adaptations. *Springer Series on Stress and Coping, 1-29*.

Kahn, C. (2006). Some determinants of the multigenerational transmission process. *Psychoanalytic Review, 93(1)*, 71–92.

Kaminer, H., & Lavie P. (1991). Sleep and dreaming in Holocaust survivors: Dramatic decrease in dream recall in well-adjusted survivors. *Journal of Nervous & Mental Disease, 179*, 664–669.

Kassai, SC., & Motta, RW. (2006). An investigation of potential Holocaust-related secondary traumatization in the third generation. *International Journal of Emergency Mental Health, 8(1)*, 35–47.

Keilson, H. (1979/1992). *Sequentielle Traumatiesierung bei Kindern.* Stuttgart: Ferdinand Enke Verlag. [English translation: *Sequential traumatization in children.* Jerusalem: Magnes Press].

Keinan, G., Mikulincer, M., & Rybnicki, A. (1988). Perception of self and parents by second-generation Holocaust survivors. *Behavioural Medicine, 14,* 6–12.

Kellermann, N. (1997). *Bibliography: Children of Holocaust survivors.* AMCHA, the National Israeli Center for Psychosocial Support of Holocaust Survivors and the Second Generation, Jerusalem. Retrieved from: http://www.judymeschel.com/coshpsych.htm.

Kellermann, N. (1999). Diagnosis of Holocaust survivors and their children. *Israel Journal of Psychiatry, 36,* 56–65.

Kellermann, N. (2001a). Perceived parental rearing behavior in children of Holocaust survivors. *Israel Journal of Psychiatry and Related Sciences, 38,* 58–68.

Kellermann, N. (2001b). Psychopathology in children of Holocaust survivors: A review of the research literature. *Israel Journal of Psychiatry and Related Sciences, 38,* 36–46.

Kellermann, N. (2001c). The long-term psychological effects and treatment of Holocaust trauma. *Journal of Loss and Trauma, 6,* 197–218.

Kellermann, N. (2001d). Transmission of Holocaust trauma: An integrative view. *Psychiatry: Interpersonal & Biological Processes, 64,* 256–67.

Kellermann, N. (2005, June). Unconditional hate: Anti-Semitism in the contemporary world. *The Jewish Magazine, 91,* Retrieved from: http://www.jewishmag.com/91mag/anti-Semitism/antisemitism.htm.

Kellermann, N. (2008a). Die Kinder der Child Survivors. In H. Radebold, W. Bohleber, & J. Zinnecker (Eds.), *Transgenerationale Weitergabe kriegsbelasteter Kindheiten.* München: Juventa, 57–73. [The children of child survivors].

Kellermann, N. (2008b). Transmitted Holocaust trauma: A curse or a legacy? On the aggravating and mitigating factors of Holocaust transmission. *Israel Journal of Psychiatry, 45,* 263–271.

Kellermann, P.F. (1992). *Focus on Psychodrama.* London: Jessica Kingsley.

Kellermann, P.F. (2007). *Sociodrama and collective trauma.* London: Jessica Kingsley.

Kellermann, PF., & Hudgins, K. (Eds.). (2000). *Psychodrama with trauma survivors: Acting out your pain.* London: Jessica Kingsley.

Kelley, DM. (1947). *22 cells in Nuremberg: A psychiatrist examines the Nazi criminals.* New York: Greenberg.

Kenan, O. (2003). *Between memory and history: The evolution of Israeli historiography of the Holocaust, 1945-1961.* New York: Peter Lang.

Kessler, RC., Sonnega, A., Bromet, E., Hughes, M., & Nelson, CB. (1995). Posttraumatic stress disorder in the national comorbidity survey. *Archives of General Psychiatry, 52,* 1048-1060.

Kestenberg, J., & Brenner, I. (1986). Children who survived the Holocaust. *International Journal of Psychoanalysis, 67,* 309-316.

Kestenberg, J., & Brenner, I. (1996). *The last witness.* Washington, DC: American Psychiatric Press.

Kestenberg, J., & Kahn, C. (1998). *Children surviving persecution: An international study of healing and trauma.* Westport, CT and London: Praeger.

Kestenberg, J. (1982). Survivor-parents and their children. In ME. Bergmann & ME. Jucovy (Eds.), *Generations of the Holocaust.* New York: Columbia University Press, 83-102.

Kestenberg, J. (1985). Child survivors of the Holocaust—40 years later: Reflections and commentary. *Journal of American Academy of Child Psychiatry, 24(4),* 378-380.

Kestenberg, J. (1998). Adult survivors, child survivors, and children of survivors. In J.S. Kestenberg & C. Kahn (Eds.), *Children surviving persecution: An international study of trauma and healing.* Westport, CT: Praeger, 56-65.

Kestenberg, JS. (1989). Transposition revisited: Clinical, therapeutic and developmental considerations. In P. Marcus & A. Rosenberg (Eds.), *Healing their wounds: Psychotherapy with Holocaust survivors and their families.* New York: Praeger, 67-82.

Klein, H. (1968). Problems in the psychotherapeutic treatment of Israeli survivors of the Holocaust. In: Krystal, H. (Ed.), *Massive psychic trauma.* New York: International Universities, 233-248.

Klein, H. (1971). Families of Holocaust survivors in the kibbutz: Psychological studies. *International Psychiatric Clinics, 8(1),* 67-92.

Klein-Parker, F. (1988). Dominant attitudes of adult children of Holocaust survivors toward their parents. In J.P. Wilson & B. Kahana (Eds.), *Human adaptation to extreme stress*. New York: Plenum, 193–217.

Kogan, I. (1995). *The cry of mute children: A psychoanalytic perspective of the second generation of the Holocaust*. London: Free Association Books.

Kohout, E., & Brainin, E. (2004). How is trauma transmitted? *International Journal of Psycho-Analysis, 85*, 1261–1264.

Kohut, H. (1978-1991). *The search for the self. Selected writings of Heinz Kohut: 1950–1981*. P. Ornstein (Ed.), four volumes. New York: International Universities Press.

Kolb, CC. (1985). Commentary. *Integrative Psychiatry, 3*, 120–123.

Kranz, T. (1999). *Unterwegs*. In *Was bleibt von der Vergangenheit: Die junge Generation im Dialog uber den Holocaust*. Mit einem Beitrag von Roman Herzog. Berlin: Ch. Links Verlag. [On the way. What is left from the past: The young generation in dialogue on the Holocaust].

Krell, R., & Sherman MI. (Eds.). (1997). *Medical and psychological effects of concentration camps on Holocaust survivors: a bibliography*. New Brunswick & London: Transaction Publishers.

Krell, R. (1982). Family therapy with children of concentration camp survivors. *American Journal of Psychotherapy, 36*, 513–522.

Krell, R. (1985a). Child survivors of the Holocaust: 40 years later. *Journal of the American Academy of Child Psychiatry, 24(4)*, 378–380.

Krell, R. (1985b). Therapeutic value of documenting child survivors. *Journal of the American Academy of Child Psychiatry, 24(4)*, 397–400.

Krell, R. (1993). Child survivors of the Holocaust: Strategies of adaptation. *Canadian Journal of Psychiatry, 38*, 384–389.

Krell, R. (1999). Facing memories: Silent no more. *Newsletter published by the Hidden Child Foundation/ADL*. Retrieved from: http://www.adl.org/hidden/v6/memories.asp.

Krell, R. (2001). The psychological challenges facing child survivors of the Holocaust, hidden or otherwise. In R. Krell (Ed.), *Messages and memories: Reflections on child survivors of the Holocaust*. Vancouver, BC: Memory Press.

Krell, R. (2006). Child survivors of the Holocaust: The elderly children and their adult lives. An introduction. In MI. Glassner & R. Krell (Eds.), *And life is changed forever: Holocaust childhoods remembered.* Detroit, MI: Wine State University Press, 11.

Krondorfer, B. (1995). *Remembrance and reconciliation: Encounters between young Jews and Germans.* New Haven: Yale University Press.

Krondorfer, B., Loewy, H., Brocke, E., Rosenthal, G., Strauß, D., Strohl, I., & Bar-On, D. (1998). Begegnung als Bearbeitungsform der nachträglichen Wirksamkeit des Holocaust. Podiumsdiskussion. In C. Staffa & K. Klinger (Eds.), *Die Gegenwart der Geschichte des Holocaust.* Berlin: Institut für vergleichende Geschichtswissenschaften, 11–142. [The presence of the history of the Holocaust.]

Krystal, H., & Danieli, Y. (1994). Holocaust survivor studies in the context of PTSD. *PTSD Research Quarterly, 5(4),* Vermont: National Center for Post-Traumatic Stress Disorders.

Krystal, H., & Niederland WG. (1968). Clinical observations on the survivor syndrome. In H. Krystal (Ed.), *Massive psychic trauma.* New York: International Universities, 327–348.

Krystal, H., & Niederland, WG. (Eds.). (1971). *Psychic traumatization: Aftereffects in individuals and communities.* Boston, MA: Little, Brown.

Krystal, H. (1981). The aging survivor of the Holocaust. *Journal of Geriatric Psychiatry, 14,* 165–189.

Krystal, H. (1993). Beyond the DSM-III-R: Therapeutic considerations in posttraumatic stress disorder. In JP. Wilson & B. Raphael (Eds.), *International handbook of traumatic stress syndromes.* New York: Plenum, 841–854.

Krystal, H. (Ed.).(1968). *Massive psychic trauma.* New York: International Universities Press.

Kuch, K., & Cox, BJ. (1992). Symptoms of PTSD in 124 survivors of the Holocaust. *American Journal of Psychiatry, 149(3),* 337–340.

Kulka, OD., & Jäckel, E. (Eds.).(2004). *Die Juden in den geheimen NS Stimmungs-berichten 1933–1945.* Düsseldorf: Droste, volume 34 of Yad Vashem Studies.

Kurtz, C. (1995). The second generation. *Jewish Action Magazine.* Orthodox Union of America.

Kuwert, P., Spitzer, C., Träder, A., Freyberger, HJ., & Ermann, M. (2006). Sixty years later: Post-traumatic stress symptoms and current psychopathology in former German children of World War II. *International Psychogeriatrics*, 1–7.

Lamet, A., & Dyer, J. (2004). Risk and resilience: Reactions of elderly Jewish Holocaust survivors to current terrorist events. *Journal of Multicultural Nursing & Health*. Retrieved from: http://findarticles.com/p/articles/mi_qa3919/is_200401/ai_n9361146/pg_1?tag=artBody;col1.

Landau, R., & Litwin, H. (2000). The effects of extreme early stress in very old age. *The Journal of Traumatic Stress, 13(1)*, 473–488.

Lang, B. (1988). *Writing and the Holocaust*. New York: Holmes & Meier.

Langer, L. (1991). *Holocaust testimonies: The ruins of memory*. New Haven, CT: Yale University Press.

Langer, L. (1995a). *Admitting the Holocaust*. New York: Oxford University Press.

Langer, L. (1995b). *Art from the ashes: A Holocaust anthology*. New York: Oxford University Press, 1995.

Langer, WC. (1972). *The mind of Adolf Hitler*. New York: Basic Books.

Latane, B., & Darley, JM. (1970). *The unresponsive bystander: Why doesn't he help?* New York: Appleton-Century-Crofts.

Laub, D., & Auerhahn, NC. (1993). Knowing and not knowing massive psychic trauma: forms of traumatic memory. *The International journal of psycho-analysis, 74*, 287–302.

Laub, D., Sussillo, M., Itzkowitz, S., Behm, A., Loew, C., Richman, S., & Metzger-Brown, E. (2007). Last witnesses: Child survivors of the Holocaust. Roundtable discussion. *Psychoanalytic Perspectives: A Journal of Integration and Innovation, 4(2)*, 51–75.

Lebert, S., & Lebert, N. (2000). *Denn Du trägst meinen Namen*. Back Bay Books. [My father's keeper: Children of Nazi leaders].

Leon, GR., Butcher, IN., Kleinman, M., Goldberg, A., & Almagor, M. (1981). Survivors of the Holocaust and their children: Current status and adjustment. *Journal of Personality & Social Psychology, 41*, 503–516.

Lester, D. (2005). *Suicide and the Holocaust*. New York: Nova Science.

Letzter-Pouw, S., & Werner, P. (2005). Correlates of intrusive memories and avoidance of memories of the Holocaust. *Israel Journal of Psychiatry & Related Sciences, 42(4),* 271–277.

Levav, I. (2009). The psychiatric epidemiology of the after-effects of the Holocaust among Israeli survivors and their offspring. In I. Levav (Ed.), *Psychiatric and behavioral disorders in Israel: From epidemiology to mental health action.* Jerusalem: Gefen, 104–130.

Levav, I., & Abramson JH. (1984). Emotional distress among concentration camp survivors: A community study in Jerusalem. *Psychological Medicine, 14(1),* 215–218.

Levav, I., Levinson, D., Radomislensky, I., Shemesh, A., & Kohn, R. (2007). Psychopathology and other health dimensions among the offspring of Holocaust survivors: Results from the Israel National Health Survey. *Israel Journal of Psychiatry, 44,* 144–151.

Levi, P. (1988). *The drowned and the saved.* New York: Summit.

Levine, HB. (1982). Toward a psychoanalytic understanding of children of survivors of the Holocaust. *Psychoanalytic Quarterly, 51,* 70–92.

Levinger, L. (1962). Psychiatrische Untersuchungen in Israel an 800 Fällen mit Gesundheitschaden-Förderungen wegen Nazi-Verfolgung. *Nervenarzt, 33,* 75–80. [Psychiatric investigations in Israel of 800 cases of health claims because of Nazi persecution].

Lev-Wiesel, R., & Amir, M. (2004). Lost childhood: Children surviving the Holocaust. In TA. Corales (Ed.), *Trends in posttraumatic stress disorder research.* New York: Nova Science, 129–156.

Lev-Wiesel, R., & Amir, M. (2000). Posttraumatic stress disorder symptoms, psychological distress, personal resources, and quality of life in four groups of Holocaust child survivors. *Family Process, 39(4),* 445–460.

Lev-Wiesel, R., & Amir, M. (2003). Posttraumatic growth among Holocaust child survivors. *Journal of Loss and Trauma, 8(4),* 229–237.

Lichtman, H. (1984). Parental communication of Holocaust experiences and personality characteristics among second-generation survivors. *Journal of Clinical Psychology, 40(4),* 914–924.

Lifton, RJ. (1979/1983). *The broken connection: On death and the continuity of life.* New York: Basic Books.

Lifton, RJ. (1986). *The Nazi doctors: Medical killing and the psychology of genocide.* New York: Basic Books.

Lifton, RJ. (1993). *The protean self: Human resilience in an age of fragmentation.* New York: Basic Books.

Lis-Turleiska, M., Luszczynska, A., Plichta, A., & Benight, CC. (2008). Jewish and non-Jewish World War II child and adolescent survivors at 60 years after war: Effects of parental loss and age at exposure on well-being. *American Journal of Orthopsychiatry, 78(3),* 369–377.

Loew, C. (2007). Roundtable discussion. *Psychoanalytic Perspectives. A Journal of Integration and Innovation, 4(2).*

Lombardo, KL., & Motta, RM. (2008). Secondary trauma in children of parents with mental illness. *Traumatology, 14(3),* 57–67.

Lomranz, J. (1995). Endurance and living: Long-term effects of the Holocaust. In SE. Hobfoll & MW. deVries (Eds.), *Extreme stress and the communities: Impact and intervention.* Amsterdam: Kluwer, 325–352.

Lomranz, J. (2000). The skewed image of the Holocaust survivor and the vicissitudes of psychological research. *Echoes of the Holocaust, 6,* 5-9.

Longerich, P. (2006). *Davon haben wir nichts gewusst!: die Deutschen und die Judenverfolgung 1933–1945.* München: Siedler. [From that we didn't know! The Germans and the persecution of the Jews 1933–1945].

Lowin, RG. (1983). Cross-generational transmission of pathology in Jewish families of Holocaust survivors. California School of Professional Psychology, San Diego. *Dissertation Abstracts International, 44,* 3533.

Lurie-Beck, JK., Liossis, P., & Gow, K. (2008). Relationships between psychopathological and demographic variables and posttraumatic growth among Holocaust survivors. *Traumatology, 14,* 28.

Marcus, EL., & Menczel, J. (2007). Higher prevalence of osteoporosis among female Holocaust survivors. *Osteoporosis International, 18(11),* 1501–1506.

Marks, S. (2009). Über Nationalsozialismus, Scham und die Folgen. In MN. Ebertz, W. Nickolai, & R. Walter-Hamann (Eds.), *Opfer, Täter und Institutionen in der nationalsoziatistischen Gesellschaft: Blicke aus der Gegenwart.* Konstanz: Hartung-Gorre Verlag, 75–88. [On National Socialism, shame and its consequences].

Märthesheimer, P., & Frenzel, I. (1979). *Im Kreuzfeuer: Der Fernsehfilm Holocaust.* Frankfurt a.M.: Fischer. [In the cross fire: The TV film "Holocaust"].

Merten, J. (1995, August, 26). Brückenschlag der Kinder: Das Schweigen durchbrechen. *Berliner Morgenpost*, p. 26. [The children's bridge-building: To break through the silence].

Metzger-Brown, E. (1998). The transmission of trauma through caretaking patterns of behaviour in Holocaust families: Re-enactment in a facilitated long-term second-generation group. *Smith College Studies in Social Work, 68(3)*, 267–285.

Metzger-Brown, E. (2007). A child survivor of the Holocaust comes out of hiding: Two stories of trauma. *Psychoanalytic Perspectives: A Journal of Integration and Innovation, 4(2)*, 51–75.

Milgram, S. (1974). *Obedience to authority: An experimental view*. New York: Harper & Row.

Mitscherlich, A., & Mitscherlich, M. (1967). *The inability to mourn*. Munich: Fischer.

Moses, R., & Cohen, Y. (1993). An Israeli view. In R. Moses (Ed.), *Persistent shadows of the Holocaust: The meaning to those not directly affected*. New York: International Universities Press, 119–153.

Moskovitz, M. (1985). Longitudinal follow-up of child survivors of the Holocaust. *Journal of the American Academy of Child Psychiatry, 24*, 401–407.

Moskovitz, S. (1983). *Love despite hate: Child survivors of the Holocaust and their adult lives*. New York: Schocken.

Motro, HS. (1996, April 19). Children of Holocaust survivors remembering in their own way. *International Herald Tribune*. Retrieved from: http://www.nytimes.com/1996/04/19/opinion/19iht-edhelen.t.html.

Müller-Hohagen, J. (1994/2002). Geschichte in uns. Psychogramme aus dem Alltag. München: Knesebeck (2. Auflage 2002 unter dem Titel Geschichte in uns. Seelische Auswirkungen bei den Nachkommen von NS-Tätern und Mitläufern. Berlin: Pro Business). [History in us].

Müller-Hohagen, J. (2005). *Verleugnet, verdrängt, verschwiegen*. Seelische Nachwirkungen der NS-Zeit und Wege zu ihrer Überwindung. München: Kösel. [Denied, repressed, silenced].

Müller-Hohagen, J. (2008). Übermittlung von Täterhaftigkeit an die nachfolgenden Generationen. In H. Radebold, W. Bohleber, & J. Zinnecker (Eds.), *Transgenerationale Weitergabe kriegsbelasteter Kindheiten*. Weinheim: Juventa, 155–164. [Transmission of perpetratorship on the following generations].

Munn, S. (2001a). The Austrian encounter. In A. Kimenyi& O. Scott (Eds.), *Anatomy of genocide: State-sponsored mass-killings in the twentieth century.* New York: Edwin Mellen Press.

Munn, S. (2001b). The Austrian Encounter. In E. Lappin & B. Schneider (Eds.), *Die Lebendigkeit der Geschichte. Dis-Kontinuitäten in Diskursen über den Nationalsozialismus.* St. Ingbert: Röhrig Universitätsverlag. [The aliveness of history. (Dis-)continuations in discourses regarding National Socialism].

Nadler, A. (2001). The victims and the psychologist: Changing perceptions of Israeli Holocaust survivors by the mental health community in the past 50 years. *History of Psychology, 4,* 159–181.

Naor, A. (2003). Lessons of the Holocaust versus territories for peace, 1967–2001. *Israel Studies, 8(1),* 130–152.

Naor, Y. (1999). The theater of the Holocaust. In SK. Levine & EG. Levine (Eds.), *Foundations of expressive arts therapy: Theoretical and clinical perspectives.* London: Jessica Kingsley.

Natan, TS., Eitinger, L., & Winnik, H.Z. (1964). A psychiatric study of survivors of the Nazi Holocaust: A study in hospitalized patients. *Israel Annals of Psychiatry & Related Disciplines, 2,* 47–76.

Ne'eman Arad, G. (1997, June). The Holocaust as an Israeli experience. *The Pennsylvania Gazette, 95(8).* Retrieved from: http://www.upenn.edu/gazette/0697/israeli.html.

Nessman, R. (2005, January 25). For Israel, the wounds of the Holocaust remain fresh. *Associated Press.* Retrieved from: http://sfgate.com/cgi-bin/article.cgi?file=/news/archive/2005/01/25/international1429EST0642.DTL.

Neumann, W. (1999). Spurensuche als psychologische Erinnerungsarbeit. Tübingen: dgvt-Verlag. [Search for traces as psychological memory work].

Niederland, WG. (1964). Psychiatric disorders among persecution victims. *Journal of Neurological and Mental Disturbances, 139,* 458–474.

Niederland, WG. (1971). Introducing notes on the concept, definition and range of psychiatric trauma. In H. Krystal & WG. Niederland (Eds.), *Psychic traumatization: Aftereffects in individuals and communities.* Boston, MA: Little, Brown, 1–9.

Niederland, WG. (1972). Clinical observations on the survivor syndrome. In RS. Parker (Ed.), *The emotional stress of war, violence, and peace.* Pittsburgh, PA: Stanwix.

Niederland, WG. (1981). The survivor syndrome: Further observations and dimensions. *Journal of the American Psychoanalytic Association, 29(2),* 413–425.

Niederland, WG. (1988). The clinical after effects of the Holocaust in survivors and their offspring. In RL. Braham (Ed.), *The psychological perspectives of the Holocaust and of its aftermath.* Boulder, CO: Social Sciences Monographs, 45–52.

Niewyk, DL. (Ed.).(1998, March 4). *Fresh wounds: Early narratives of Holocaust survival.* Chapel Hill, NC: The University of North Carolina Press.

Nutkiewicz, M. (2003). Shame, guilt, and anguish in Holocaust survivor testimony. *The Oral History Review, 30(1),* 1–22.

Ohry, A., & Shasha, SM. (2006). Late morbidity among Holocaust survivors: myth or fact? *Harefuah, 145(4),* 250–253.

Oliner, SP., & Oliner, PM. (1988). *The altruistic personality: Rescuers of Jews in Nazi Europe.* New York: Free Press.

Padover, SK (2001). *Lügendetektor. Vernehmungen im besiegten Deutschland 1944/45.* Econ Tb. [Lie-detector: Interrogations in defeated Germany].

Parens, H., Mahfouz, A., Twemlow, SW., & Scharff, DE. (Eds.).(2007). *The future of prejudice: Psychoanalysis and the prevention of prejudice.* Lanham, MD: Rowman & Littlefield.

Pauley, BF. (1996). Austria. In SD. Wyman (Ed.), *The world reacts to the Holocaust.* Baltimore/London: The John Hopkins University Press, 473–513.

Perry, BD. (1999). Memories of fear: How the brain stores and retrieves physiological states, feelings, behaviors, and thoughts from traumatic events. In J. Goodwin, & R. Attias (Eds.), *Images of the body in trauma.* New York: Basic Books.

Picard, M. (1946). *Hitler in uns selbst.* Erlenbach: Rentsch. [Hitler In Ourselves].

Pillar, G., Malhotra, A., & Lavie, P. (2000). Post-traumatic stress disorder and sleep—what a nightmare! *Sleep Medicine Reviews, 4(2),* 183–200.

Podietz, L., Zwerling, I., Ficher, I., Belmont, H., Eisenstein, T., Shapiro, M., & Levick, M. (1984). Engagement in families of Holocaust survivors. *Journal of Marital and Family Therapy, 10,* 43–51.

Pollack, M. (2004/2006). *The dead man in the bunker: Discovering my father.* London: Faber. [German: Der Tote im Bunker].

Pollak, A. (2005). *Opferstaat und Tätergesellschaft. Das Jubiläumsjahr als Schaubild des Umgangs mit der NS-Vergangenheit in Österreich.* Retrieved from: http://www.kbk.at/refugius/symposien/pollak2005.html.

Porat, D. (1986). *Trapped leadership.* Tel Aviv: Am Oved.

Prince, RM. (1985). Second generation effects of historical trauma. *Psychoanalytic Review, 72(1),* 9–29.

Pross, C. (2001). *Wiedergutmachung: Der Kleinkrieg gegen die Opfer.* Berlin: Philo Verlagsgesellschaft. [Compensation: The little war against the victims.]

Radebold, H. (2000). *Abwesende Väter und Kriegskindheit. Fortbestehende Folgen in Psychoanalysen.* Göttingen: Vandenhoeck & Ruprecht. 3. Aufl. 2004. [Distant fathers and war childhood].

Radebold, H. (2005). *Die dunklen Schatten unserer Vergangenhet.* Stuttgart: Klett-Cotta. [The dark shadows of our past].

Radebold, H. (Ed.)(2003/2004). *Kindheiten im II. Weltkrieg und ihre Folgen,* volume 92. Giessen: Psychosozial Verlag. [Childhood in World War II and their consequences].

Ratiner, C. (2000). Child abuse treatment research: Current concerns and challenges. In RM. Reece (Ed.), *Treatment of child abuse: Common ground for mental health, medical, and legal practitioners.* Baltimore: Johns Hopkins University Press, 362–370.

Reulbach, U., Bleich, S., Biermann, T., Pfahlberg, A., & Sperling, W. (2007). Late-onset schizophrenia in child survivors of the holocaust. *The Journal of Nervous and Mental Disease, 195(4),* 315–319.

Robinson, S, Rapaport-Bar-Sever, M., & Rapaport J. (1994). The present state of people who survived the Holocaust as children. *Acta Psychiatrica Scandinavica, 89,* 242–245.

Robinson, S., & Hemmendinger, J. (1982). Psychosocial adjustment 30 years later of people who were in Nazi concentration camps as children. In CD. Spielberger, IG. Sarrason, & N. Milgram (Eds.), *Stress and Anxiety,* vol. 18. New York: Hemisphere.

Robinson, S. (1979). Late effects of persecution in persons who as children or young adolescents survived Nazi occupation in Europe. *Israel Annals of Psychiatry and Related Disciplines, 17(3)*, 209–214.

Robinson, S., Hemmendinger, J. Netanel, R., Rapaport, M., Zilberman, L., & Gal, A. (1994). Retraumatization of Holocaust survivors during the Gulf War and SCUD missile attacks on Israel. *British Journal of Medical Psychology, 67(4)*, 353–362.

Robinson, S., Rapaport, J., Durst, R., Rapaport, M., Rosca, P., Metzer, S., & Zilberman, L. (1990). The late effects of Nazi persecution among elderly Holocaust survivors. *Acta Psychiatrica Scandinavica, 82(4)*, 311–315.

Robinson, S., Rapaport-Bar-Sever, M., & Rapaport, J. (1997). Orphaned child survivors compared to child survivors whose parents also survived the Holocaust. *Echoes of the Holocaust, 5.*

Rommelspacher, B. (1995). *Schuldlos—Schuldig? Wie Sich Junge Frauen Mit Dem Antisemitismus Auseinandersetzen.* Hamburg: Konkret Literatur. [Guilty—Not Guilty? How young German women concern themselves with anti-Semitism].

Rosen, J., Reynolds, CF., Yeager, AL., Houck, PR., & Hurwitz, LF. (1991). Sleep disturbances in survivors of the Nazi Holocaust. *American Journal of Psychiatry, 148,* 62–66.

Rosenbaum, AS. (Ed.). (1996). *Is the Holocaust unique? Perspectives on comparative genocide.* Boulder, CO: Westview.

Rosenberg, R. (1998). *Explaining Hitler: The search for the origins of his evil.* New York: Random House.

Rosenberger, L. (1973). Children of survivors. In EJ. Anthony & C. Koupernik (Eds.), *The child in his family: The impact of disease and death.* New York: Wiley, 375–377.

Rosenthal, G. (Ed.) (1997). *Der Holocaust im Leben von drei Generationen. Familien von Überlebenden der Shoah und von Nazi-Tätern.* Gießen: Psychosozial.

Rossberg, A., & Lansen, J. (2003). *Das Schweigen brechen. Berliner Lektionen zu den Spätfolgen der Schoa.* Berlin-New York: Peter Lang. [Breaking the silence: Berlin lessons about the late consequences of the Shoah].

Rothberg, M. (2000). *Traumatic realism: The demands of Holocaust representation.* Minneapolis, MN: University of Minnesota Press.

Rowland-Klein, D., & Dunlop, R. (1998). The transmission of trauma across generations: identification with parental trauma in children of Holocaust survivors. *Australian and New Zealand Journal of Psychiatry, 32(3),* 358–369.

Sabini, J., & Silver, M. (1980). Destroying the innocent with a clear conscience: A socio-psychology of the Holocaust. In J. Dimsdale (Ed.), *Survivors, victims, and perpetrators: Essays on the Nazi Holocaust,* 329–359. Reprinted in NJ. Kressel (Ed.), (1993). *Political psychology: Classic and contemporary readings.* New York: Paragon House, 192–217.

Sadavoy, J. (1997). Survivors: A review of late-life effects of prior psychological trauma. *American Journal of Geriatric Psychiatry, 5(4),* 287–301.

Sagi-Schwartz, A., Van Ijzendoor, MH., & Bakermans-Kranenburg, MJ. (2008). Does intergenerational transmission of trauma skip a generation? No meta-analytic evidence for tertiary traumatization with third generation of Holocaust survivors. *Attachment & Human Development, 10(2),* 105–121.

Sagi-Schwartz, A., Van IJzendoorn, MH., Grossmann, KE., Joels, T. Grossmann, K., Scharf, M., Koren-Karie, N., & Alkalay, S. (2003). Attachment and traumatic stress in female Holocaust child survivors and their daughters. *American Journal of Psychiatry, 160,* 1086–1092.

Salpeter, E. (2001, January 31). The Holocaust belongs to everyone. *Haaretz.*

Santayana G. (1905). *The life of reason or the phases of human progress,* volume 1. Prometheus Books.

Sartre, J-P. (1946). *Anti-Semite and Jew.* New York: Schocken. [French: Reflexions sur la Question Juive].

Scharf, M. (2007). Long-term effects of trauma: Psychosocial functioning of the second and third generation of Holocaust survivors. *Development and Psychopathology, 19(2),* 603–622.

Schiff, H. (1995). *Holocaust poetry.* New York: St. Martin's Press.

Schreiber, S., Soskolne, V., Kozohovitch, H., & Deviri, E. (2003). Holocaust survivors coping with open heart surgery decades later: posttraumatic symptoms and quality of life. *General Hospital Psychiatry, 26(6),* 443–452.

Schützenberger, AA. (1998). *The ancestor syndrome.* London: Routledge.

Schützenberger, AA. (2000). Health and death: Hidden links through the family tree. In PF. Kellermann. & K. Hudgins (Eds.), *Psychodrama with trauma survivors: Acting out your pain.* London: Jessica Kingsley, 283–298.

Schwartz, S., Dohrenwend, BP., & Levav I. (1994). Nongenetic familial transmission of psychiatric disorders? Evidence from children of Holocaust survivors. *Journal of Health Social Behavior, 35,* 385–402.

Sears, RR., Maccoby, EE., & Levin, H. (1957). *Patterns of child rearing.* New York: Harper & Row.

Segal, J. (1986). *Winning life's toughest battles: Roots of human resilience.* New York: Ivy.

Segev, T. (2000). *The seventh million: The Israelis and the Holocaust.* New York: Henry Holt.

Seifter Abrams, M. (1999). Intergenerational transmission of trauma: Recent contributions from the literature of family systems approaches to treatment. *American Journal of Psychotherapy, 53(2),* 225–231.

Seritan, AL., Gabbard, GO., & Benjamin, L. (2006). War and peace: Psychotherapy with a Holocaust survivor. *American Journal of Psychiatry, 163(10),* 1705–1709.

Shalev, A. (2002, April 9). Holocaust memorial day address at Yad Vashem. *Jerusalem Post,* p. 5.

Shamai, M., & Levin-Megged, O. (2006). The myth of creating an integrative story: The therapeutic experience of Holocaust survivors. *Qualitative Health Research, 16(5),* 692–712.

Shanan, J., & Shahar, O. (1983). Cognitive and personality functioning of Jewish Holocaust survivors during the midlife transition (46–65) in Israel. *Archives für Psychologie, 135,* 275–294.

Shanan, J. (1989). Surviving the survivors: Late personality development of Jewish Holocaust survivors. *International Journal of Mental Health, 17,* 42–71.

Sharansky, N. (2004). 3D test of anti-Semitism: Demonization, double standards, delegitimization. *Jewish Political Studies Review, 16,* 3–4.

Shefler, G., Brom, D., Greenberg, D., & Witztum, E. (Eds.). (2007). *Trauma, loss, and renewal in Israel: Selected papers of Prof. Haim Dasberg.* Jerusalem: Herzog Hospital.

Sheleg, Y. (2001, June 29). Profits of doom. *Haaretz.*

Shlonsky, A. (1972–1973). *The complete works of Avraham Shlonsky.* Tel Aviv: Sifriat Poalim.

Shmotkin, D., Blumstein, T., & Modan, B. (2003). Tracing long-term effects of early trauma: a broad-scope view of Holocaust survivors in late life. *Journal of Consulting & Clinical Psychology, 71(2),* 223–234.

Shmotkin, D., & Lomranz, J. (1998). Subjective well-being among Holocaust survivors: an examination of overlooked differentiations. *Journal of Personal Social Psychology, 75(1),* 141–155.

Shoshan, T. (1989). Mourning and longing from generation to generation. *American Journal of psychotherapy, 43(2),* 193–207.

Shuval, JT. (1957). Some persistent effects of trauma: Five years after the Nazi concentration camps. *Social Problems, 5(3),* 230–243.

Sicher, E. (1998). *Breaking crystal: Writing and memory after Auschwitz.* Chicago: University of Illinois Press.

Sichrovsky, P. (1987). *Schuldig Geboren.* Koln: Kiepenheuer & Witsch. [*Born guilty: Children of Nazi families.* 1988.] New York: Basic Books.

Sigal, JJ. & Weinfeld M. (1989). *Trauma and rebirth: Intergenerational effects of the Holocaust.* New York: Praeger.

Sigal, JJ. & Weinfeld, M. (2001). Do children cope better than adults with potentially traumatic stress? A 40-year follow-up of Holocaust survivors. *Psychiatry, 64(1),* 69–80.

Sigal, JJ. (1998). Long-term effects of the Holocaust: Empirical evidence for resilience in the first, second, and third generation. *Psychoanalytic Review, 85,* 579–585.

Sikron, M. (1957). *Immigration to Israel from 1948 to 1953.* Jerusalem: Falk Center.

Simenauer, E. (1978). A double helix: Some determinants of the self-perpetuation of Nazism. *Psychoanalytic Study of the Child, 33,* 411–425.

Sindler, AJ., Wellman, NS., & Stier, OB. (2004). Holocaust survivors report long-term effects on attitudes toward food. *Journal of Nutrition Education and Behavior, 36(4),* 169–224.

Smith, HW. (2002). *The Holocaust and other genocides: History, representation, ethics.* Nashville: Vanderbilt University Press.

Solomon, SD., & Johnson, DM. (2002). Psychosocial treatment of posttraumatic stress disorder: A practice-friendly review of outcome research. *Journal of Clinical Psychology, 58,* 947–959.

Solomon, Z., & Prager, E. (1992). Elderly Israeli Holocaust survivors during the Persian Gulf War: A study of psychological distress. *American Journal of Psychiatry, 149,* 1707–1710.

Solomon, Z. (1998). Transgenerational effects of the Holocaust: The Israeli research perspective. In Y. Danieli (Ed.), *International handbook of multigenerational legacies of trauma.* New York & London: Plenum, 69–84.

Solomon, Z., Neria, Y., & Ram, A. (1998). Mental health professionals' responses to loss and trauma of Holocaust survivors. In JH. Harvey (Ed.), *Perspectives on loss: A sourcebook.* Philadelphia: Brunner/Mazel, 221–230.

Sorscher, N., & Cohen LJ. (1997). Trauma in children of Holocaust survivors: Transgenerational effects. *American Journal of Orthopsychiatry, 67,* 493–500.

Spiegel-survey (1992). Mehr Verdrängt als bewältigt: Die Einstellung der Deutschen und der Juden zueinander. *Spiegel Spezial, 2,* 61-73. [More repressed than worked through: The attitudes of the German and the Jews to one another].

Spiegelman, A. (1991). *Maus: A survivor's tale.* New York: Pantheon Books.

Staffa, C., & Klinger, K. (1998). *Die Gegenwart der Geschichte des Holocaust.* Berlin: Institut für vergleichende Geschichtswissenschaften. [The presence of the history of the Holocaust].

Staffa, C., & Spielmann, J. (Eds.).(1998). *Nachträgliche Wirksamkeit: Vom Aufheben der Taten im Gedenken.* Berlin: Institut für Vergleichende Geschichts-wissenschaften. [The late effects: On the traces of deeds in memory].

Staffa, C. (1998). Arbeitsgruppen 1: Tradierund und Kommunikation. In CS taffa & K. Klinger (Eds.), *Die Gegenwart der Geschichte des Holocaust.* Berlin: Institut für vergleichende Geschichtswissenschaften, 71–110. [The presence of the history of the Holocaust].

Stark, H. (1978). Other Gestapo men explain. In R. Chartock & J. Spencer (Eds.), *The Holocaust years: Society on Trial,* 127–128.

Staub, E. (1989). *The roots of evil: The origins of genocide and other group violence.* New York: Cambridge University Press.

Staub, E. (1999). The roots of evil: Social conditions, culture, personality, and basic human needs. *Personality and Social Psychological Review, 3(3),* 179–192.

Stessman, J., Cohen, A., Hammerman-Rozenberg, R., Bursztyn, M., Azoulay, D., Maaravi, Y., & Jacobs, JM. (2008). Holocaust survivors in old age: the Jerusalem longitudinal study. *Journal of American Geriatric Society, 56(3),* 470–477.

Strous, RD., Weiss, M., Felsen, I., Finkel, B., Melamed, Y. Bleich, A., Kotler, M., & Laub, D. (2005). Video testimony of long-term hospitalized psychiatrically ill Holocaust survivors. American *Journal of Psychiatry, 162(12),* 2287–2294.

Suedfeld, P. (1997). Reactions to societal trauma: Distress and/or eustress. *Political Psychology, 18(4),* 849–861.

Suedfeld, P. (1998). Homo invictus: The indomitable species. *Canadian Psychology, 38,* 164–173.

Suedfeld, P. (2002). *Life after the ashes: The postwar pain, and resilience, of young Holocaust survivors.* United States Holocaust Memorial Museum: Center for Advanced Studies. Washington, DC, 1–24.

Suedfeld, P. (Ed.) (2001). Light *from the ashes: Social science careers of young Holocaust refugees and survivors.* Ann Arbor: University of Michigan Press.

Suedfeld, P., Krell, R., Wiebe, R., & Steel, GD. (1997). Coping strategies in the narratives of Holocaust survivors. *Anxiety, Stress, & Coping, 10,* 153–179.

Swiss Banks (2000, September 11). Holocaust Victims Assets Litigation. *Special Master's Proposal.*

Terno, P., Barak, Y., Hadjez, J., Elizur, A., & Szor, H. (1998). Holocaust survivors hospitalized for life: The Israeli experience. *Comprehensive Psychiatry, 39(6),* 364–367.

Terr, L. (1990). *Too scared to cry: Psychic trauma in childhood.* New York: Harper & Row.

Thomsett, MC. (1997). *The German opposition to Hitler: The resistance, the underground, and assassination plots, 1938–1945.* New York: McFarland.

Thygesen, P. Hermann, K., & Willanger, R. (1970). Concentration camp survivors in Denmark: persecution, disease, disability, compensation: A 23-year follow-up. *Danish Medical Bulletin, 17,* 65–108.

Titelman, D. (2006). Primo Levi's loneliness: psychoanalytic perspectives on suicide-nearness. *Psychoanalytic Quarterly, 75(3),* 835–858.

Trappler, B., Cohen, CI., & Tulloo, R. (2007). Impact of early lifetime trauma in later life: depression among Holocaust survivors 60 years after the liberation of Auschwitz. *American Journal of Geriatric Psychiatry, 15(1),* 79–83.

Turner, HA., Finkelhor, D., & Ormrod, R. (2006). The effect of lifetime victimization on the mental health of children and adolescents. *Social Science & Medicine, 62,* 13–27.

Turner, RJ., & Lloyd, DA. (1995). Lifetime traumas and mental health: The significance of cumulative adversity. *Journal of Health and Social Behavior, 36(4),* 360–376.

Updegraff, JA., & Taylor, SE. (2000). From vulnerability to growth: Positive and negative effects of stressful life events. In J. Harvey & E. Miller (Eds.), *Loss and trauma: General and close relationship perspectives.* Philadelphia, PA: Brunner-Routledge, 3–29.

Urban, S. (2004). Anti-Semitism in Germany today: Its roots and tendencies. *Jewish Political Studies Review, 16(3-4).* Retrieved from: http://www.jcpa.org/JCPA/Templates/ShowPage.asp?DRIT=3&DBID =1&LNGID=1&TMID=111&FID=625&PID=863&IID=1072&TTL= Anti-Semitism_In_Germany_Today:_Its_Roots_And_Tendencies.

Urban, S. (2008). Representations of the Holocaust in today's Germany: Between justification and empathy. *Jewish Political Studies Review, 20(1-2).* Retrieved from: http://www.jcpa.org/JCPA/Templates/ ShowPage.asp?DRIT=5&DBID=1&LNGID=1&TMID=111&FID=625 &PID=0&IID=2219&TTL=Representations_of_the_Holo-caust_in_ Today's_Germany:_Between_Justification_and_Empathy.

Valent, P. (1995a). Documented childhood trauma (Holocaust): Its sequel and applications to other traumas. *Psychiatry, Psychology and Law, 2,* 81–89.

Valent, P. (1995b). Survival strategies: a framework for understanding secondary traumatic stress and coping in helpers. In C.R. Figley (Ed.), *Compassion fatigue: Secondary traumatic stress disorder in helpers.* New York: Brunner/Mazel.

Valent, P. (1998). *From survival to fulfillment: a framework for the life-trauma dialectic.* Philadelphia: Brunner/Mazel.

Valent, P. (2002). *Child survivors of the Holocaust.* New York/London: Brunner-Routledge. Originally published 1993 in Port Melbourne, Vic.: Heinemann.

Van der Hal-van Raalte, E. (2007). *Early childhood Holocaust survival and the influence on well-being in later life.* PhD dissertation, Universiteit Leiden.

Van der Hart, O., & Brom, D. (2000). When the victim forgets: Trauma-induced amnesia and its assessment in Holocaust survivors. In A. Shalev, R. Yehuda, & AC. McFarlane (Eds.), *International handbook of human response to trauma,* New York: Kluwer Academic, 233–248.

Van der Kolk, BA., McFarlane, AC., & Van der Hart, O. (1996). A general approach to treatment of posttraumatic stress disorder. In B. A. van der Kolk, A. C. McFarlane, & L. Weisaeth (Eds.), *Traumatic stress: The effects of overwhelming experience on mind, body, and society.* New York: Guilford, 417–440.

Van IJzendoorn, M.H., Bakermans-Kranenburg, M.J., & Sagi-Schwartz, A. (2003). Are children of Holocaust survivors less well-adapted? No meta-analytic evidence for secondary traumatization. *Journal of Traumatic Stress, 16,* 459–469.

Volkan, V. (1997). *Bloodlines: From ethnic pride to ethnic terrorism.* Boulder, CO: Westview.

Völter, B., & Dasberg, M. (1998). Similarities and differences in public discourse about the Shoah in Israel and West and East Germany. In G. Rosenthal (Ed.), *The Holocaust in three generations: Families of victims and perpetrators of the Nazi regime.* London: Continuum, 27–31.

Von Schirach, R. (2005). *Der Schatten meines Vaters.* München: Carl Hanser. [The shadow of my father].

Von Westernhagen, D., (1965). *Children of the perpetrators.* Collective guilt international perspectives series: Studies in emotion and social interaction. NR. Branscombe (Ed.), University of Kansas. [German: *Die Kinder der Täter. Das Dritte Reich und die Generation danach.* München, 1987].

Waite, RGL. (1977). *The psychopathic god: Adolf Hitler.* Cambridge, MA: Dacapo Books.

Wardi, D. (1992). *Memorial candles: Children of the Holocaust*. London: Routledge.

Weisaeth, L., & Eitinger, L. (1993). Posttraumatic stress phenomena: Common themes across wars, disasters and traumatic events. In JP. Wilson, & B. Raphael (Eds.), *International handbook of traumatic stress syndromes*. New York: Plenum, 69–77.

Weiss, H. (2005). *Mein Vater, der Krieg und ich*. Köln: Kiepenheuer & Witsch. [My father, the war and I].

Weiss, M., & Weiss, S. (2000). Second generation to Holocaust survivors: enhanced differentiation of trauma transmission. *American Journal of Psychotherapy, 54,* 372–385.

Welzer, H. (2005). *Täter. Wie aus ganz normalen Menschen Massenmörder werden*. Frankfurt a.M.: Fischer. [Perpetrators: How fully normal people became mass murderers].

Welzer, H. (2009). *Die Deutschen und ihr "Drittes Reich."* In Ebertz, M.N., Nickolai, W. & Walter-Hamann, R. (Eds.). Opfer, Täter und Institutionen in der nationalsoziatistischen Gesellschaft: Blicke aus der Gegenwart. Konstanz: Hartung-Gorre, 60–74. [The Germans and their "Third Reich"].

Welzer, H., Moller, S., & Tschuggnall, K. (2002). *Opa war kein Nazi*. Nationalsozialismus und Holocaust im Familiengedächtnis. Frankfurt a.M.: Fischer. [My grandfather was not a Nazi. National-socialism and Holocaust in the family remembrance].

Wiesel, E. (1978). *A Jew today*. New York: Random House.

Wiesel, E. (1997). Foreword. In R. Krell & MI. Sherman (Eds.), *Medical and psychological effects of concentration camps on Holocaust survivors*: A bibliography. New Brunswick & London: Transaction.

Williams, MB., & Sommer, JF. (Eds.). (2002). *Simple and complex post-traumatic stress disorder: Strategies for comprehensive treatment in clinical practice*. New York: Haworth Press.

Wilson, JP., Smith, WK., & Johnson, SK. (1985). A comparative analysis of PTSD among various survivor groups. In CR. Figley (Ed.), *Trauma and its wake*. New York: Brunner/Mazel.

Winnik, HZ. (1967). Psychiatric disturbances of Holocaust ("Shoah") survivors. Symposium of the Israel Psychoanalytic Society. *Israel Annals of Psychiatry and Related Disciplines, 5(1),* 91–100.

Wiseman, H., & Barber, JP. (2008). *Echoes of the trauma: Relational themes and emotions in children of Holocaust survivors.* New York: Cambridge University Press.

Wiseman, H., Barber, JP., Raz, A., Yam, I., Foltz, C. et al. (2002). Parental communication of Holocaust experiences and interpersonal patterns in offspring of Holocaust survivors. *International Journal of Behavioral Development, 26(4),* 371–381.

Wiseman, H., Metzl, E., & Barber, J. (2006). Anger, guilt, and intergenerational communication of trauma in the interpersonal narratives of second-generation Holocaust survivors. *American Journal of Orthopsychiatry, 76,* 176–184.

Witztum, E., & Malkinson, R. (2009). Examining traumatic grief and loss among Holocaust survivors. *Journal of Loss and Trauma, 14,* 129–143.

Wolf, C. (1989). *Kindheitsmuster.* Essen: Blaue Eule. [Childhoodpatterns].

Wolffsohn, M. (Ed.).(1995). *Die Deutschland Akte: Juden und Deutsche in Ost und West: Tatsachen und Legenden.* Munich: Ferenczy bei Bruckmann. [The German act: Jews and Germans in east and west].

World Health Organization (1992). *International Classification of Diseases and Related Health Problems* (ICD-10), Tenth Revision, World Health Organization, Geneva, Switzerland.

Yablonka, H. (1999). *Survivors of the Holocaust: Israel after the war.* New York: New York University Press.

Yablonka, H. (2004). *The state of Israel vs. Adolf Eichmann.* New York: Schocken (translated from Hebrew).

Yehuda, R. (1999a). Parental PTSD as a risk factor for PTSD. In R. Yehuda (Ed.), *Risk factors for posttraumatic stress disorder.* Progress in psychiatry series, American Psychiatric Association, Inc., 93–102.

Yehuda, R. (1999b). Biological factors associated with susceptibility to posttraumatic stress disorder. *Canadian Journal of Psychiatry, 44(1),* 34–39.

Yehuda, R. (2006). Psychobiology of posttraumatic stress disorder: A decade of progress. In R. Yehuda (Ed.), *SciTech Book News,* 1071. New York: Blackwell.

Yehuda, R., Bell, A., Bierer, L. M., & Schmeidler, J. (2008). Maternal, not paternal, PTSD is related to increased risk for PTSD in offspring of Holocaust survivors. *Journal of Psychiatric Research, 42,* 1104–1111.

Yehuda, R., Bierer, LM., Schmeidler, J., Aferiat, DH., Breslau, I., & Dolan, S. (2000). Low cortisol and risk for PTSD in adult offspring of Holocaust survivors. *American Journal of Psychiatry, 157(8),* 1252–1259.

Yehuda, R., Schmeidler, J., Wainberg, M., Binder-Brynes, K., & Duvdevani, T. (1998a). Vulnerability to posttraumatic stress disorder in adult offspring of Holocaust survivors. *American Journal of Psychiatry, 155(9),* 1163–1171.

Yehuda, R., Schmeidler, J., Elkin, A., Wilson, S., Siever, L., Binder-Brynes, K., Wainberg, M., & Aferiot D. (1998b). Phenomenology and psychobiology of the intergenerational response to trauma. In Y. Danieli (Ed.), *International handbook of multigenerational legacies of trauma.* New York: Plenum.

Yehuda, R., & Giller EL. (1994). Comments on the lack of integration between the Holocaust and PTSD literatures. *PTSD Research Quarterly, 5(4).* Vermont: National Center for Post-Traumatic Stress Disorders.

Yehuda, R., Schmeidler, J., Labinsky, E., Bell, A., Morris, A., Zemelman, S., & Grossman, RA. (2009). Ten-year follow-up study of PTSD diagnosis, symptom severity, and psychosocial indices in aging holocaust survivors. *Acta Psychiatrica Scandinavica, 119(1),* 25–34.

Yehuda, R., Kahana, B., Southwick, SM., & Giller, EL. (1994). Depressive features in Holocaust survivors with post-traumatic stress disorder. *Journal of Traumatic Stress, 7(4),* 699–704.

Yehuda, R., Kahana, B., Schmeidler, J., Soutwick, SM., Wilson, S., & Giller, EL. (1995). Impact of cumulative lifetime trauma and recent stress on current posttraumatic stress disorder symptoms in holocaust survivors. *American Journal of Psychiatry, 152(12),* 1815–1818.

Zertal, I. (2005). *Israel's Holocaust and the politics of nationhood.* Cambridge: Cambridge University Press (translated from Hebrew).

Ziegler, M., & Kannonier-Finster, W. (1997). *Österreichisches Gedachtnis. Über Erinnern und Vergessen der NS-Vergangenheit.* Wien-Köln-Weimar. [Austrian remembrance. On remembering and forgetting the NS-past].

Zilberfein, F. (1996). Children of Holocaust survivors: Separation obstacles, attachments, and anxiety. *Social Work and Health Care, 23(3),* 35–55.

Zloof, D., Yaphe, J., Durst, N., Venuta, M., & Fusman, R. (2005). Emotional resilience or increased vulnerability? A survey of the reactions of Holocaust survivors to the threat of terror in Israel. *Giornale Italiano Psycopatologia, 11*, 347–353.

Zlotogorski, Z. (1985). Offspring of concentration camp survivors: A study of levels of ego functioning. *Israel Journal of Psychiatry and Related Sciences, 22(3)*, 201–209.

Zohar, AH., Giladi, L., & Givati, T. (2007). Holocaust exposure and disordered eating: A study of multi-generational transmission. *European Eating Disorders Review, 15(1)*, 50–57.

INDEX

Amcha – National Israeli Center for Psychosocial Support of Survivors of the Holocaust and the Second Generation

www.amcha.org

**Amcha is supported by
the Conference of Jewish Material Claims Against Germany**